The Paradox of Regulation

In memory of Adam Sutton 15.6.1950–6.9.2010

The Paradox of Regulation

What Regulation Can Achieve and What it Cannot

Fiona Haines

Associate Professor, University of Melbourne and Adjunct Senior Research Fellow, Australian National University

Edward Elgar
Cheltenham, UK • Northampton, MA, USA

Published by
Edward Elgar Publishing Limited
The Lypiatts
15 Lansdown Road
Cheltenham
Glos GL50 2JA
UK

Edward Elgar Publishing, Inc.
William Pratt House
9 Dewey Court
Northampton
Massachusetts 01060
USA

A catalogue record for this book is available from the British Library

Library of Congress Control Number: 2011924288

Mixed Sources
Product group from well-managed
forests and other controlled sources
www.fsc.org Cert no. SA-COC-1565
© 1996 Forest Stewardship Council
FSC

ISBN 978 1 84844 863 6 (cased)

Typeset by Cambrian Typesetters, Camberley, Surrey
Printed and bound by MPG Books Group, UK

Contents

Abbreviations

AASB	Australian Accounting Standard Board
ABC	Australian Broadcasting Corporation
ACCC	Australian Competition and Consumer Commission
AFP	Australian Federal Police
AIFRS	Australian International Financial Reporting Standards
ALP	Australian Labor Party
APRA	Australian Prudential Regulatory Authority
AQIS	Australian Quarantine and Inspection Service
ASIC	Australian Securities and Investments Commission
ASIC	Aviation Security Identification Card
ASIO	Australian Security and Intelligence Organisation
AUASB	Australian Auditing Standards Board
AVID	Aviation Identification
BRTF	Better Regulation Task Force
CBA	Cost Benefit Analysis
CLERP 9	Corporate Law and Economic Reform Program 9
CoAG	Council of Australian Governments
CSI	Container Security Initiative
CTFR	Counter Terrorism First Response
Customs	Australian Customs Service
DFAT	Department of Foreign Affairs and Trade
DIPNR	Department of Infrastructure, Planning and Natural Resources (NSW)
DOTARS	Department of Transport and Regional Services (later renamed Office of Transport Security (OTS))
DOFI	Direct Offshore Foreign Insurers
ERA	Esso Resources Australia (also referred to as 'Esso')
ESC	Essential Services Commission (Victoria)
ESV	Energy Safe Victoria
ETD	Explosives Trace Detection
FCR	Financial Condition Report
FITB	Future Income Tax Benefits
FRP	Financial Reporting Panel
HAZOP	Systematic Hazard Analysis (lit. Hazard and Operability Study)

HIH	HIH (Insurance) Pty Ltd
IASB	International Accounting Standards Board
ICA	Insurance Council of Australia
ICAA	Institute of Chartered Accountants of Australia
IFRS	International Financial Reporting Standards
ISPC	International Ship and Port Facilities Code
KPI	Key Performance Indicators
MHF	Major Hazard Facility
MHU	Major Hazards Unit of Victorian WorkSafe
MNC/MNE	Multinational Corporation/Enterprise
MSIC	Marine Security Identity Card
MUA	Maritime Union of Australia
NCTC	National Counter Terrorism Committee
NOHSC	National Occupational Health and Safety Commission
NOPSA	National Offshore Petroleum Safety Authority
NSW	New South Wales
NT	Northern Territory
OCL	Outstanding Claims Liabilities
OCP	Outstanding Claims Provisions
ODRC	Optimised Depreciated Replacement Cost
OECD	Organisation for Economic Co-operation and Development
OHS	Occupational Health and Safety
ONA	Office of National Assessments
OTS	Office of Transport Security
PAIRS	Probability and Impact Rating System
RPT	Regular Public Transport
SOARS	Supervisory Oversight and Response System
TSP	Transport Security Plan
VIC	Visitor Identification Card
VWA	Victorian WorkCover Authority that housed WorkSafe the Occupational Health and Safety regulator

Acknowledgements

This research has constituted a considerable part of my professional and personal life for the past six years. It has benefitted enormously from the support and collaboration from colleagues, research participants and friends. The project began as part of a research partnership with my dear friend and long-time collaborator Adam Sutton. His contribution to this work is considerable and I owe him an enormous debt of gratitude for many of the ideas and concepts elaborated on in this book. Indeed, had it not been for his devastating illness and subsequent retirement from academic life in 2008 this would have in all probability been a joint project with both our names clearly identified with this work. In fairness to Adam, however, I did not want his name linked with any weaknesses in the work (he was a most fastidious taskmaster in our joint projects!), so I have decided to dedicate the book to him rather than continue the joint authorship we had intended for this work when starting out in 2005. We were most fortunate in this work to secure the services of Chris Platania Phung who began work on the project as a research assistant but whose contributions went far beyond the confines of that role and far beyond the point at which the money ran out! Thank you, Chris.

The manuscript benefitted greatly from a six-month research fellowship I undertook at RegNet at the Australian National University in 2009. It was during this time that the analysis of risk presented here was refined and improved, indeed work on this book was a primary task whilst at RegNet. Ideas, feedback and supportive critiques were provided by the many excellent scholars, graduate students and colleagues at RegNet, in particular Neil Gunningham, John Braithwaite, Valerie Braithwaite, Peter Drahos, Hilary Charlesworth, Mary Ivec, Janet Hope, Kyla Tienhaara, Petrina Schiavi and Kylie McKenna. I was also able to complete final chapters during my sabbatical from the University of Melbourne in the first six months of 2010. Many colleagues have provided extensive and most welcome feedback on various chapters in the book. Most particularly, I would like to thank Kit Carson, Christine Parker, Caron Beaton-Wells, Gary Wickham and Nesam McMillan. The work as a whole also benefitted from fruitful discussions with Nancy Reichman, Susan Silbey, Cate Lewis and Jens Zinn. Peter Ferguson provided excellent copyediting support and Karen Gillen also in preparing the index. To all of you my grateful thanks.

I am also indebted to those who agreed to provide information to me in the course of this research. This included regulators, consultants, those from industry and community members who allowed me to attend meetings during 2008. Certainly, the work of public servants, particularly in those bureaucracies represented here, is pressured and often difficult. Without the consent of those within the regulatory agencies to give of their time and expertise, this research would have been far poorer. The same is true for those within industry. I am also most grateful to those managers, supervisors, technical workers and shop floor staff who agreed to participate in this research and to help me understand the demands of compliance. I have endeavoured to be true to the sentiment expressed in all the interviews and to build on the material each provided, which allowed me vivid and fruitful insight into the regulatory worlds you inhabit. Thank you.

Finally, I would like to thank my husband Bruce for his invaluable assistance. As an engineer he kept me honest with my discussions and elaboration around the Longford explosion and his work as a risk consultant provided invaluable insights into the world of compliance. Finally, he painstakingly read draft manuscripts (plural!) to ensure the work is clear and accessible. I could not have asked for better support both professionally and personally.

This research was supported by an Australian Research Council Grant DP0557431. The University of Melbourne also provided assistance. This financial support was essential to the successful completion of the research and this book.

1. Introduction

This book was written at a time of heightened concern about the global economy, global warming and, within Australia at least, how to deal with devastating bushfires in Victoria and floods in Queensland. Fran Bailey, a local Australian Federal politician was the latest to repeat the well-worn phrase 'such devastation must never happen again' in response to the fires that swept though Marysville, a regional town in her electorate where 34 residents lost their lives. These events were just the latest examples of successive crises that motivate governments and communities to want to learn from their current suffering so that future harm can be avoided. In each arena, the frenzy of policymaking begins. At the centre of many such initiatives is the drive to regulate and control the capricious risk and create an environment where lives, communities, environments or finances are safe (Braithwaite and Drahos 2000; Hancher and Moran 1998). Such regulatory responses are diverse: from strengthened building regulations to provide protection from the expected increased intensity of bushfires to a cap on executive salaries to ensure the pain of recession is shared more evenly. What these responses have in common, however, is the goal of avoiding, or at least reducing, the risk of future harm.

I would argue that much can be learnt about regulation from studying the crises of the recent past. It is here that the problems and possibilities of a regulatory solution to the risk problem become clear. It is then possible, when emotions are less intense, to ask why certain paths were chosen and not others, to determine, in light of the challenges of implementation, what the regulatory approaches devised actually accomplished and whether the reform momentum was sustained.

To understand the strengths and limitations of regulation requires more than a close-grained analysis of a recent disaster and identification of what rules, if implemented could prevent a recurrence of tragedy. I argue the urge to regulate must be placed alongside perennial demands that we are over-regulated. In the lull between disasters, prominent debates revolve around how contemporary societies are being swamped by the proliferation of regulations that threaten individual liberties, dampen entrepreneurial zest and blunt our competitive edge. This demand for more and more protection is an indication, we are told, of how risk averse we are becoming and how the 'nanny state' has

been revived in the guise of the regulatory state and the regulatory enforcement officer.

It is this paradox of regulation, namely the presence of conflicting imperatives that is important to understand. Significant benefit can be gained from
exploring what these seemingly inconsistent demands can tell us about the
shape of our society. This is a study that teases apart the underlying pressures
and needs that result in governments espousing in one moment 'this must
never happen again' and in the next bemoaning the complexity of laws and
regulations that seek to control risk. In doing so, the reality of regulation as at
once a technical, political and social project comes to the fore. As such a
project, the problems and possibilities of avoiding harm and controlling future
risk through regulation become clearer.

The analysis in this book suggests that a lack of effective regulatory techniques may rarely form the central weakness of a regulatory risk reduction
strategy. Rather, the analysis here suggests the limited effectiveness of regulation is caused by two different factors. First, regulation as the quintessential
instrumental form of policymaking is both politically and technically attractive, but can be thwarted when the risk to be reduced is not amenable to
narrow, targeted interventions. Nonetheless, regulation may remain popular as
it allows claims that progress has been made and that, this time, the lessons
from tragedy have been learnt. Secondly, the analysis here suggests that even
when regulation can be effective in avoiding catastrophe it needs sufficient
political support to ensure its implementation; but not overweening political
intervention that prevents the regulator framing the regime in the optimal
direction.

Three separate disasters form the bedrock of the analysis. The first, an
industrial explosion at the Longford Gas Plant in Gippsland, Victoria, took the
lives of two people and cut gas supplies to the State for two weeks in 1998.
Such an event was devastating to the families of those who died, costly for the
local businesses across the state that suffered a loss of gas supply and an
inconvenience to those Victorians forced to shower in cold water or wait in
queues for kindly hotel operators to allow them to use their facilities. The
second, the terrorist attacks of 11 September 2001, in the United States of
America, was as global in its impact as Longford was parochial. The final
catastrophe was the collapse of HIH Insurance, to date the largest financial
collapse in Australia; a corporate demise resulting in losses totalling some $3
billion AUD. In each case, the changes to regulation within Australia were of
primary concern.

These particular disasters give life to the analysis of the paradox of regulation. Essentially, this is a book about regulation and risk. It traces the impact
of political pronouncements of 'Never again!' that resonated in the wake of
these three disparate events. In each case, these injunctions were followed by

regulatory reform. In the case of Longford this resulted in a ground up reworking of what it meant to control catastrophic risk of explosion and fire, but only in the state most closely affected. Following September 11 the regulatory demands placed on sea and airports poured forth from government in the wake of the event, creating a new breed of regulators drawn from the military, rather than industry or the professions, and a level of surveillance in some locations (but not other equally vulnerable sites) that would astonish George Orwell himself. The collapse of HIH occurred during a maelstrom of reform already occurring in the financial industry. Financial regulatory agencies were tentatively reshaping at the behest of the Australian Commonwealth Government to bring their activities in line with contemporary ideas of risk-based regulation, a regime argued to both increase the efficiency and effectiveness of financial regulation. The severity of the impact of the collapse of HIH, however, pointed to weaknesses in risk control and sent shockwaves through the two regulators most closely affected, the Australian Securities and Investments Commission (ASIC) and the Australian Prudential Regulatory Authority (APRA).

I argue throughout this book that regulation embodies the promise of modernity. It creates the vision of technical mastery over threats (whether from technology, terrorists or financial mismanagement). It offers hope of learning from the past to control the hazards of the future. This technical project is both optimistic and seductive. It has led to an explosion of didactic literature that bristles with opportunity. Human agency will prevail; we can be fruitful, multiply and subdue (the threats of) the earth.

Regulation as a modernist project, then, involves the development of processes and styles of enforcement that are argued to ensure greater and greater levels of compliance that will minimise a risk, or avoid a specified harm. Indeed, there are regulatory successes that can be identified and promoted. Yet, regulation often appears as not only the solution, but also the problem. Chapter 2 explores the literature on regulation, teasing apart the technical, social and political elements that comprise this literature. It is a literature that encompasses not only the reform impetus and the techniques considered appropriate to deal with risk but also the nature of the compliance challenge on the ground. The first part of the chapter explores the literature around reform and technique (exploring the ideas of responsive regulation and meta-regulation for example) and then goes on to explore literature on compliance and the problems of the 'law/practice' gap. Through the analysis of regulation the instrumental character of regulation and its political core is revealed.

Chapter 3 explores the ways in which the study of risk as a 'knowable harm' has developed. As many regulatory reform manuals attest, the first challenge of reform is to define the problem, the risk or the harm. It is this instrumental orientation that forms an essential element to regulation (Black 2002). But, while regulation provides the means to achieve a given end, it remains silent on what ends are most important or able to be reached through a regulatory strategy. A natural complement to the regulatory literature is that on risk and in particular literature that endeavours to identify the specific nature of the harm, its impact and likelihood of occurrence, and specific methods that will reduce that risk. Analyses of risk often are accompanied by an assessment of which threats need greatest attention. Technical understandings of risk provide a logical complement to regulatory control. This form of risk is defined in the book as 'actuarial risk'. By actuarial risk, I mean the physical, environmental and financial impact that is highlighted by the event and calculated as likely to occur in the future. This form of risk is often developed and defined by scientists, engineers, economists and actuaries who develop models of the likelihood and impact of a given hazard being realised.

Clearly, many contest the assumptions that underlie both the regulatory and the risk management project centred on an actuarial understanding of risk. The subsequent sections of Chapter 3 work through the critiques of an actuarial understanding of risk. In working through this literature, I argue that it is unhelpful to understand risk as an essentially singular construct. Rather, three distinct ideal-types of risk affect the regulatory challenge: one actuarial, the second socio-cultural and the third political. The concept of socio-cultural risk is developed through the insights of Durkheim (1964) and Mary Douglas (1992) and their ideas of how risk is centred on concerns with social order. The idea of political risk is developed from the work of Habermas (Borradori 2003; Habermas 1979; 1989a; 1989b; 1989c; 1996) and is comprised of the dual threat to political legitimacy that arises either from a government's inability either to manage the economy in a manner that provides the necessary resources for government, or from an incapacity to reassure the population about their own security and doubts about the capacity of government to provide such security. The lesson from this chapter is that regulation may well be asked to reduce three distinct risk challenges.

Chapter 4 describes the three events that set in train regulatory reforms within Australia. The purpose here is to draw on both primary and secondary sources to provide an insight into the significance of each event. The aim of this chapter is to analyse how the physical and financial crises laid bare through each disaster were interpreted. These interpretations encompassed the underlying physical and technical causes of each disaster, as well as the significance placed on each event by the public and media of the time and by the political elite. Each of the disasters had a distinct actuarial, socio-cultural and political profile that framed what regulatory response was desirable and against what particular form of risk it should be primarily directed. The lessons here were clear, actuarial assessments of cause needed to be set alongside economic and political constraints and opportunities that resulted from each disaster.

Chapter 5 assesses the regulatory reforms that emanated from the three events. This chapter reveals how regulatory reform was propelled by the crisis event, but then modified and attenuated by the location of the event, whether it was embedded within what were seen as essential industries and what reforms were considered necessary to reassure the citizenry that their security needs were paramount. In contrast to much of the regulatory literature that assumes considerable agency on behalf of the regulator to choose a response that could address the actuarial risk raised by the disaster, this analysis demonstrates the limits to the regulator's authority. Each of the three ideal types of risk: actuarial, socio-cultural and political moulded and shaped the regulatory response to disaster. Understanding the interplay between them provides insights into what productive role regulation can play in the contemporary era, and what it cannot.

As much socio-legal literature has emphasised, however, the gap between the reforms and what actually happens on the ground, in terms of actual compliance, can be considerable. Three chapters (6, 7 and 8) are devoted to assessing the impact of the regulatory reforms, described in Chapter 5, through research on the way hazardous industrial sites, air and seaports responded to their new regulatory responsibilities. These chapters reveal two critical elements to these responses: firstly, that the kind of actuarial risk to be reduced does make a difference in terms of the capacity of regulation to reduce the risk of future disaster and secondly, that support for the regime was important not only for developing an effective regulatory regime, but also how seriously it was adhered to by regulated sites. Where the actuarial risk severely challenged the capacity of regulation to reduce such risk (because of the agency of the perpetrator of the harm), there was a need to develop a narrative around how the next incident may occur, and what the causal influences could be, to 'tame' the response and the compliance challenge. In these chapters it became clear that the task of reducing the risk of a future industrial disaster was more amenable to a regulatory approach than the tasks of reducing the risk of a terrorist attack or financial collapse. This potential was best realised when there was effective and knowledgeable leadership that took seriously a collaborative approach to risk reduction. In contrast, the security regime that followed 11 September 2001 faced major challenges since security and surveillance could always be seen as insufficient when faced by a determined protagonist. Finally, the response to financial reforms post-HIH pointed to the essential ambiguity in an actuarial assessment of financial risk. Such ambiguity was on the one hand seen as a desirable condition that encouraged the necessary flexibility needed within a financial system and that nurtured the entrepreneurial spirit. Yet, on the other hand ambiguity was the problem, a condition to be dispelled through greater transparency and accountability. In the face of this ambiguity, the financial reforms were vulnerable to creative compliance and regulatory arbitrage and also viewed by some as clumsy demands that generated poor financial outcomes.

Chapter 9 concludes by bringing together the analysis of the literature together with the insights of the empirical research. This chapter argues that regulation has considerable strengths in reducing the risk of future harm. At best, it can tame actuarial risk and generate confidence in the regulator while also creating a positive dynamic where a 'race to the top' in risk reduction occurs. But the environment where it is most successful is perhaps rarer than we had imagined. To be successful, regulation must embrace actuarial, socio-cultural and political risk reduction through a common regulatory project. Critically, improving risk reduction outcomes involves more than just sweeping to one side the socio-cultural and political risk concerns that were so clearly important in shaping the effectiveness of the regulatory reforms that followed each of these events. Socio-cultural concerns about community and individual vulnerability are, as sociologists would argue, intrinsic to assessments of risk and demands for security. They are substantive and significant. Socio-culturally based fears often lie behind the perennial demand for a strong command and control regulatory response from government. Governments in contemporary society need to take these security concerns seriously.

Hence, scholars promoting governance approaches to risk reduction will need to continue to take government seriously. Regulatory reform is perennially attractive to contemporary governments as they demonstrate their sincerity in providing a sufficient response to tragedy and future threat, but it is a response heavily shaped by an equally pressing demand for them to release the chains around the creativity of the market. Yet, regulation may fail in its promoted aim of increasing safety, security or financial integrity, particularly where the actuarial risk is difficult to encompass within a regulatory framework. The lessons within this book suggest that the regulatory response to disaster is unlikely to carry the full weight of prevention of future tragedy, a load it is often asked to bear. Rather, it must sit alongside commensurate efforts to ensure skilled and knowledgeable actors are available to work in areas of high risk and to ensure that entrepreneurial zest leads to public benefit. Strategies to engender political legitimacy should not be allowed to result in divisive social policies that rest on unrealistic regulatory goals. Neither should we accept that a 'free' market tethered only by specific (but numerous) constraints will, almost magically, generate the future we need.

2. The regulatory paradox

'Like a smouldering fire the Liberals let the deregulation agenda in this country lie dormant for most of their eleven years in office. I intend to re-ignite it.' Lindsay Tanner (Australian Labour Party), Minister for Finance and Deregulation[1]

'... Not once have we heard any of them (The Liberal/National opposition) discuss exactly why the world economy has been plunged into crisis over the past two years. Not once have they mentioned the disastrous policies of the Bush administration and the Republican congress in the United States over the past decade. These included the massive and irresponsible tax cuts for the wealthiest section of the population, the reckless deregulation of the financial system ...' Senator David Feeney (Australian Labour Party (Victoria))[2]

'We therefore need a frank analysis of the central role of neo-liberalism in the underlying causes of the current economic crisis. We also need a robust analysis of the social-democratic approach to properly regulated markets and the proper role of the state.' Kevin Rudd, Australian Prime Minister (Australian Labour Party)[3]

Well-designed and properly implemented regulation can bring about good results. Yet a critical assessment of when and how regulation can bring about beneficial ends and when it fails to do so is challenging. This is because the appropriate level of regulation considered necessary, when it is required and how it should be enforced, is vigorously contested. Political debates rage around the need to protect and control, and almost simultaneously a competing demand for a loosening of controls, for a simplification and reduction in the regulatory obligations on business and the community more generally. This suggests that ensuring good regulation is implemented is going to need more than a technical and empirical analysis of regulatory design and its successes and failures (important as these are). To make sense of what regulation can achieve, it is necessary to take seriously the challenges of regulatory reform, as well as how well it performs. There are two interrelated literatures that can assist in developing an understanding of the challenges facing 'good regulation' from inception to implementation; scholarship on regulation and compliance (the subject of this chapter) and risk in the next.

Careful assessment of research and analysis around regulation, regulatory reform and regulatory compliance reveals important elements to the challenge of developing good regulation. In approaching this literature, a useful starting point is to map how the conceptualisation of regulation itself is changing. The extent of what is considered regulation is expanding, while at the same time the tasks that regulation is set to undertake appears to be narrowing. So, there has been a broadening of the term regulation to encompass activities and actors outside of the state and as expressed through law and subordinate legislation. Regulation is argued to be better conceptualised as governance where control originates from various public and private actors and is given effect not only through law, but also by private agreements, the implementation of non-government standards, accreditation schemes and a multitude of other potential control mechanisms. At the same time as the regulatory actors extend, an instrumental conception of regulation has come to dominate debate. Notwithstanding the multiple sources and methods of control, regulation is defined as an attempt to bring about a clearly defined end. Regulation should be 'problem focussed' and goal-oriented. Paradoxically, the focus on goals and how they may be reached ties regulation back to the capacity for enforcement, and, notwithstanding the shift to governance, takes our understanding of what successful regulation looks like back to the importance of law and law enforcement.

These trends towards governance, instrumentality and an emphasis on 'appropriate' enforcement are prominent within policy reform documents, research and writing designed to improve regulation. Across these literatures better regulation is that which has tightly defined goals (instrumentalism), and uses pressures outside of government to achieve those goals (governance not just government). Policy prescriptions and literature on regulation share a desire to see regulation as tightly defined and 'problem focussed'. Research in the area provides evidence that sharply targeted and suitably enforced regulation under certain circumstances can achieve set goals.

But differences emerge between reform policies and academic research that point to competing philosophies underpinning the project to promote 'good regulation'. Such disagreements point to the inherently political nature of regulation. Disparate values inform what regulation 'should' be asked to do, and what it can achieve. Conflict surrounds what adequate enforcement entails, for example, as well as tensions between policy and research on what a switch to governance actually consists of. For the policy community, a governance approach suggests that adequate standards of risk reduction often will be found within the intentions and actions of the regulated community. 'Good regulation' is thus 'light-handed', since these good intentions may easily be brought to bear in bringing about sufficient levels of improvement and a minimal level of government involvement. The academic literature, however, shares no such view that the result of regulation will necessarily be felt as a 'light touch' by all concerned. Here, governance approaches arguably can result in the antithesis of light-handed regulation requiring significantly greater levels of attention to risk reduction than that required under previous 'command and control' regimes.

Attention to the areas of consensus and points of conflict concerning what innovative, well-targeted and effective regulation looks like in practice can lead us to a broader assessment of the demands on regulation in contemporary society. Clearly, what is argued to constitute a viable 'governance' approach to meeting set goals is not value free. Tensions arise around whether market competition does or does not sit at the centre of a governance strategy. Disputes further develop around whether markets and/or competition are the principal drivers bringing greater health and wellbeing to all. Differences concerning what regulation is needed, the level of competition that should be promoted or prevented and the strength of the regulatory controls required can be understood as key sites of material and ideological conflict. This should alert us to the potential that the successful passage of a regulatory reform initiative itself may be a significant signal of success or failure in of itself, quite divorced from its actual effect on the target regulated audience. Arguably, these contests should not be seen as merely an unwanted side-effect but as an intrinsic component of regulation in contemporary society. The politics of the process may be as important to society (and certainly as important to understand) as the actual impact the ensuing regulations do or do not have.

The centrality of politics and the growing emphasis on regulatory performance brings attention back to the instrumental nature of regulation. Regulation is understood as a means to an end. However, as Weber argued nearly a century ago, the method of enshrining values in rules, a key component of the regulatory project, is a fraught one. Ritualism (following rules with little sense of why they are there) and creative compliance (using rules to escape the purpose the rules are trying to serve – as in elaborate tax avoidance schemes), both problems Weber well understood, remain key challenges. But, arguably a more intransigent problem stems from the Weberian insight that good outcomes from regulation cannot inspire the broader public as to their worth. The Achilles heel of dedicated intellectual engagement in defining the exact nature of the regulatory problem and the most effective method of amelioration cannot, in itself, bring about the necessary social and political commitment to its own project.

PATTERNS IN THE REGULATORY LANDSCAPE

Nearly two decades ago, Ian Ayres and John Braithwaite (1992) pointed to what they called a state of regulatory flux, in their broad sweep of the activities of regulatory agencies in the United States. They highlighted the way that deregulation was often followed by an escalation of punitive measures and an increase in levels of fines against firms. Over a decade and a half later, the impression of the regulatory landscape is one of multiple regulatory cycles in diverse policy contexts in constant motion, moving from a loosening of regulatory control to a subsequent tightening and back. Arguably, the only firm conclusion possible from these 'wheels within wheels' is that future change in terms of regulatory reform is guaranteed.

However, there is some sense of direction that emerges, not withstanding differences in detail between geographic location and industrial sector (Jordan, Wurzel and Zito 2005). Trends can be seen in three interrelated areas: first, regulatory control as extending beyond government, secondly a dominance of regulation understood as instrumental ('problem-solving') projects and finally a shift in what is considered the preferred style of government regulation and enforcement.

For a number of current commentators and writers on regulation, regulation is now argued to be less about government and more about governance (Braithwaite 2000; Freeman 1999; Gunningham, Thornton and Kagan 2005; Hancher and Moran 1998; Rose and Miller 1992; Scott 2004; Shearing 1993). As a governance project, regulation draws on influences beyond government in order to secure higher standards. Multiple players should be brought in to 'shape' regulatory space so that the rules of the market can be seen to serve the regulatory goal (Shearing 1993 but see Haines 1997). This orientation of regulation as governance allows for a proliferation of potential initiatives drawing on the support of third parties such as insurers or non-government organisations, allowing for negotiated public and private agreements and employing market-based instruments such as taxes and market incentives in order to achieve enhanced levels of risk reduction.

Under a governance paradigm the prominence of the law and the role of the state in the task of regulation declines, such that all that remains of the regulatory project is its instrumental orientation (Black 2002). This characterisation of regulation as intrinsically concerned with instrumental goals is noteworthy. It signals a shift in emphasis away from regulation as a set of rules that constitute a market (for example in economic regulation a two-airline policy or limiting the number of banking institutions, that is, defining who can trade in a given market) to regulation as intervention in the market in order to redress market 'failure' (Baldwin and Martin 1999). Regulation most often is perceived as an instrument designed to solve a problem, a goal-oriented practice for the purpose of reducing a tightly-defined and specific harm (Teubner 1998).[4]

This instrumental orientation to regulation brings to the fore regulation as policing. Regulation is tied to enforcement. The connection between regulation and policing has been noted by a number of scholars (Braithwaite 2008; Carson 1985; Wells 2001), yet it is a connection that makes most sense when regulation is understood as instrumental law. Regulation encompassing law enforcement under a neo-liberal paradigm also can be seen to have a distinct character. It is less about punish and more about persuade, or better still get the private sector to voluntarily achieve high standards (Grabosky 1994).

However, two of these three elements – the shift to governance and the emphasis on eschewing deterrence in preference for compliance – have met considerable resistance. Within academia, a prominent strand of writing asserts that greater protection requires more, not less, emphasis on law and the state, elements that can and should be centre stage in any regulatory regime. Further, the criminal law vigorously enforced should be a routine component to a regulatory strategy. The decline of the state and the emphasis on compliance and partnership is to be decried. Writers such as Laureen Snider (2000), for example, write of the need for an 'obituary' of corporate crime, viewing the shift to governance as a reversal of recognition of the harm wrought by corporate malfeasance. Together with writers such as Frank Pearce and Steve Tombs (Pearce and Tombs 1990; Tombs 2002) they argue that regulation as governance is a retrograde step, resulting in a lowering of standards and opening up new opportunities for the powerful to profit at the expense of the powerless. Overall, and especially within the criminological literature, the commitment to a project of criminalisation of corporate harm remains undiminished (Friedrichs 1996; Glasbeek 2002; Rosoff, Pontell and Tillman 2004; Wells 2001).

Such condemnation of the 'crimes of the powerful' has had some effect on policy – particularly when combined with sustained activism by both unions and other non-government organisations around some signal event. Contrary to those who point to the decline of the state (Scott 2004), tougher penalties in a range of regulatory arenas have emerged (Baldwin 2004). At least as a faint echo of standard 'law and order' policy responses in the area of street crime, higher fines and the possibility of imprisonment has found its way into certain areas of industrial harm (Baldwin 2004; Gobert 2005; Haines and Hall 2004). Certainly, in high-profile cases of financial fraud, lengthy jail terms for white-collar offenders can and do occur, (in the United States at least), with the 24-year sentence handed down to Jeffrey Skilling, former CEO of Enron, arguably the most high-profile example. Indeed, as this book was finalised, Bernard Madoff was sentenced to 150 years jail.

Those determined to 'reignite the fires' of deregulation, then, face considerable obstacles from the combined effects of diversified sources of regulatory control, a proliferation of regulatory techniques and, in some areas, higher penalties and greater stringency in enforcement. Even if only a narrow definition of regulation is adopted, namely instrumental forms of control tied to the state, there is evidence that government attempts to deregulate overall has resulted in more regulation (Banks 2005; Levi-Faur 2005; Sunstein 1990b). Part of the story of escalation is the long-recognised assessment that deregulation in the form of privatisation generated a proliferation of regulations aimed at ensuring competitive markets (Ayres and Braithwaite 1992; Levi-Faur 2005). But it also appears that additional instrumental regulatory controls beyond those aimed to enable competition have increased emanating from disparate state and international governmental bodies (Braithwaite 2008; Levi-Faur 2005). To this enumeration of government regulation needs to be added the wealth of non-government and self-regulatory initiatives such as certification regimes and corporate social responsibility programmes (McNichol 2006; Meidinger 2006). Overall, and despite the stated intentions of governments to deregulate and simplify more regulation, not less, seems to be the result.

THE PURSUIT OF 'GOOD REGULATION'

This complex, shifting picture generates ongoing pressure to create better systems of regulation, regimes that can work more efficiently and effectively in the public interest. Proponents argue that better regulation and enforcement practices, greater coherence, firmer connectedness between various regimes and higher levels of integrity between regime and its actual capacity to achieve set goals need to be established. Then, it is argued, regulation can allow both greater levels of productivity and wealth while reducing the harmful 'side-effects' of competitive markets.

Analysing the arguments around 'good regulation' also has much to offer in helping our understanding of the roles that regulation is being asked to play in contemporary society. There are two distinct sets of writing here, one largely found in government documents and the other in academic texts. Both share the view that good regulation can provide the way forward in a manner that reduces risk while also minimising the impact on business and so to free up their entrepreneurial spirit in generating profit and contributing to the public good. There are areas of consensus between these bodies of work but also areas of tension and conflict. Both are worthy of close attention.

The View from the Bureaucracies

The elaboration of what constitutes 'good regulation' within most government publications is found within documents aspiring to a world of less regulation. It is intriguing to explore this literature, since its efforts are largely designed as regulation of regulators, meta-regulation in Bronwen Morgan's (2003) sense of that term. The overall impression from reading through various examples of government documentation concerned with producing 'better regulation' is a sentiment 'enough, stop and think *before* you reach for the regulatory toolbox!' Each of the not inconsiderable documents produced by bodies such as the Organisation for Economic Co-operation and Development (OECD), the Better Regulation Task Force (BRTF) in the United Kingdom and the Council of Australian Governments (CoAG) emphasise the problems regulations can create for business.

What actually constitutes 'good regulation' according to this literature is, however, elusive. The UK BRTF tellingly entitled 'Regulation – Less is More', and the CoAG report entitled 'Best Practice Regulation' essentially points to the processes that should be followed should a new regulation be proposed. These documents orientate themselves towards a 'survival of the fittest' approach. Regulation should be made to jump multiple hurdles. Good regulation is that which makes it through to the other end, transformed in a process of evolution which creates a race of efficient, demonstrably effective rules, in the words of the OECD, 'regulatory structures and processes [that] are robust, transparent, accountable and forward looking.' (OECD guiding principles, p.1). Good regulation is thus a natural outcome of rigorous regulatory reform processes.

The initial flourishing of regulatory reform initiatives held an implicit (and occasionally explicit) assumption that most regulatory proposals (as well as the existing stock of 'outdated' regulation) would be eliminated through mandatory regulatory reform processes (Morgan 2003). Libertarian views of laissez faire markets held sway where consumers would reign supreme, unfettered by self-interested government bureaucrats. The zeitgeist was that markets were self-regulating and would regulate better than any government. Former President George W. Bush captured this sentiment pithily, saying 'even an imperfect market produces better results than arrogant experts and grasping bureaucrats' (cited in Chen and Hanson 2004 p.19). While in reality regulations may have proliferated, the 'meta-script' (Chen and Hanson 2004) animating reform was that self-regulating markets generate the most beneficial public outcomes. Only when the market had 'failed' was there justification to intervene.

Over the nearly two decades of deregulatory initiatives a subtle shift in emphasis has taken place (Carroll 2008). Certainly, the demand to 'cut red tape' is still front and centre of reform models and there exists a long line of ostensible swords that can cut the Gordian knot of overwhelming regulatory demands: cost benefit analysis, 'one in one out' requirements, standardised methods of assessing costs (the standard cost model), setting percentage figures to reduce the administrative burden (by 10 per cent, 25 per cent, and so on).

But to focus on this alone is no longer a sufficient reading of the intention of regulatory reform. Rather, current attempts at regulatory reform can be likened in its attempt to create 'An Honest Politicians Guide' (or rather approach) to regulation. Just as Morris and Hawkins (1970) aimed to do with criminal justice reform, regulatory reform units now desire a rational, transparent, accountable process that identifies the most efficient, yet also demonstrably effective method in achieving a given policy goal. Like its earlier criminological counterpart, the emphasis is on government keeping out of engaging in partisan morality and self-interested 'puffery', while delivering effective policies in the public interest. The goal is to engender a 'regulatory spiral' rather than a 'regulatory cycle' (Kahn 1990) where better design of regulation targeted in appropriate areas clearly reduces unwanted risks.

'Good' regulation is back in fashion. Successive experiences of industrial crises and, in particular, the current economic crisis, have generated support for regulation. Arguments that 'this is not the time to fire the police force ...' (p.349) made by commentators such as Alfred Kahn (1990) after the Savings and Loans Crisis now appear to have greater resonance. Regulation is part of the progression to a better future, one with possibly more regulation, but instrumental control that is more efficient and effective. Kahn's words in light of current efforts around regulatory reform appear particularly apt:

> ... the lesson I take from recent history is that the evolution of regulatory policy will never come to an end. The path it takes – and we should make every effort to see that it takes – however, is the path not of a full circle or pendulum, which would take us back to where we started, but of a spiral, which has a direction. This is in a sense only an expression of preference for seeking consistently to move in the direction of the first-best functioning of a market economy, rather than the second- or third-best world of centralized command and control ... (1990 pp.353–4).

In the wake of the 2008–9 economic crisis the emphasis is once again on better regulation, not deregulation. Deregulation is a bad word. Getting rid of regulation without reconstructing better, more effective, regulation is part of the problem. As a rueful Barak Obama reflected:

> Unfortunately, instead of establishing a 21st century regulatory framework, we simply dismantled the old one ... we have overseen 21st century innovation – including the aggressive introduction of new and complex financial instruments like hedge funds and non-bank financial companies – with outdated 20th century regulatory tools ... Presidential Address to the Cooper Union[5]

What regulation is and is not appropriate, however, remains vigorously contested. This debate is not just concerned with economic and financial regulation, but all forms of regulation through what is labelled the 'anti-competitive effects' of regulations promoting (amongst other things) health, safety and the environment (Chen and Hanson 2004). Tensions stem from what is understood as the most effective institutional arrangements and regulatory controls that should comprise a 'market economy'. There are those who remain committed to the public choice school (Stigler 1971) and champion regulatory elimination as a worthwhile goal, while others consider regulation as an intrinsic part of contemporary capitalism. This diversity can be seen in the response to the recent financial crisis where for some the crisis stemmed from too much regulation and government intervention (Freidman 2009), while for others the problem was too little of both (Stiglitz 2009). Certainly, differences may stem in part from differences between capitalist economies (Hall and Soskice 2001a; Levi-Faur 2005; Marshall, Mitchell and Ramsay 2008; Wailes, Kitay and Lansbury 2008); however, even within so-called liberal market economies (such as the UK, US and Australia) (Hall and Soskice 2001b) there are contrasting views on how 'vibrant' yet 'sustainable' markets are best nurtured and the role regulation plays in bringing about desirable outcomes.

But this tension needs to be understood as being more complex than a binary opposition between those who see minimal or no regulation as ideal and those who see a strong positive role for regulation in a market economy. Ambiguity about the connection between a cost to business and the cost to competition is fuelled by conflicting and competing views. In Stigler's (1971) original thesis, business gained from regulation and so by definition a regulatory cost to business could not be synonymous with the cost to competition. An assessment of the impact of regulation on competition needed to be separate from the cost of regulation on business. Public choice perspectives see existing businesses as supportive of regulation (even of the social kind) as a useful strategy to keep competitors out of a market. It is not the altruism of business that lies behind any support for regulation here but a self-interested exercise in controlling the market. The distinction between a cost to competition and a cost to business is found in the detail of some regulatory reform processes, not surprisingly since it is a process designed largely by economists. Current guidelines for the preparation of regulatory impact statements (RIS), for example in Victoria, do recognise the difference here. The RIS requirements separate out the cost/benefit analysis from what is termed a 'competition assessment' in recognition of the differences between the two.

These nuances, however, tend to be lost in the political debate, where any cost on business is seen as a drag on (usually international) competitiveness. A cost to business is seen as by definition to be a drag on competition. In the process, public choice assumptions are turned on their head. The only exception here is when political attention is turned to the cost on small business, where there is some recognition that regulation may drive small business out of the market.

Competing views and values lead to ambiguities that cloud what regulatory reformers, politicians and commentators argue to be 'good regulation'. 'Good regulation' is alternatively an oxymoron to public choice perspectives (except, perhaps, competition regulation), minimal and 'light handed' for regulatory reformers and effective in the pursuit of the health and environmental wellbeing for others.

This does not, however, get us much further in understanding what, in the eyes of regulatory reform protocols, good regulation actually consists of. There are some guidelines here. A key attribute of good regulation according to such documentation does not relate to content but rather to accessibility. Good regulation is that which is accountable, consistent and transparent. To make it so, the regime and the regulator should provide clear reasons and justification underpinning the regulations; they should engage in adequate consultation with their stakeholders; their actions should be subject to review and appeal and they should be working under a clear legislative mandate (CoAG 2007; Government of Victoria 2007; Regulation Taskforce 2006). In terms of content, this means regulations should be drafted in 'plain language' and clearly communicate to those affected what they are required to do.

The second set of criteria for good regulation revolves around the targeting of what the particular problem is that requires regulatory attention. Regulation, as the OECD understands it, is that which 'serves clearly identified policy goals' (OECD n.d. p.3). What sufficient targeting is can range from simply a statement of the need for the regime to be in line with stated government policy (OECD n.d.), to a more explicit demand of demonstration that 'a problem' (not just a policy goal) exists (Regulation Taskforce 2006) and finally on problems that are specific, measurable, achievable, realistic and relevant and time dependent the so called 'SMART' approach to regulation (Government of Victoria 2007 p.3.5). The regulatory regime should work like a precision instrument in targeting and ameliorating the 'problem'. The Victorian model even goes one step further in requiring regulatory proposals to include an analysis of the cause of a problem in order to clarify how regulation will address the causes and reduce the identified harm (Government of Victoria 2007).

Enforcement is required to be consistent with this problem-based approach. Enforcement policies and practices should be orientated towards those 'whose activities give rise to the most serious risks' (Regulation Taskforce 2006 p.52). In contrast to the 'zero tolerance' mantra that accompanies many 'law and order' approaches to street crime, good regulation is that which is enforced only when 'serious' risks arise.

Finally, regulation should achieve its objectives in the least costly manner. To do so, policy documents state that the regulatory response should be proportional to the risk posed. Alternatives to direct government intervention should be considered from the full range of governance alternatives before a prescriptive rule is proposed. The rationale is that the regulatory focus should be on achieving good outcomes. Good outcomes relate to addressing and reducing the problem so outcome-based regimes (that actually focus on measuring these outcomes) are considered superior to those that rely principally on processes or prescriptive rules. The emphasis on cost brings into play a range of techniques for an assessment of cost. It is apparent, however, in some guides that considerable effort has gone into assessing the costs of regulation, yet there is little attempt to assist in enumerating or outlining the benefits (Regulation Taskforce 2006; cf. Government of Victoria 2007).

The View from Regulatory Scholars

A parallel literature on what constitutes good regulation, particularly regulation of the instrumental kind, is found within academic literature. That such a literature should develop at a time when government policy is focussed on how to neatly excise the harms associated with competitive markets from their benefits should come as no surprise. The discovery that markets can regulate and create higher standards (Grabosky 1994; Shearing 1993) and that regulation can be counterproductive (Grabosky 1995; Sunstein 1990b) demonstrates a neat confluence between the aspirations of policymakers and academic writing.

This academic literature has a number of similarities to the policy documentation discussed above. A 'problem-solving' orientation to regulation is common to both (Gunningham and Grabosky 1998; Gunningham and Johnstone 1999; Sparrow 2000). Similarly, too, a common orientation is found concerning the essence of good regulation as measured by its capacity to focus ultimately on outcomes (Black 1997). Regulation that works is that which demonstrably and measurably reduces risk. Outcome-based approaches, rather than policies that focus on specifying detailed rules or, to a lesser extent, proper processes are most desirable (Black 1997; Coglianese 2003; Sunstein 2005). A significant development here is meta-regulation, understood as the regulation of self-regulation[6] where processes internal to a regulated organisation are steered to achieve the regulatory outcome desired (Parker 2002).

There is also a fair degree of congruence with the policy literature in terms of the need for a coherent enforcement strategy. Perhaps the approach with the greatest affiliation is John Braithwaite's notion of 'responsive regulation' where more persuasive measures precede punitive approaches to non-compliance (Ayres and Braithwaite 1992). The rationale behind such an approach is the basic premise that in the majority of circumstances the intent of the regulated individual or organisation is honourable, that most want to comply most of the time. Enforcement strategies should capitalise on this goodwill and not undermine it, by creating defiance and counterproductive behaviour (Parker 2002; Tyler 2006b). Considerable research has been undertaken into the various 'motivational postures' (V. Braithwaite 2009) of the regulatee and the ways in which enforcement can most easily bring about compliance with a range of different regulated individuals and organisations. Such a responsive approach can also be combined with a risk-based approach to enforcement, labelled 'meta-risk management', where the most intransigent and costly problem is that given the most careful attention (Braithwaite 2003a; Sparrow 2000).

At the more punitive end of the enforcement spectrum, too, there has been a range of studies reporting on a plethora of sentencing and court-based options for improving levels of compliance. A variety of techniques, from enforceable undertakings, on-the-spot fines and what might be termed 'smart sentencing' options (such as corporate probation) should prosecution be necessary create the capacity for a response to non-compliance best able to bring about the desired behaviour (for a comprehensive overview see Australian Law Reform Commission 2002; Baldwin and Martin 1999; Gunningham and Grabosky 1998; Morgan and Yeung 2007; Yeung 2004).

There is also a shared emphasis between policy and academic literature on governance as extending beyond government. In the academic sphere this includes ways that government can develop regulatory regimes designed to enable the use of multiple, complementary tools from both within and outside of government (Coglianese and Nash 2006; Grabosky 1997; Gunningham and Grabosky 1998). Studies draw attention to ways in which regulatory regimes can capitalise and further direct the self-regulatory imperatives within the corporation (Parker 2002). In arguably its most complete conception, good regulatory governance is that where networks of actors push standards ever-upward from below and meta-regulatory (in Parker's definition of the term) efforts of government demand higher and higher standards from above (Braithwaite 2008; Braithwaite and Drahos 2000).

Perhaps rather too obvious but still critical here is the orientation of both the policy and the academic regulatory literature on the virtuous capacity of markets and in particular the virtues of competition (Braithwaite 2008; Kahn 1990; Sunstein 1990a; 2005). In this writing, there can be a race to the top in standards, not an inevitable race to the bottom (Braithwaite 2008; Majone 1998). However, distinct from proponents of free markets and laissez faire capitalism, what is being argued for here is a mixed economy, a social democratic project. For one leading writer in the field, John Braithwaite, the connection of markets and the need for competition stems in part from his history as a consumer advocate (Braithwaite 2008). Much of Christine Parker's (see for example Parker 1999a; Parker 2002) work revolves around the activities of the Australian Competition and Consumer Commission and their efforts to generate and maintain competitive markets within Australia. Overall, scholarly writing retains a strong normative commitment to how capitalist markets can and should be made to work better. This should not, however, be taken as a single-minded belief that competition will be virtuous, rather that it can be. Markets of vice clearly exist and are recognised (Braithwaite 2008). But, markets of vice can be 'flipped' into markets of virtue; capitalism can be regulated so as to serve the public interest.

This substantive commitment to making markets work in the public interest creates a number of the distinctions found in this literature when compared with the regulatory reform documentation of government. For example, there is a more explicit emphasis on the inclusion in a regulatory regime of those most affected by the *harm* rather than simply those who will be affected by the cost of the regulatory regime (Ayres and Braithwaite 1992). Under a notion of 'tripartism' the inclusion of community groups, consumers, nursing home residents, workers and unions are understood to have a key role to play in enhancing the integrity of any regulatory regime in raising standards.

The substantive focus also is found in the commitment to ever-increasing standards of health, consumer and environmental protection[7]. This leads to a distinct orientation towards how business can be made to work in the public interest. In the regulatory research literature, within the social sciences at least, regulation is part of the solution rather than part of the problem as public choice economics would suggest. Indeed, some go further and dispute there is any such thing as a free market. Markets are always regulated; they always are found in settings where various pressures and priorities constitute those rules (Shearing 1993). The key is, through regulation, to tip the incentives in the desired direction.

The striking difference in the definition of the term 'regulatory capture' provides a useful illustration of the contrasting values attached to the stated goals of the regulatory regime. For the public choice economist, regulatory capture occurs when government creates regulation that controls entry to a market thus feathering the nest of both existing industry players and the regulator whose regime rises in importance and resources (Stigler 1971). Such a definition has nothing to say about whether the regulations concerned do, or do not, result in increased health and safety standards, environmental standards or any other risk-reduction goal. That is irrelevant. The difference from criminological definitions of regulatory capture could not be wider. For the criminologist, regulatory capture is where business gets away with lower environmental/safety/health standards (whatever the particular focus) because the regulatory enforcer has come from industry and so 'forgives' their minor (or not so minor) transgressions (Clinard and Yeager 1980; Makkai and Braithwaite 1998). Regulatory capture is defined by reference to lower standards and turning a blind eye to the law. In the former, public choice definition regulatory standards per se of health, and so on, are of no concern. Regulatory capture is avoided by deregulation. For the criminologist regulatory capture is overcome by more effective, often tougher, law enforcement.

The substantive commitment of writers in regulation to the regulatory goal and not just the workings of the market also are found in the growing emphasis on networks consisting of NGOs and innovative businesses that can 'ratchet up' regulatory standards (Braithwaite and Drahos 2000). The pursuit of better and better outcomes, of ameliorating the problems with markets of 'vice' and the race to the bottom in terms of standards (Braithwaite 2008) can and should be addressed. The concerted efforts of actors outside of government by virtue of savvy media skills and generally high levels of community approval can push standards ever higher (Braithwaite 2008; Braithwaite and Drahos 2000; Shearing and Wood 2003).

Not surprisingly, then, good regulation in this academic body of work does not align itself with ideas of 'light handed' regulation, a term as we saw above that is central to regulatory reform initiatives and economic writing on regulation. Indeed, in reading much of this literature it is clear that ideal forms of regulation can be as far from 'light handed' as it is possible to get. For example, while Christine Parker's (2002) Open Corporation might build on the idea of the regulation of (corporate) self-regulation, the detailed account provided in the book leaves one in no doubt that should a practice of regulating an 'open corporation' take place and be done successfully, the result would likely be anything but 'light handed'!

These differences between the various literatures around good regulation essentially point to the critical involvement of values and politics in regulatory reform. Political contests arise stemming from the different views held about the proper role of the market, from concerns that the market and competition may not, after all, protect the vulnerable, or that it will be swamped by self-interested unreasonable regulatory demands. Essentially, as Offe (1984) found with the welfare state, the regulatory state faces similar challenges of commodification and the pursuit of the public good through the market, and decommodification commitment to values and ideals (such as health, human rights and environmental wellbeing) and a determination to preserve the intrinsic quality of such values. At the level of regulatory reform 'good regulation' is given the unenviable task of mediating such a process.

DOES GOOD REGULATION WORK?

Learning from Studies of Compliance

A separate assessment, however, needs to be made of whether this flurry of policymaking aimed at generating good regulation that actually can generate compliance and risk reduction on the ground has borne fruit. It is important not to confuse the proliferation of demands at government level for 'better' regulation, the employment of a multiplicity of governance strategies or changes to penalties with inevitably good or bad outcomes.[8]

What, then, does research tell us about the success of 'good regulation'; that is, clearly targeted, well designed, that draws on the good intentions of the regulated community and that is appropriately enforced? The simple response is that, in a variety of circumstances, good regulation can and does work in increasing compliance, reducing risks and raising standards (Braithwaite 2003a; Gunningham and Grabosky 1998; Sunstein 1990a). Targeting regulation to solve the most critical problems and the least compliant companies and individuals can work well (Braithwaite 2003a). A potential problem should be noted with this work, however, in that evaluation studies work best when there is a clear measurement of outcomes (money received through increased tax compliance, lower levels of pollutants, reduction in injuries, and so on) (Braithwaite 2003a; Eckert 2004; Gray and Scholz 1993; Roos and Roos 1972), so the success of regimes with clear, measurable outcomes may, in part, be an artefact of the needs of the evaluation methodology itself. Nonetheless, there is strong evidence that regulation can be effective in certain circumstances.

What about the need for enforcement? Does effective regulation need to be enforced? Here the results are mixed, and the clear answer is 'it depends'. There is some evidence that simply having a regulatory requirement can, independently from enforcement lead to increased standards (Eggert and Ellegard 2003; Gunningham, et al. 2005), and that inspections with no further regulatory action may also have some, albeit small, improvement on performance (Eckert 2004). But, there is clearly an issue of context here, with other studies showing that an absence of enforcement means that regulatory requirements are routinely ignored (Nyborg and Telle 2006; Thornton, Kagan and Gunningham 2008). Evaluation of the effectiveness of enforcement in occupational health and safety shows enforcement to be an important element of lower injury rates (Gray and Scholz 1993). Such a finding is silent, however, on whether such enforcement is considered criminal or not (Haines and Hall 2004). Indeed, as I have argued elsewhere criminal prosecution may well have a more important role in responding to victims' needs for justice and in changing public perceptions about non-compliance and its resulting devastation. Criminal prosecution, then, acts to denounce rather than deter (Haines and Hall 2004). Overall, however, adequate enforcement often appears as an important component of a robust regulatory regime.

This finding is further strengthened when attention is turned to the effectiveness of governance strategies that draw on self-regulatory impulses at varying distances from government. Governance when realised as government-sponsored voluntary programmes where 'the market' does the work does not appear to be promising. Here, research contains some important lessons. Voluntary programmes may work in encouraging those industry leaders who pride themselves in their capacity to reduce their impact on the environment, for example (Coglianese and Nash 2006; Gunningham 2009; Koehler 2007). But it is difficult to gauge whether improvements actually stem from the programme or the orientation of the firm to show continuously improving standards (Coglianese and Nash 2006; Gunningham 2009). Further, encouraging the uptake of voluntary programmes to those with a lower substantive commitment may lead to a cancelling out of early gains (Koehler 2007). Overall, there appears little to commend a government-sponsored voluntary programme as a regulatory strategy that has robust integrity in improving standards (Coglianese and Nash 2006; Koehler 2007; Parker 1999b).

Governance approaches that are generated largely outside of government auspices also have mixed results, although some approaches may be promising. There are examples of industry self-regulation that have been effective such as the nuclear power industry in the wake of Three Mile Island (Rees 1994). Responsible Care, a self-regulatory initiative of the chemical industry, however, has a much more mixed score card (Gunningham 2009; Gunningham and Grabosky 1998; Koehler 2007). Others, such as ISO 14000 the initiative of the International Organization for Standardization and the Forestry Stewardship Council accreditation scheme, where there is external auditing appear, though, to have some success (Gunningham and Grabosky 1998; Koehler 2007; Meidinger 2006).

However, the 'gap' between the aspirations of the regulatory regime and the reality on the ground remains significant in many areas. Further, it is recognised that the capacity of regulation and enforcement to bridge that gap alone is too optimistic. Simply put, the concerns of the regulated workplace may be at some distance from those of the regulator. Attention may be directed elsewhere (Heimer 2008). The independent pressures on the regulated industry and firm that either enhance or undermine regulatory compliance and an improvement in standards is critical to consider (Haines 2005). Key amongst these is the economic pressures on a given business. If the profit levels are so tight that improved standards and/or compliance is not compatible with staying in business, then lower standards and non-compliance is the likely result (Gezelius 2002; 2003; Haines 1997; Holley and Gunningham 2006; Kagan, Gunningham and Thornton 2003; Thornton, et al. 2008).

Norms and the social setting of compliance are also important. Where there is strong social disapproval for non-compliance or where local community groups are vigorously monitoring the activities of their local chemical plant or pulp mill compliance and improved standards are likely (Gezelius 2002; 2003; Gunningham, et al. 2005; Kagan, et al. 2003). Finally, the legitimacy of the law and the regulator is important to consider. Where a government and their regulatory regime are seen as legitimate, then a normative orientation towards compliance is enhanced (Gezelius 2002; 2003).

Overall, then, the effectiveness of a regulatory regime is contoured by the independent pressures and opportunities that exist within a particular regulated context. While these various pressures may improve compliance and elevate standards, there are clearly plenty of examples where they do not. Clearly, regulation alone may be relatively powerless where economic conditions are tough, normative expectations of compliance are non-existent and the perceived legitimacy of government law.

But effective regulation, too, needs to be regulation that remains in place once it has proved its worth. Effective regulation needs to be resilient in the face of those determined to see its removal. Clearly, political philosophies and projects have the capacity to undermine the longevity of effective regulation. Neil Gunningham's (2009) historical overview of environmental regulation in Australia points to the very real impact of a neo-liberal agenda of small government on the form government-initiated regulation took in that country. He argues that the push to reduce, deregulate and build on a governance approach led to a significant shift away from 'command and control' regulation based around mandating specific technologies and a punitive approach to non-compliance, towards a more educative, persuasive regulatory style that sought to maximise the voluntary efforts of firms to reduce their impact on the environment. His assessment is that these reforms led to worse outcomes since they only influenced those firms who had high standards to begin with. These reforms were, he argues, part of a neo-liberal programme committed to a public choice interpretation of the self-interested bureaucrat and the inherent self-regulatory capacity of the market. Such reforms had, at least temporarily, the effect of turning the state's attention away from concentrated attention of the overall impact of business on the environment.

How resilient effective regulation is to business and political pressure, then, is clearly an important consideration in what regulation can achieve and what it cannot. Indeed, there are numerous examples of the way political pressure and lobbying as well as political self-censorship results in ineffective or non-existent regulation. Examples here are found in securities (Reichman 1998) environmental (Christoff 2006; McCright and Dunlap 2003; Pearce 2007; Thornton, et al. 2008) and mine safety regulation (Curran 1993). This would suggest that regulation that does not have political support would be likely either to not exist, or to be significantly flawed.

Instrumentalism, Regulation and Modernity

Answering the question 'does good regulation work?' though, takes us into broader terrain and in particular to take a close look at the challenges of instrumentalism as a principal method of progressing human and environmental wellbeing. As argued above, a key rationale for the need to regulate is the amelioration of some tightly defined harm or the raising of standards, whether aimed at improving safety, environmental health or the standard of financial reporting. The pursuit of instrumental goals is a dominant understanding of the purpose of regulation.

The emphasis on an instrumental purpose behind regulation, of 'problem solving' is not surprising. Regulatory reform may occur for a range of reasons including industrial restructuring; privatisation and the potential harmful side-effects of new technology can generate regulatory reform, as can broader political programmes for harmonisation (Ayres and Braithwaite 1992; Black 2005a; Levi-Faur 2005). Yet, regulation often arises in the context of some regulatory 'crisis' (Hancher and Moran 1998) such as a high-profile incident (Black 2005b; Boin and t'Hart 2003; Paterson 2000) and is designed to 'solve' that crisis or prevent recurrence of disaster.

Once designed and implemented, regulation, as it has been well-aired in various literatures can be counter-productive (Grabosky 1995; Lin, Beck, Stewart and Garbutt 2007; Sunstein 1990b). A significant challenge, though, may result *not* because regulation is poorly targeted, but because regulation by definition concentrates on a series of narrow goals. It is this instrumentalism that may well be the source of a number of problems. So, a narrow focus on cartel enforcement, for example, may in the long term result in greater concentration of industry and lower the competitiveness of markets (Braithwaite 2008). Ultimately, the result is mega-corporations which, as is argued in the current crisis, are 'too big' to let fail. So, some financial regulation may be successful at achieving its aims, yet the cyclical nature of financial crises (Calavita, Pontell and Tillman 1997; Clarke, Dean and Oliver 2003; Ferguson 2008; Kindleberger and Aliber 2005) again casts doubt on the capacity of targeted regulation to decrease levels of financial harm wrought by corporations. This pattern is repeated in other areas. Whilst it may be true that through carefully targeted regulation, work (for some) has become a much safer activity and place (Braithwaite 1985), it is unclear whether the workplace overall has become a healthier or happier place. In many jurisdictions, for example, levels of asbestosis and mesothelioma continue to rise (Kazan-Allen 2005). Further, the impact of psycho-social diseases such as stress, which has a clear impact on physical and mental health is largely unmeasured and unavailable (LaMontagne, Shaw, Ostry, Louie and Keegal 2006). Safety at work is notoriously difficult to measure, and attempts to measure the disease burden from work as a whole are few and far between. As we have seen above the impact of regulation on the environment also has had targeted successes, but the overall impact of industry on the environment reveals a much less clear picture, particularly in the face of challenges around anthropogenic climate change (Garnaut 2008; Guruswamy 1991; Popper, Lempert and Bankes 2005).

If this is true, then, it simply may not be possible to surgically remove the harms from a given activity and leave only the benefits as the rationale behind more and more tightly targeted regulation would suggest. For example, the harm targeted by regulation might be closely intertwined with certain publicly desirable benefits. Removing the harm may not be possible without undermining the benefits of the original activity (Sutton and Haines 2003). The capacity of regulation to act as a 'surgical bombing raid' without collateral damage may be limited. Hence, the regimes that do occur may pursue goals that on the one hand seem to have obvious merit but are those that are seen as acceptable by all parties and do not create problems in their wake. Further, the harms and benefits of both economic activity and regulation are unevenly distributed. Where benefits accrue to those with economic and political resources and the harms to those with fewer resources to draw on, change to redress the balance in either markets or regulation is less likely (Sutton and Haines 2003).

However, the commitment to an instrumental 'problem solving' ethos is an enduring one in contemporary society. The ubiquity of regulation with this rationale brings to the fore a realisation that instrumentalism may usefully be understood as intrinsic to modernity (Teubner 1998). It is, if you like, the quintessential tool of the enlightenment, part of ongoing rationalisation and ordering processes of contemporary society. But, as suggested above, it may well be one with some corrosive effects (Habermas 1989a).

Seen in this light, it is worth reflecting further on the challenges associated with instrumentalism as the basic premise behind regulation. Here, I take as a starting point Weber's analysis of instrumentalism as an ongoing process of rationalisation. There are several features of note here. In Weberian terms rationalisation involves in part a tighter and tighter definition of both means and ends. It is a process fraught with paradoxical possibilities (Weber 1964 [1947]; 1991 [1925]). Rationalisation, for Weber, was the transformation of a value (in the case of regulation the value attached to the reduction of some form of risk) into a formal rule-based system (in this case a regulatory regime) (Gerth and Mills 1991 [1948] pp.43–51; Giddens 1995; Weber 1964 [1947]; 1991 [1925]). When a particular crisis occurs: an explosion occurs at a chemical facility or some form of critical infrastructure is attacked by a terrorist group, a consensus is formed around reducing that risk. Reducing the potential for future disaster is valued, and the need to translate this valuing of human life, or prevention of financial disaster is transformed into a set of regulations.

Yet, for Weber, problems were inevitable. Indeed, his central thesis was that value commitments when institutionalised as formal laws, the rules and protocols inevitably fall prey to the problem of 'the iron cage', where rules proliferate and yet the spirit of the law persists in escaping the letter. There are two related problems: the first is ritualism where compliance with rules becomes perfunctory and lacks the capacity to generate meaningful change and the second arises where the rules created are used as a vehicle in the pursuit of alternative ends.

Both ritualism and strategic compliance are endemic challenges for those committed to seeing substantive improvements resulting from regulation. The challenge of perfunctory attention being given to a process that is designed to engage participants in a serious, thoughtful, consideration of risk and risk reduction is well canvassed in the regulatory literature. Commentary, research and analysis highlights the problem of ritual compliance both for those wishing to see the regulatory reform process taken seriously (Carroll 2008) and for compliance challenges in a diverse range of regulatory regimes (see for example, Braithwaite 2008; Hopkins 2002b; Parker and Lehmann Neilsen 2006). Auditing and monitoring regimes, in particular, are seen as vulnerable to ritual compliance (Power 1997)

Recognised problems of ritualism extend beyond the regulatory literature. Indeed, much of the thrust of institutionalist writing takes this aspect of rationalisation as a cue and demonstrates how rules are developed and designed not to be effective at the level of compliance but in bolstering the legitimacy of the rule-maker (Meyer and Rowan 1977; Powell and DiMaggio 1991).

Yet, regulation and compliance encompass not only the institutional processes that affect the rule maker, but distinct institutional frameworks and influences on those charged with compliance (Haines 2009a). Where the legitimacy of regulations is in doubt from those with economic and knowledge resources, the rules then can become pawns in an entirely different game. Compliance based on a strategic form of rationality surfaces (Habermas 1989a). Clearly, this problem is well evident in tax, where those at the top who choose not to pay tax have a good (and legal) chance of not doing so (Braithwaite 2003b). Rules and regulations in a range of financial settings are the tools for some to creatively comply (McBarnet and Whelan 1999; Shah 1996) to generate ever-more creative ways of making money. Instrumental approaches thus enable non-compliance by creating the loopholes through which the unscrupulous may pass.

But there are other dimensions to rationalisation that are important here. Rationalisation, Weber understood, was an intellectual project where expertise develops in multiple fields to refine both goals and means (Giddens 1995). Here, regulation as rationalisation is a process of intellectualisation. An understanding of the challenges of the regulatory endeavour here would emphasise the way regulatory reform and regulatory compliance seeks out expertise in order to ascertain the exact cause of risk/harm to be addressed and hence the most effective risk reduction measure. Indeed, this seems entirely positive and a desirable outcome.

The potential paradox here, from a Weberian perspective is that good outcomes may fail to inspire the broader public. There is, associated with this intellectual engagement, the problem of disenchantment. The necessary clinical dissection of cause and effect, for Weber, stripped away the central concerns of the population for an appreciation of meaning and social significance. What was required was for politicians to provide the necessary passion to adopt and employ the methods demanded by the clinical assessment or analysis (Giddens 1995; Weber 1991 [1948]). Political passion, then, is critical to regulation. Without it a regulatory project, however effective in reducing a specific risk, will be seriously weakened as it fails to inspire the broader public.

A related element here is Weber's position that value conflict was not amenable to rational debate. The expertise developed could not convince those with competing value positions of the rightness of their view. This is because we build our rationality around our values. Hence, a Weberian approach would emphasise how rational debate cannot resolve value differences around which harms should attract regulatory attention and which should not. Again, this position emphasises the centrality of politics and in particular perhaps charisma and the importance of politicians as 'statesmen' and 'stateswomen' in providing a sense of direction and coherence to a regulatory project. If the choice of where to regulate and what to regulate is more about values than a rational assessment, the act of regulation may be more about the creation of meaning and significance, and less about actual effectiveness on the ground.

Directing attention back to the earlier discussion of 'good regulation' suggests that decisions around what comprises 'good regulation' are not the result of rational debate and assessment alone. Arguably, what passes as good regulation in the policy documentation discussed above rather can be viewed as a rationalistic approach to accommodating multiple demands and value positions with an overlay of demands for 'accountability' and 'transparency' that reassure a wary audience that government may be doing something that threatens their beliefs, values or interests.

From an optimistic frame of reference, (and with a prior particular value position, Weber would suggest) it is possible to see the shift away from an uncompromising neo-classical free market stance and towards a 'rational evidence-based' programme that enshrines a greater commitment to humanistic values as a positive development. It is entirely consistent with the enlightenment project of creating the good society through the rational efforts of humankind. The 'invisible hand' of the market is to be disciplined by the visible, accountable and transparent hand of the regulator. A good society is achieved by regulatory control of the market, in the words of former Prime Minister Kevin Rudd the vision is of a 'social-democratic approach to properly regulated markets and the proper role of the state ...' Social democrats, then, conceptualise society as existing beyond the market. Regulation or rather regulatory reform and deregulatory imperatives no longer can ride roughshod over hard-won rights. One concrete example of this is the way regulatory reform processes in some jurisdictions (such as in the State of Victoria) include requirements to take account of human rights charters and legislation. Further, regulation can and should be oriented to give effect to those rights (Darian-Smith and Scott 2009).

From a more sceptical stance, however, it is possible to read developments in regulatory reform as an example of institutional hypocrisy, of policymaking that has resulted from political negotiations over conflicting value positions that simply result in policies that are impossible to implement (Brunsson 2002). Regulation is the result of ideological conflict, where the rule represents a temporary truce (Gibbs 1996; Haines and Gurney 2003). The tangible results are regulatory regimes that encompass incompatible objectives: such as the demands that good regulation be both 'flexible' and 'consistent and predictable'. Regulators who are in the political spotlight may well come in for criticism for attempting to be flexible, and then being charged with being inconsistent, or when opting for consistency and being criticised for being inflexible. Such non-commensurable aspirations, then, may well be ripe for exploitation by different sections of society each vying for their values and interests to be evident in the eventual regime.

If this has any truth to it, requiring regulators to take more, and yet more, issues into consideration in designing and giving effect to regulation is to ask too much. Regulation simply may not be capable of dealing with the complexity of current financial markets (Kahn 1990) or with the significant harms generated by contemporary market-based economies. Really responsive regulation (Baldwin and Black 2008), for example, may simply be an aspiration too far. At the very least, we should be alert to how we may assist regulators to deal with complexity and political gamesmanship. Solutions may not lie in assuming regulators have more agency than they actually do to solve such complexity or, as regulatory reformers tend to do, suggesting that simple answers can be found to highly complex problems (Walker 2008).

CONCLUSION AND IMPLICATIONS FOR THE STUDY

Regulation appears well characterised as a paradox. It came to prominence at a time when political emphasis lay on the capacity of markets and competition to bring the greatest public benefit. Arguably, predictions were that less and less regulation would be needed as markets and, in particular, competition brought benefits in the form of greater economic wealth and a greater array of products and services that could reach across the globe.

But this has not happened. Rather multiple regulatory regimes have proliferated and debates continue to rage around what level of regulatory control, emanating from what source and in what particular form should be adopted at any one time and in response to an array of regulatory crises. Part of this proliferation can be understood as a widening of the definition of the term as regimes of control extending beyond government and at times without any government involvement are brought under scrutiny as new forms of 'regulation'. Not all of the rapid expansion of regulation can be understood in terms of semantics and a changing focus of attention, however. This chapter pointed to complex and competing pressures that give contemporary regulatory regimes their dynamic character. The shift to governance approaches including government sponsored voluntary programmes, an emphasis on the powers of self-regulation and a lesser prominence given to 'command and control' approaches is met with resistance and demands for greater state involvement, of more law and tougher law enforcement.

Part of the dynamism here is found in the pursuit of 'good regulation', where policymakers and scholars develop forms of regulation that are argued to be both more efficient and more effective. Within the regulatory reform field, this remains largely a project of ensuring less regulation, albeit perhaps with a corollary that whatever regulation we do end up with must be the most efficient sharply defined and transparent set of rules and requirements. Yet, distinct differences are found in the animating values and views that result in programmes aimed at generating robust and well-honed rules. To this is added the distinct contribution of regulatory scholars who, whilst sharing a belief in the capacity of markets to bring benefit, differ from reformers in key ways. Gone are conceptions of light-handed regulation. Regulation is an important tool in the pursuit of health, environmental sustainability and in making markets work to the benefit of most. A commitment to the substantive goals espoused by a regulatory regime makes the contribution of regulatory scholars distinct.

Such scholarship draws attention to evidence that appropriately targeted, sufficiently enforced regulatory regimes can be effective in achieving their goal. But, there are significant contextual factors to consider. Important to the success of a regime are economic and normative considerations, for example, as well as beliefs in the legitimacy and authority of both the regulator and the government.

This chapter argued, however, that greater attention to the paradox inherent within regulation as an instrumental endeavour is warranted. Instrumentalism has become the defining feature of regulation and, as shown by evaluation, with some justification. But, there are chronic challenges. The finely honed goals of particular regimes can create myopia where broader, more entrenched challenges can arise. Drawing on Weberian insights, the latter part of the chapter pointed to the challenges of creative compliance but perhaps more significantly the limits to the intellectual project on regulation in assisting decisions about which problems and what regulations are appropriate and when. Such an analysis pointed to the centrality of politics to the regulatory project. Technical assessments of regulatory effectiveness or appropriateness, then, may have only a small role to play in showing the way forward.

The implications of the analysis above for the empirical study in this book are as follows. The discussion above suggests the need to develop an understanding of the challenges of compliance in light of those that surround reform since underlying both may be a complex relationship between political and instrumental goals. That is, fruitful empirical work may assist us in understanding how reform and compliance are both separate but also interrelated elements of regulation. So, it may help us understand not only more about the conditions under which good regulation can arise as well as those under which compliance is best achieved, but also how challenges in reform affect compliance and how challenges in compliance lead to further reform efforts. In short, the empirical analysis presented in this book attempts to unravel what the conditions are that are best to enable and nurture the emergence of effective regulation and how these same conditions affect compliance and the relationship between the two. To assist in this analysis the goals of regulation are first placed in a broader context to enable an understanding of precisely what kinds of problems, instrumental and political, regulation is asked to solve.

NOTES

1. Speech to the Sydney Institute 26 February 2008.
2. 12 February 2009 http://www.aph.gov.au/hansard/senate/dailys/ds120209.pdf
3. *The Monthly*, February 2009.
4. Of course, instrumental forms of regulation also have a long history, exemplified by the regulation of working hours and health and safety arising out of the industrial revolution (see W.G. Carson (1974) 'Symbolic and Instrumental Dimensions of Early Factory Legislation: A Case Study in the Social Origins of Criminal Law'. In: Hood, R. (ed). *Crime, Criminology and Public Policy: Essays in Honour of Sir Leon Radnowicz.* London: Heinemann, 107–138. Marvel, H.P. (1977). 'Factory Regulation: A Reinterpretation of Early English Experience'. *The Journal of Law and Economics*, 20 (2):379–402) to the regulation of weights and measures for many centuries before that. However, arguably what characterises current debates on regulation is the almost exclusive emphasis on the pursuit of instrumental goals.
5. Available at http://my.barackobama.com/page/community/post/samgrahamfelsen/gGBNsq (accessed 8 March 2009).
6. And in contrast to Bronwen Morgan's (2003) definition where meta-regulation is the regulation of the regulators as discussed above.
7. Clearly, this view shares similarities with the emphasis of many occupational health and safety and environmental regulators with 'continuous improvement'.
8. Clearly, the definition of 'good outcomes' also can vary between those who would look to the outcomes in terms of economic indicators of employment and economic growth and those who would take greater account of evaluations of a reducing of environmental harm, enhanced standards of health and safety, greater levels of tax compliance and so on. Arguably, it is the success or otherwise of regulatory reform that should manifest in economic indicators, and the success of the regulatory regime in terms of reducing risk on the ground. Hence, I am concerned here with the instrumental impact of regulation in terms of the environment, safety and so on.

3. Risk and the task of regulation

Bournemouth Borough Council has barred its pools from lending arm-bands and rubber rings to children. They might get an infection blowing them up, it seems, and the Council might be liable if they punctured. Better that the children drown uninfected but with the Council in the clear. Better that they risk swimming with no arm-bands (their own fault) than that the Council risks blame from the (much lower) risk that the supplied arm-bands might leak ... *The Oxford Agenda*[1]

More than 200 schools have been closed in south-eastern Australia as the government warned of an intensified fire risk ahead of the weekend. A lack of rain and a predicted change in wind has made conditions the most dangerous in recent weeks. *BBC News Channel*[2]

Former Vice President Dick Cheney said Sunday that President Obama had made the country less safe, asserting that the new administration's changes to detention and interrogation programs for terrorism suspects would hamper intelligence gathering. Mr. Cheney said the moves suggested that terrorism was now being treated as a law enforcement problem. "He is making some choices that, in my mind, will, in fact, raise the risk to the American people of another attack," Mr. Cheney said of Mr. Obama in an interview on the CNN program 'State of the Union.' *New York Times*[3]

The central argument of this chapter is that close attention to the breadth and complexity of risk provides a fruitful complement to the previous chapter's emphasis on the enduring presence of instrumentalism and politics in regulation. The quotes above attest to the breadth of circumstances where something or someone is identified as 'risky', which seems to complicate rather than clarify issues around regulation. Can we understand, for example, the risk of infection from blowing up a rubber ring in the same way as we understand the risk of bushfire in an increasingly arid Australia, or the risk of a terrorist attack? This chapter argues we can, but to do so requires a nuanced understanding of the connection between risk and regulation, one that can tease apart what risks regulation is used to control and against which risks it is most likely to be effective.

Certainly, the control of undesirable risk is a central justification for regulation (Hutter 2001; 2005). Further, the decades of regulatory reform aimed at a 'best practice' model, outlined in Chapter 2, suggest that a wide variety of risks can be subjected to scientific and technical analysis in order to determine when regulatory intervention is necessary and what techniques would best suit the risk in question. According to this approach, expert scrutiny will provide the facts to allow bureaucrats to make rational decisions so that serious risks will be suitably controlled and regulation eschewed when risk is low. In this world of rational policymaking, the risk of infection from blowing up a rubber ring would be adequately assessed in light of the need to learn to swim, the loss of life from bushfire eliminated and overall security enhanced.

Yet, are all risks commensurable? Commensurability would appear to be essential for the connection between risk and regulation to be robust. Indeed, discussions around risk and regulatory reform are based on the assumption that it is not only possible but *necessary* to measure and compare across the spectrum of risks facing society at any one time, in order to prioritise resources (see for example Sunstein 2005; Viscusi 1992). Risks, from infection at the local swimming pool to global terrorism are seen as amenable to a common process: assessment and measurement of the threat and a technical assessment of the most cost-effective means of risk reduction. This, it is argued, enables effective prioritisation of risks and allows for the most efficient employment of scarce resources (Sunstein 2005).

Clearly, however, bringing about this state of affairs has proved challenging. *The Oxford Agenda* above expresses frustration at the way 'minor' risks are targeted, how the risk of infection threatens to swamp children's capacity to take the necessary risks in learning to swim. Fear of legal liability, it is argued, distorts the political process and leads to risk aversion – in particular aversion to the 'wrong' kinds of risk. Such pessimism fits well with the discussion in the previous chapter centred on the proliferation of regulation in the face of longstanding attempts to reduce government intervention. Despite vociferous arguments by some that greater scientific rigor is required and that many of the risks we face may not warrant heavy-handed government intervention (see for example Viscusi 1992) regulation has increased. For those who would agree with the sentiment expressed in *The Oxford Agenda* above, this threatens our capacity to take the necessary risks that can enhance our overall wellbeing.

This chapter explores whether more effective regulation might result from a greater emphasis on risk assessment and risk management. Should we redouble our efforts to ensure rigorous risk analyses are undertaken before we regulate, ones that can strip away 'irrational' assessments of risk? There is considerable support for such a strategy. Indeed, the second quote above expressing the heightened risk around bushfires in the summer of 2009 in Victoria points to the need for a greater understanding of the threats from bushfire and the need to devise better ways of protecting communities from the devastation of such fires. Strident arguments were made in the wake of the devastation about sentimental emotional attachments to native vegetation and 'city slicker' green sensibilities that stood in the way of the need to protect life and property. In short, that 'cold, hard facts' were needed to inform the most effective solution (Institute of Foresters of Australia 2009; Packham 2009).

The argument presented below suggests that there are problems with placing an exclusive emphasis on the capacity of scientific and technical assessments of risk in providing sufficient information to generate good regulatory outcomes. One obvious problem is where a rigorous risk assessment cannot be made with a reasonable degree of accuracy (such as in the case of terrorism). But, even where the relevant assessment is easier to obtain there are doubts regarding whether this information will be persuasive in bringing about effective policies aimed to enhance human wellbeing. There are reasons to question whether scientific or technical assessments can provide a sound basis to ensure that tougher controls will be forthcoming where the risk is deemed by the experts to be sufficiently high, or that less regulation will eventuate where the assessment points to little justification for such action.

The shortcomings to an overreliance on technical assessments of risk lie both with the political nature of regulation and with too narrow a framing of how risk and regulation are connected. As we saw in Chapter 2, carefully targeted regulation may well be effective in reducing some risks, but this does not guarantee that such regulation will be forthcoming. Political needs intervene. Further the analysis of regulation in Chapter 2 argued that instrumental regulation may not be the most appropriate means to address the specific problem a society faces at any particular time. Regulation's instrumental form may render it limited in tackling certain social problems. Yet, regulation may still be imposed despite the lack of a sound basis for believing the new regulatory regime will actually solve the problem.

Close attention to the nature of risk can help us to understand the seemingly 'irrational' quality to regulatory intervention that is too much regulation where none would seem warranted and too little where it could be extremely valuable. Debates around risk are much richer than statements about the impact and likelihood of occurrence of a particular hazard and what effective control looks like. These debates hold important clues about what is meant when something is referred to as 'risky' or 'a risk'. Analysis of the various meanings of risk reveals potentially important connections between 'risk' and regulation. For this reason, public debates about risk should not be too easily dismissed as part of the problem of the propagation of 'irrational' beliefs about what is risky and what is not.

For example, pronouncements about risk need to be analysed in light of their intended audience. It is important to analyse how risk is used to situate a speaker within a particular community or nation. Take former Vice President Dick Cheney's concerns as expressed at the beginning of this chapter. He is surely implying more than the Obama administration is putting US security at risk by not undertaking a rigorous assessment of the threat posed by terrorism.

Critical here is his appeal to the 'American public' on the parlous nature of their security since President Obama came to office, and a claim that the Republican side of politics could (and did) provide a greater level of safety from outside threat.

In drawing attention to the political and social nature of risk, however, I do not wish to disregard technical and scientific assessments and reconfigure risks as essentially socially constructed and/or irredeemably subjective (either at the level of individual psyche or cultural sensibility). Rather, I would take my cue from authors such as Latour (2005) Murphy (2001) and Sayer (1997) in preserving the independence of what I term actuarial risk, such as the physical or financial threat explicitly identified by a particular party (sometimes labelled the 'hazard') together with the assessment of the probability of such a threat coming to fruition. In Latour's words such a physical potential (often as experienced in the past) acts and has an influence, in this case on regulatory policy. Such a reality cannot be replaced by political reconstruction or cultural expectations.

The analysis below suggests that risk may usefully be understood as a complex of three independent yet intersecting ideal types: one actuarial, the second socio-cultural and the third political. Actuarial risk forms the dominant motif for an understanding of risk as it is conceptualised within a regulatory analysis. But, it is an incomplete conceptualisation of risk and hence the ways risk and regulation relate to one another. Social and cultural norms also are important. Durkheim's (1964) insights into how various 'taboos' provide meaning essential to maintaining social cohesion resonate as much with contemporary societies as with those of the past (Douglas 1992). What is seen as risky or rather dangerous are threats to 'proper' order and place. Opinions and concerns with what is risky and what is not fundamentally are tracing and retracing the contours of a given society. To illustrate, the commentators of *The Oxford Agenda* see threats to *risk-taking* as dangerous, because they threaten our way of life where children learn to take risks – and that is what it means to be human (perhaps in this case to be English!). The writer here is communicating about the risks to 'our way of life' as much as writing of actuarial risk (arguably more so). This does not mean the actuarial risk does not exist, infections from swimming pools do occur and people who cannot swim may drown if left stranded in deep water; but there is much more being expressed here about risk than these specific actuarial risk concerns of infection and drowning.

As Douglas (1992) argues these normative and reciprocal expectations around order are ripe for political manipulation. Indeed, her argument is they are always political. Politicians and various interest groups within society aim to generate popular concerns and hence to influence social mores (and retain or gain power) (Douglas 1992; Erikson 2005; Gusfield 1963). But, just as I would want to retain actuarial risk as a distinct type, so too I would argue to keep socio-cultural risk as separable from political risk. In particular, the contests around and manipulation of socio-cultural risk needs itself to be subject to scrutiny and understood in light of the contemporary challenges faced by governments within capitalist democracies. Political risk involves threats to authority, in particular governments. Here I take my cue from Habermas (Habermas 1979; 1989c; 1996). Exhortations around threats and risks can be devices to enable a political administration to secure mass loyalty. Populist measures provide one means to do so. But, political risk is more than just securing mass loyalty (that is, legitimation) by ascribing who 'we are' and who 'we are not'. It also arises from an incapacity to steer the economy in order to provide the necessary financial resources to the state (Habermas 1979; 1989c). The potential and problems with managing a capitalist economy form a fundamental component of political risk.

In summary, I suggest that actuarial, socio-cultural and political risk need to be analysed separately. Each is generated from independent sources within society and each one affects how regulation develops and a regulatory framework's capacity to generate positive outcomes. Critically, such an analysis must not reduce the complexity of risk into simple binary categories of 'real/imagined', 'rational/irrational' or 'objective/subjective' where one group argues that they understand through rational calculus the real, objective risk at hand, whilst others (perhaps emotionally driven) fall victim to irrational fears borne of a limited subjective frame of reference. In contrast, the argument here is that each of these risk types has integrity. Attempts to dismiss one or more ideal types as 'irrational' or 'subjective' (or alternatively 'arrogant', 'elitist' and 'condescending') is to oversimplify the nature of risk in contemporary society and the role regulation plays in risk management. In the pursuit of good regulation, it is not possible to take account of one aspect of risk only.

I would shy away, however, from creating three distinct categories and placing a particular risk unambiguously and uniquely as 'actuarial', 'socio-cultural' or 'political'. There is no neat dividing line delimiting where one form of risk ends and another begins. Actuarial risk, socio-cultural risk and political risk are better understood rather as ideal types so as to retain the way they push and pull 'necessary' and 'adequate' and 'effective' regulation in various ways but without ignoring the connections between each. Further, I would draw from Latour (2005) to argue that the connection between risk types (as actors) is key. The connection between these various types of risk as well as their independent effects on regulation are important to trace.

It is important to explore in some detail the parameters of each type of risk introduced above. In doing so, the strengths of a regulatory response and the challenges each risk poses to 'good regulation' become clearer. Detailed analysis also helps tease apart both the strengths and the weaknesses to prominent methods (such as cost benefit analysis) for deciding where regulatory resources are best utilised. From this discussion a more collaborative approach appears as promising, yet it also faces considerable hurdles. To meet all three risk challenges – actuarial, socio-cultural and political – the potential for collaboration may still be premised on a political vision that can provide space for productive debate that enhances the capacity of regulation used appropriately and designed in a manner to be effective.

ACTUARIAL RISK

At the heart of actuarial risk is the reality of harm: in the case of industrial disasters, this is the explosion or fire that results in loss of life, injury and environmental pollution; in the case of the terrorist's bomb, it is similarly the deaths and injuries that ensue. Such harm that arises from the realisation of an actuarial risk may be self-evident, but it also may be elusive. Actuarial risks can surprise us; they can elude our best attempts to capture them and reveal where they lie. To help us cope with this, there exist bodies of knowledge developed over time that relay to us a more accurate picture of what to be wary of and where we might safely go about our everyday business without concern. But, actuarial risks can remain uncertain, with causal mechanisms incompletely understood, or unrelentingly complex with the resulting body of knowledge imperfect and open to multiple legitimate interpretations.

Who is most at risk, and the process of avoiding actuarial risks also can be counter-intuitive. This is even the case where the potential harm is self-evident since the methods of avoiding actuarial risks may be anything but. Examples are not hard to find; three I mention here. An obvious example is the way many of us might intuitively run for shelter under a tree in a thunder storm, only to be killed by the tree as it falls when struck by lightening. An actuarial risk assessment could recommend staying out in the rain during an electrical storm if there is no robust building to shelter in; we would get wet but we would be safer from a lightning strike. Secondly, despite the greater concern being with the threat to physical safety of young women out at night, equal if not greater risk of harm exists for young men (ABS 2005). Parents concerned with such safety could be better advised to keep their sons under equally as tight supervision as their daughters. Despite this, daughters often remain more tightly controlled. A third example is provided by asbestos, the silent killer that is (in my home country Australia) ubiquitous. Under certain circumstances, removing some forms of asbestos from a building where the fibres have been well-secured in resin or covered with paint can create a much higher risk than leaving it well alone. Knowing the location of the secured asbestos and keeping the material well-maintained can be a better way to ensure the fibres do not become airborne rather than disturbing them. Despite this, demands for removal of all asbestos from some public buildings (even when well-secured) can arise. Well-known risks, then, do not necessarily lead to 'obvious' avoidance strategies.

This Machiavellian quality of actuarial risk gives rise to strident arguments about which of our fears are rational and which are not. Rational fears are argued to be those based on a 'realistic' assessment of risk. Often we are dependent upon experts to tell us what is safe in terms of actuarial risk. They tell us, for example, that it is safer to take an aeroplane than to take the same journey by car. Yet many of us fear flying whilst remaining quite at ease driving on the road. Other experts are then on hand to tell us why there is a difference between our fears and 'real' levels of risk. Psychological studies of risk perception (see for example Slovic 1987) have been developed to investigate why we are more afraid of actuarial risks in some circumstances than would seem warranted and less so in others.

Building Actuarial Knowledge: Risk Assessment and its Challenges

The assumption behind expert analysis of actuarial risks is that an objective assessment of the level of risk of a particular adverse event (its 'riskiness') is possible. There are several basic stages to such an assessment: an identification of the hazard (the adverse event or the harm), an elaboration of the causal mechanisms that result in the realisation of that adverse event, a calculation of probability that the event will occur and finally an estimation of overall risk, where the likelihood and the severity of the impact are combined. Some would argue for inclusion of a further step, namely an assessment of exposure and/or vulnerability of the likely affected population or region (Renn 2008 p.69).

Accurate risk assessments then are heavily dependent on requisite expertise with the capacity to develop sufficient knowledge about impact, cause and probability. Various techniques to aid the development of such knowledge are used including probabilistic methods for large technological systems (such as modelling interactions between causal mechanisms for explosion within a major hazard facility for example, or plume modelling for the dispersion of an airborne pollutant), dose-response effects leading to calculations of LD50, or the dose at which 50 per cent of experimental animals die, exposure assessments and epidemiological analyses amongst others (Renn 2008).

Clearly, the actuarial risks we are dealing with in this book extend beyond the technological risks that form a considerable component of the literature on actuarial risk. The risks of collapse of a financial system do not provide the possibility for a neat set of laboratory experiments, nor does the actuarial risk of experiencing a terrorist attack. Nonetheless, expertise in the calculation of probabilities and consequences for both of these risks has been developed (Bernstein 1996; Black 2005a; Willis 2005; Willis, Morral, Kelly and Medby 2005). So, despite the acknowledged difficulty and high levels of uncertainty attached to such assessments, actuarial calculations (based on various models) exist that attempt to capture the likelihood and impact of various risks to financial integrity and of the risk of a terrorist attack.

Yet, there are differences here between assessments of various types of actuarial risk. For the world of finance, for example, there is a more explicit emphasis on the benefits of risk-taking (Bernstein 1996), building on the expectation that for those who take risks the rewards should accrue. Indeed, as we saw in Chapter 2 the debate around deregulation often is premised on the need for entrepreneurs to take financial risks in order to reap rewards both individually and for the benefit of the economy as a whole (see also Lupton 1999; O'Malley 2004). The benefits of taking risks, however, jar with a common regulatory orientation, for example within occupational health and safety, that those who take risks in their business should protect others from the harms they may generate (Haines and Sutton 2003). The desirability or otherwise of risk-taking, and by whom, may differ between actuarial risks that then shape how assessments are made. Differences can be found, too, between areas where there is an emphasis on quantitative skills and other arenas where professional judgement and a reluctance to quantify levels of actuarial risk are found (O'Malley 2004). In areas of finance, for example, risk management has been argued to move between a science and an art in recognition of its elusive and labile nature (Bernstein 1996). In the counter-terrorism arena, too, intelligence work and expert acumen are seen as critical to an effective overall assessment of actuarial risk (Willis 2005; Willis, Morral, Kelly and Medby 2005). In these areas actuarial risk assessments centrally involve identifying either 'dangerous' people and/or complex motives that lie behind human behaviour that pose particular challenges. Oversimplifying or ignoring the impact of human behaviour here may have catastrophic consequences. In the recent economic crisis the weakness of risk models underpinning assessment of financial integrity that ignored human behaviour were only too painfully revealed. In a wonderfully entitled piece 'The Model Made Me Do it' Matthew Stewart (2008) writes of the mistaken assumption underpinning financial risk assessment techniques:

> ... that financial markets operate in the manner of a physical process, subject to the iron laws of statistics, like atoms bouncing around in a thermodynamic equilibrium.[4] This beguiling analogy makes it too easy for geeks like me to lose sight of a timeless truth: If atoms could talk to one another, then the laws of thermodynamics would get broken every day by clouds of stampeding gases.

Actuarial Risk and Uncertainty

It is important to tease apart chronic challenges to actuarial risk assessments. Essentially, these relate to uncertainty, but uncertainty that comes in more than one form (Renn 2008 pp.75–8). Put simply, it may be relatively clear what it is we don't know; a situation Ortwin Renn labels simply 'uncertainty'. But, there may be complex interconnections between cause and effect with multiple causal networks and feedback loops. Here, we don't know what we don't know. Ecosystems and complex chemical interactions within industrial processes may suffer from high levels of complexity where uncertainty surrounds not only a single causal pathway but a composite 'soup' of multiple intersecting possible causal pathways. Then, there is the uncertainty of interpretation. Where uncertainty and/or complexity are present then there may well be more than one interpretation possible from the same pool of data, a situation Renn (2008) labels as 'ambiguous'. Uncertainty, complexity and ambiguity often surround debates on actuarial risk.

The different levels and combinations of uncertainty, complexity and ambiguity create different characteristics to individual actuarial risks. These characteristics appear to some as personalities, indeed Renn (2008 pp.161–6) draws on Greek mythology to classify actuarial risk. The result is evocative. He points to the risk class 'Damocles' where the extent of damage is high, but the probability of occurrence low. The visual image of the Sword of Damocles hanging by a thread speaks volumes on the actuarial risk posed by nuclear power, for example. Add to this Sunstein's (2003; 2005) findings that where impact is high, calculations of probability are often seen as meaningless and hence disregarded. Contrast Damocles to the risk class Pandora where there is considerable uncertainty around probability combined with the possibility of high damage. Think here of nanotechnology – tiny molecules able to pass the blood brain barrier. Or risk class Cassandra where both probability and impact are high – but the regulatory authority is not interested or not concerned. This would seem to be a classic description to the risks of anthropogenic climate change as well as the relentless and dramatic loss of biodiversity. Then there is Medusa, where both probability and impact are low, but there are high levels of public concern. Renn (2008) cites electromagnetic fields as an example of this class. To complete the analogy, there are the risk classes of Pythia and Cyclops, the former where uncertainty surrounds both probability and impact and the latter where there is clear knowledge of high impact but a one-dimensional understanding of probability.

Clearly, classification of actuarial risk in light of the levels of uncertainty and public perception of the risk in the manner above does not in itself generate better outcomes. But, as Renn (2008) points out, it does create the opportunity to discuss how different actuarial risks (in Renn's terminology 'risk classes') may well require different strategies of amelioration. There may well be cases where more research to try to clarify at least some of the uncertainty is needed. Or, in other classes what is needed is to find better methods of communication around risk and building confidence in the institutions created to ascertain levels of risk of one kind or another. This form of actuarial risk classification may also shed light on when there is likely to be an amplification of a particular actuarial risk or an attenuation of it within the public realm (Kasperson and Kasperson 1996). In the case of the Cassandras and Medusas more research may not be a top priority (indeed in the case of Cassandras it may be a classic bureaucratic or political stalling strategy (Bedsworth and Kastenberg 2002), but communication with and persuasion of key audiences is critical.

Uncertainty and Science

It is important here, however, to take a closer look at uncertainty. Within public debate, there is often recourse to a scientific 'fact' about a particular risk where scientific analysis 'proves' a particular state of affairs. Within the framework of science, however, actuarial assessments are accountable to the scientific method and with this terrain comes acknowledgement of uncertainty and fallibility. By their very nature, assessments of the riskiness of particular forms of actuarial risk sit on an uncertain foundation. Science understands itself as uncertain (Bedsworth and Kastenberg 2002; Beyea and Berger 2001; Popper, et al. 2005; Tilley 1980). The risk analyst's task is to use the scientific method to appreciate more accurately the nature of the hazard itself, the causal mechanisms for such an occurrence and the probability of such a situation arising. For many within the scientific community, assertions of 'fact' about the riskiness of a given chemical, for example, are often misleading since the essence of the scientific method is 'falsifiability' (Beyea and Berger 2001); what we know today about a given risk is contingent on tomorrow's experiment proving otherwise.

   This uncertainty, however, is not infinitely malleable. The scientific method almost always results in knowledge that is precarious, but it is not arbitrary since the aim is to allow an understanding that moves ever-closer to the object of enquiry (Tilley 1980). Scientists then are understood as '… imperfect eyewitnesses to the scientific enterprise' (Beyea and Berger 2001 p.364). Further, levels of uncertainty may not materially affect the need to take action in terms of regulation or risk management. Citing uncertainty as an 'a priori' reason not to act is disingenuous. We know, for example, that at some point unless sufficient precautions are taken a chemical plant will explode if there is sufficient build-up of flammable gasses in a confined area, with exposure to a source of ignition. Uncertainty may exist about the exact conditions that may precipitate a runaway chemical reaction resulting in a conflagration, but that does not detract from the fact that unless temperatures are kept within safe limits for a given chemical (including the temperature parameters of storage and processing vessels) and sources of unwanted ignition are eliminated then an explosion will result.

Uncertainty means, however, that expert views on particular forms of actuarial risk will change over time – risks may become more or less 'risky'. The uncertainties around a particular risk may, to an extent at least, be resolved by additional research. So, a risk that may be understood to belong to the class Pandora, for example, by virtue of uncertainties around both probability and impact may move towards Pythia (where uncertainties are, to an extent at least bounded even though there remains large margins for error), Medusa (where public concern is found but where the actuarial risks are small) or to Cassandra where the actuarial risks are high in both probability and impact. Measures put in place may also affect the threat posed by any actuarial risk (Renn 2008 pp.168–72). These may alter future assessments because of the risk controls undertaken, changing circumstances or because of increasing scientific or technical knowledge able to result in more accurate assessment of the particular risk.

However, Renn's (2008) approach may still rather oversimplify the problem of uncertainty, notwithstanding his emphasis on the need to take account of ambiguity, complexity and the unknown. There may well be particular challenges to be faced, for example, where actuarial risk involves intention to take risks or to harm. Chapter 2 pointed to the gaming involved in creative compliance strategies to elude risk controls. A risk assessment around a terrorist attack, too, may face similar difficulties with active circumvention of measures designed to reduce actuarial risk of attack. Secondly, uncertainty itself may be desirable. Pat O'Malley (2004), for example, argues that there is a need to take much greater account of uncertainty as a central feature of actuarial risk. In his view, there is not an inexorable movement towards greater certainty but rather a tension between risk and uncertainty. For some, uncertainty is not to be dispelled but embraced:

> Doubtless (risk) is a very salient principle; but the promotion of neoliberalism and entrepreneurial governance has also pressed a new *telos* of creative uncertainty to the foreground. Rather than concerning ourselves about a possibly futile exercise in measuring whether risk is 'spreading', we should recognise that risk and uncertainty are *both* being valorised in new ways and forms. (p.174)

Not only are techniques of risk assessment fragile, then, but uncertainty itself may be both desired and desirable.

Actuarial Risk and Legitimacy

In contemporary society, the legitimacy of actuarial risk calculations as a basis for adequate risk management also has been questioned. They are criticised as being based more on the support of powerful interests and imprecise science with only lip-service paid to a rigorous understanding of cause and effect (Bedsworth and Kastenberg 2002; Cantor 1996; Chen and Hanson 2004; Gable 1992). Further, even where cause and effect are under scrutiny, the problems of complexity and ambiguity confound scientific knowledge. The work of Ulrich Beck is central here. Beck (1992) argues that contemporary risk problems no longer can be understood through the lens of the simple elegant causal models so favoured by traditional science. Rather, the impact of contemporary industrial life on the earth's ecosystem is characterised by multiple causality and feedback loops such that the paradigm of science and its emphasis on parsimony is rendered suspect. Indeed, those who experience problems first hand may have greater insight into the complexity of cause and effect than distant scientists (Wynne 1996).

It should be clear, however, that most critics (Beck (1992) included) are not arguing for a constructivist account of actuarial risk to the extent of denying the existence of significant impacts that result from modern industrial processes – often quite the reverse. What is under scrutiny is the 'objectivity' of what is labelled by experts as 'risky'. Political and economic interests materially effect what is understood as risky and in need of control (Clarke and Short 1993; Short and Clarke 1992). Further, scientific models of causality can understate both potential impact and the complexity of cause. Critiques of expert assessments of actuarial risk argue that the requisite knowledge is not discernable through science alone. Multiple possible explanations exist for any given hazard, and critical material and political interests are at stake in the determination of which causal pathway is seen as the 'correct' one.

For critics, then, actuarial risk assessments are at base social constructions (for helpful overviews see Clarke and Short 1993; Lupton 1999). The scientific and technical legitimacy that identified risks are provided with do not arise in a purely objective manner, but are selected (some would say shaped and created) from an infinite possibility of 'risks'. What we understand as risks are in essence 'risk objects' (Hilgartner 1992), where technical and social elements are tightly bound in networks and relationships. Such 'risk objects' can be generated both by activists seeking change and governments and other organisational actors seeking to retain the status quo. Each is concerned with power and influence over norms and laws (Short and Clarke 1992).

These criticisms of the problems with the concept of a technical, scientific interpretation of risk that forms the essence of actuarial risk have considerable merit. They alert us to the way a dominant narrative around a particular actuarial risk may be at odds with its inherent characteristics. They reinforce not only that the scientific or technical understanding of risk is socially constructed (many scientists may well agree with their characterisation as 'imperfect witnesses' (Beyea and Berger 2001)), but also that the risks may also be systematically distorted. Actuarial risks remain, however. They exert independent influence on individuals and the environment and are, to varying extents, appreciable through systematic scientific or technical inquiry. They are not, as critics have demonstrated, bound by that (always imperfect) knowledge! Nonetheless, we are critically dependent on that knowledge to protect us from a myriad of actuarial risks we encounter everyday.

SOCIO-CULTURAL RISK

A demonstration of how actuarial risks are, or are not, 'biased' or 'distorted' may be too limited in understanding the connection between risk and regulation. Indeed, a focus on the irrational, socially constructed or biased nature of actuarial risk assessments, may well conflate fundamentally different types of risk, types that require teasing apart. Greater illumination may be found in investigating what other forms of risk may be at play in the identification of behaviours or technologies as 'risky'. For example, public debate and concerns about threats to community include risks clearly distinguishable from those captured (or even attempted) by scientific or technical actuarial risk assessments. Concerns about risk also are centred on threats to 'our community', 'society', 'our country', 'our neighbourhood'; threats to the well-being of the communal whole. Here risk has a socio-cultural base. Such risks are often experienced as signs of 'danger' (Douglas 1992) events or behaviours identified as a threat to social order by a particular community at a particular time (Douglas 1992; Durkheim 1964). Classic examples of socio-cultural risks relate to ingesting certain drugs (categorising some as 'desirable' and others as illicit and dangerous), eating particular foods (but not others) as well as what constitutes 'risky' or 'deviant' behaviour, acceptable and unacceptable forms of religious belief, and so on (Sutton 2000).[5]

Concerns about socio-cultural risk are not, however, 'irrational'. Far from it, they spring from the reality of human existence as a social endeavour. As social creatures the well-being of the broader group is essential for the well-being of each individual, since each individual relies on the group for protection, sustenance, meaning and identity. The socio-cultural patterning of norms, risks and expectations performs a critical function in both the maintenance of social integration and the protection of individuals within a given society (Durkheim 1964). Further, in order to avail ourselves of the protection afforded by the group each individual needs to signal their membership to that group. This is done by expressing concern for the broader society in accordance with socio-cultural norms (Douglas 1966). Expressing feelings of unease or outrage about particular issues provides individuals with one way to signal concern for (and membership of) the society they live in. Individuals who express alarm at certain 'risky' behaviours, the possibility that previously 'unthinkable' events might now be realised on home soil or express fears of the increased influence of an alien belief are acting as moral citizens. Expressions of concern cannot be understood as irrational (since losing protection of the society leads to a precarious existence for any individual) nor purely as an expression of individual actuarial calculation of a narrowly-specified threat. Finally, the contours of socio-cultural risk provide community members with a 'route map' by which to navigate through the perils of individual life (Douglas 1966). This map necessarily must entail some categorisation, as individual risk assessments (both in terms of the actuarial risk posed by each activity of the day, as well as a risk assessment of the socio-cultural threats through acting in a particular way) for each and every act quickly would lead to societal paralysis. Socio-cultural risks and the norms underpinning them provide a way through the complexity of life and public concern about how to minimise such risks provides citizens with a sense of identity and belonging (Douglas 1992). To dismiss these concerns as irrational or subjective is to miss the point.

The challenge of maintaining at least some sense of social order, then, is of central concern to all within a community. Of course, this begs the next question: what kind of social order? Undoubtedly, there are many possibilities and realities, some more desirable than others with a wide variation of preferences amongst individual members of any society for any particular system of order. Indeed, many treatises are devoted to outlining the nature of social order most amenable to human wellbeing, balancing freedom and obligation in various ways. The concern here, though, is not to establish what kind of order (although that is clearly very important), but to make the case that *some* order is inevitable and desirable. Some forms of order are repressive, others exclusive and intolerant, others premised on individualism and rights (Douglas 1966; 1992; Hood 1998). The argument being made here, however, is that being human inevitability gives rise to the problem of social order and hence the inevitability of socio-cultural risk. It is not possible to live in a society without socio-cultural risk.

Socio-cultural Risk, Identity and Respect

Socio-cultural risk may not, however, follow the same rules as actuarial risk. It may well have an emotional as much as an intellectual logic. Feeling threatened, being reassured or being respected, arguably are intertwined with perceptions of socio-cultural risk. Our interdependence is centre stage and with that our interaction with government and other sources of authority are critical. So, just as psychological assessments of risk may be helpful in under-standing actuarial risk perception, so too psychology has something to offer our understanding of socio-cultural risk. How people are responded to when they express concern about a particular issue, problem or risk may provide some insight into the dynamics surrounding socio-cultural risk. Social psycho-logical research suggests that experiences with authority shapes individual levels of trust, feelings of loyalty, and the legitimacy offered to that authority (Tyler 2006a; Tyler and Blader 2003). Processes that are considered just and fair engender individual commitment to the goals of a group. In sociological terms, then, just processes may increase an individual's sense of belonging and being valued. This may increase social integration and reduce socio-cultural risk.

Translating this into the risk setting, what is relevant is that interacting with authority may be important to socio-cultural risk management, but also may be somewhat independent from actuarial risk management outcomes. In debates around risk and regulation both socio-cultural and actuarial concerns may be at play and both may need to be addressed.

The critiques of the work of Tyler and his colleagues also can help tease apart several issues of relevance to socio-cultural risk. The first is the way Tyler and his colleagues appear to use their ideas around procedural justice as strategic tools to engender acceptance of the outcome by complainants. That is, just procedures are good because they lead to good outcomes in terms of satisfaction of the complainant and greater legitimacy for authority. To writers such as Tankebe (2009) this focus is problematic. Processes that involve respect and being heard should be valued because of their intrinsic qualities, not because it makes the authority more legitimate. It has substantive value, not merely strategic importance. It is about sincerity and reciprocity. Tankebe is basing his argument here on a value rational perspective of potential impor-tance to our discussion on socio-cultural risk. Keeping levels of socio-cultural risk in check may require responses that resonate with those expressing some concern about substantively held beliefs. Respectful processes may lose legit-imacy when simply reduced to strategic tools. Strategic tactics are 'polluting' of such values and may be threatening and demeaning (Espeland 1998; Habermas 1989a). Socio-cultural norms centred on meaning and identity may not purely be understood in light of their political and strategic importance.

Socio-cultural Risk, Material Interests and the Role of Values

The second critique of importance relates to the way a focus on process under-mines broader claims to distributive justice (see for example Fox 1999). A focus on procedural justice, critics argue, turns attention away from just outcomes. To an extent, this is the opposite of Tankebe's critique. Rather than see the problem with Tyler's work as generating insincerity around what is valuable about interpersonal relationships, Fox understands procedural justice fundamentally as concerned with the generation of 'false consciousness', since individuals become reconciled to their unequal and marginalised position in society. In Bourdieun (2001) terms, procedural justice makes individuals care about things that have no intrinsic value; procedurally just processes are ephemeral and empty, their only value is to the powerful who are able to discipline the powerless to accept their lot gratefully. The exchange here is of symbolic goods, an artificial creation where calculation is to be eschewed. In this, Bourdieu weaves together Marxist notions of false consciousness with Weberian analyses of value rationality.

This challenge by Fox (1999) has two potential interpretations. Firstly, different values and interests are found within a society, so socio-cultural norms can never be taken at face value. This clearly is important since it would be unsustainable to argue that value conflict does not exist within a society. Within any society there exists perennial debates and contests around what values should be seen as 'society's' values, contests often (but not always) associated with material interests. Dominant norms may also reflect, in Mary Douglas's terms, a system at war with itself, by virtue of the internal contradictions borne of categories of order that cannot ever remain pure (Douglas 1966; Sutton 2000). The argument being made in this chapter, however, is that within various societies there is a call to a broader sense of order, for an overarching framework of belonging, nonetheless a framework that may encompass groups with quite different value positions and which comprise conflicting norms and values.

The second critique is potentially quite different, however, and is centred on a belief that values don't really exist. Rather values are a proxy for interests and power and influence that determine whose 'values' are heard and whose are not. Whilst an appeal to values may certainly be related in some way to material interests, I feel it is premature in the debate on risk undertaken here to conflate the two. To do so would provide a very narrow view of human societies and the concerns expressed through risk debates:[6] rather I would take a Weberian approach and argue that both interests and values must be taken into account as important. Further, this suggests a discussion about socio-cultural risk cannot be reduced to one only based on material interests.

Social Change and Socio-cultural Risk

Rapid social change also engenders heightened socio-cultural risk. Socio-cultural norms are in considerable flux in contemporary globalised societies.

The narratives of risk and taboo that are the visible expression of social norms (Douglas 1966; 1992; Durkheim 1964) have been challenged by economic, social and demographic change (Garland 2001). Some argue that this has resulted in risks now defined by their threat to the individual rather than collective wellbeing (Douglas 1992). For others rapid social change has created greater reflexivity, a concern and awareness about risk (Beck 1992; Giddens 1991). Yet others point to diverse responses to rapid change including rejection by some groups and societies of the cosmopolitan values that accompany globalisation. There is an active rejection of globalisation and its accompanying values and expectations and a reassertion of 'proper' values as a project to 'purify' their own society or community (Mittleman 1994). Indeed, all of these eventualities may be found in different social groups as they grapple with the problem of creating identity in a changing world.

The impact of social change also sheds significant light on the experience of being vulnerable as distinct from our level of exposure to actuarial risk (for example from the risk of being killed or injured at work, or contracting a particular disease). So, for example Giddens (1991) has argued that contemporary society is characterised by the perception of greater insecurity in the face of greater security. In terms of the discussion here, contemporary 'risk society' is characterised by higher levels of socio-cultural risk because of a heightened sense of vulnerability. Globalisation brings with it increased freedom yet heightened interdependencies that increase our feelings of vulnerability and reduce our capacity to feel secure (Giddens 1991). William Freudenberg (1993) argues, for example, contra Durkheim, that increasing interdependency heightens perceptions of risk. The reason for this is that interdependency increases our vulnerability to the actions of others, most of whom we have no personal relationship with whatsoever. What is expressed through socio-culturally inspired risk debates are concerns with the level of interdependency and hence vulnerability to the decisions of others.

In conclusion, then, socio-cultural risk is generated from within a given place. It arises from the need for social cohesion and a sense of individual belonging. It is inevitable. It is not static, but it exerts an independent influence on debates around risk. It is based on values and those values provide both some level of overarching order to a society, as it provides some level of meaning to the individual. But, this does not mean that keeping socio-cultural risk at acceptable levels is unproblematic and uncontested – far from it. Socio-cultural risk concerns are used for strategic gains (Douglas 1992); they are strategic as well as substantive. Repression, expulsion and injustice can arise through political contests that ensue. Further, the impact of the increasing complexity of society and the interconnectedness between societies across the globe holds particular challenges as our vulnerability to the actions of others increases. Socio-cultural risk always gives rise to the need for reassurance and the need for such reassurance arguably is greater as our sense of vulnerability increases.

UNDERSTANDING POLITICAL RISK

The obvious question arises, then, where does this reassurance come from? To whom do individuals and groups turn when they feel threatened either from actuarial or socio-cultural risk concerns? An obvious candidate here, particularly in the context of law and regulation, is the elected government. This is not to say there are not other sources for reassurance – family, social networks, and so on – as clearly there are. However, the elected government, or governments (since we may be involved in multiple intersecting governments: local, state, federal, and so on) are a key source of authority we expect to provide for our security – and is particularly relevant in the context of how regulation may be used to reassure in a socio-cultural rather than only an actuarial sense. That governments are perceived to fail in providing security is a major source of risk for any elected political representative and for a particular political administration as a whole.

The Twin Challenge in the Control of Political Risk

Political risk, that is risk to an elected government of a failure to secure legitimacy, may well be central to understanding the relationship between regulation and risk. Regulatory reform results from government-initiated processes and enforcement is most often a responsibility of government. It seems likely that risk to government must be a critical component of risk, one present in many of the debates about risk and regulation. At play in determining political risk is the perceived adequacy of the government's response. Since reassurance involves addressing socio-cultural as well as actuarial concerns, there may well be a need for a political response to be judged a genuine expression of concern (that is, substantive in its orientation) rather than simply a strategic ploy or self-interested gambit (that is, 'they are really just afraid of their legal liability or their own backsides but not really us' as indicated in the quote from *The Oxford Agenda* at the beginning of this chapter). If political risk is correctly understood as a risk to political authority the sources of such risk need to be analysed in light of the political task itself. Responding to socio-culturally and actuarially based anxieties from their constituency would seem a necessary and critical role of government.

Political risk and the need for governments to reassure citizens in order to reduce that risk can also be understood at different levels. At a most immediate level, this need to reassure can be understood in terms of the need for a particular elected administration to secure enough loyalty to be voted back into power. This might be a thin reading redolent of the notion of a legitimation crisis of contemporary governments (Habermas 1979; 1989c). But, there may also be deeper issues at play, issues that Gary Wickham (2006; 2010) argues relate to the need to appreciate and value 'the social' as a complex interplay of politics, law and the economy. Here, the narratives that are constructed by politics, through law and bureaucratic administration in response to critical events may themselves then increase in significance (see also Fisher 2007). In political risk terms, then, the incapacity to reassure and to retain legitimacy may threaten not only a particular government but the legitimacy of government per se. In such a case the nascent conflicts within any society may then erupt in more serious forms of violence.

Governments are required to do more, however, than provide a coordinated response to public concern with actuarial risks and to find ways to work with the community in addressing socio-cultural risk concerns. For capitalist democracies at least, this is not the case. There is the critical question of the resources needed to develop and implement the necessary policies, including any regulatory reforms deemed as necessary. To a considerable extent the financial resources to do so ultimately are generated by the private, capitalist market. Revenue to government comes from multiple sources: levying taxes, royalty payments, investments (in the market) and selling bonds amongst others. Ultimately, then, the necessary revenue comes from the economy, hence the need to ensure a vibrant capitalist market.

Economic concerns, then, form the second critical component of political risk. The economy can be capricious. It is subject to cycles of economic growth and decline. Governments are involved in 'managing the economy' and make strenuous efforts to smooth out this cyclical nature. This involves taking unpopular measures (raising taxes, or reducing spending, for example) that can independently raise political risk. Critically, maintaining economic growth and investment within a capitalist system is seen as dependent on entrepreneurial investment ('risk taking'), so threats by entrepreneurs to take their money elsewhere or to stop investing are listened to carefully. Heightened political risk, as Habermas (1979; 1989c; 1998) has long argued arises from problems with the economy, problems with reassurance or both. In short:

> The state apparatus thus has two simultaneous tasks. It has to levy the necessary taxes from profit and income and employ them so efficiently as to prevent any crises from disturbing economic growth. In addition the selective raising of taxes, the recognizable priority model of their utilization, and the administrative performance have to function in such a way as to satisfy the resulting need for legitimation ... (Habermas 1989c p.275)

Economic Challenges and Political Risk

There are several interrelated elements to consider here in terms of the economic dimension of political risk. The first is the level of independence of the capitalist market and the generation of wealth from the activities of the state. The second is the threat posed to legitimation of the government by virtue of their attempts to 'manage' the economy. The third is the challenge posed by economic globalisation. Finally, there is the ambiguity of government in relationship to uncertainty.

The degree to which the local economy is able to be influenced by the state remains strongly contested. For Marx (1990) capitalism had its own dynamic, one that the state was in no position to influence (indeed the state was often understood as complicit here). Marxist writers such as David Harvey (1989) argue that the state process of allocation of resources (for attempting to reassure the population, for example) can never be separated from the inherent challenges of the capitalist economy. The state is beholden to the contradictions within the capitalist form of exchange such that its lack of control over the market is inevitable. Indeed, he argues that the state is often complicit in exacerbating such contradictions in the interests of protecting capital. Governments historically have exacerbated these tensions, for example by stimulating speculative investments and irresponsible risk-taking through loosening controls over incorporation (Glasbeek 2002). Drawing on Marx, Harvey (1989) writes of how, in the face of their own limitations, governments then proceed to argue that the market is able to control itself. Financial instruments (such as systems of credit) seem, mistakenly, to form a solid basis for regulation of the economy. Ultimately this strategy is to no avail since: '… in speculative booms, a financial system which starts out by appearing a sane device for regulating the incoherent tendencies of capitalist production, ends up becoming "the main lever for overproduction and over-speculation"' (p.107–8).

Those drawing from a Marxist base argue that the inherent instabilities within the market always elude the state's capacity to manage the inevitable periodic crises to the economy generated by the capitalist mode of production. Such a view seems to have considerable strength, as we witnessed in 2008 the trauma unleashed by the collapse of investment banks and related financiers who promised financial and economic security through financial instruments somewhat ironically labelled as 'securitisation'.

Others disagree with this assessment of governmental impotence in the face of raw capitalist power with its inherent instabilities. Many argue government intervention has assisted in the stabilisation of the market and allowed for the growth of the welfare state. In this intervention various governments have been able, at least to some degree (Habermas 1979; 1989c; 1998) to control the market whilst not threatening their own resource base. Control over the economic cycle, however, was and is never total (Ferguson 2008; Kindleberger and Aliber 2005).

That some level of control is possible, however, is supported by the reality that there are different levels of exposure to economic crises between countries and diversity in the relationship between various governments and the private market. There were (and still are) significant levels of control exerted by various countries over local employers in the private, market sphere. Governments vary in their attempts to control wealth production in the service and maintenance of their own welfare state (Hall and Soskice 2001b; Mares 2003).

The intervention of governments in order to manage the economic cycle and redistribute the benefits of wealth creation more evenly has significant consequences for political risk. In short, the problems of the economy (whether they are caused by governments or not) are seen as a political responsibility. So an economic crisis is a threat to political legitimacy and hence heightens political risk (Habermas 1989c; 1996). Further, managing the economy itself requires governments to undertake unpopular measures (raise general taxes, lower business tax, cut spending, and so on) (Habermas 1979; 1989c). In particular, cutting back on government spending during a cyclical upswing is made more difficult as the general expectations of the population for security also rise.[7]

The rise of economic globalisation and the relative decline of state-based control of national economic fortunes also pose political risk challenges. The integration of various nation states into the global economic system (through the process of economic globalisation) arguably has lessened their control over their own economic fortunes. In order to reap the benefits from trade, the journalist and author Thomas Freidman (1999) has argued that states must don a 'golden straightjacket' and respond to the demands of the global markets by reducing trade barriers and taxes. This can place them in a difficult position as they become more dependent on the international marketplace and yet are seen by citizens as responsible for levels of economic prosperity and the employment it brings (Habermas 1989c). In the face of global competition, governments are less able, also, to redistribute wealth and levels of inequality rise (Habermas 1989c; cf. Hall and Soskice 2001a). Herein lies a contradiction where citizens may expect more of their democratically elected governments in terms of choices they should make to enhance the wellbeing of citizens whilst at the same time global competitiveness restricts choices around taxation, royalties and direct controls on local markets aimed to enhance citizen wellbeing directly (Stiglitz 2001).

This emphasis on globalisation, neoliberalism and the market finally brings the problem of uncertainty back into view. If O'Malley (2004) is right and uncertainty is indeed a desirable element of risk when viewed from the perspective of entrepreneurialism and economic vibrancy then political risk requires uncertainty to be present in order to protect its economic base (and that of the citizenry). At the same time, political risk management requires strenuous efforts to be made to peel uncertainty back in order to control the actuarial risks that are exposed through disasters and catastrophes. The political response to disaster, then, may well not be able to be premised on 'never again' if, in taking the necessary measures to minimise uncertainty, the government may seriously undermine its own financial base.

I want to be clear, though, the analysis above is not premised on a moral judgement of the justice or otherwise of particular decisions based on conserving uncertainty and promoting entrepreneurialism. Further, what is undertaken by governments is a political risk *assessment* with all the possible distortion that entails of particular material and political interests at play shaping what is, and what is not, viewed as a threat to their legitimacy and financial security. Uncertainty may well be borne by those with the least resources to bear its consequences. So, uncertainty and justice, as with order and justice, may well have a problematic relationship. Political risk, then, results from the inability of the government of the day to successfully manage the economy and promote economic growth and/or by failing to reassure the community that they (the political leaders) will protect them from a range of actuarial and socio-cultural risks. In whatever arena political risks arise, should individual politicians or whole government regimes fail in the task of either economic management or public reassurance it is their legitimacy to govern or wield authority that is at stake. Risks to legitimacy, then, sit at the heart of political risk (Habermas 1979; 1989c).

TRACING THE RELATIONSHIPS BETWEEN RISK TYPES

Central as each type of risk may be to enhancing our understanding of regulation, how they interact also is important to understand. As discussed above, political risk by its nature involves responding to socio-cultural and actuarial risk concerns. Governments must reassure us about our security and their capacity to protect us from particular socio-cultural and actuarial threats in order to reduce their levels of political risk. But they must also encourage *risk-taking* in order to stimulate economic growth and encourage investment. Whole industries are dependent upon community members 'trying something new' and taking a risk on purchasing (and consuming) a new good or service (such as flying rather than taking a train to a destination, changing employment, living in a high-rise city apartment or consuming processed food) risk taking that may both challenge socio-cultural norms and create new forms of actuarial risk.

Complexities to the relationship between the three ideal types of risk arise also as trust in government declines. As Habermas (1979) has argued, the progressive loss of faith in politicians and their capacity to generate good outcomes for the citizenry has led to a legitimacy problem. Put simply, politicians need to work harder and promise more 'identifiable' outcomes in order to retain public loyalty. This can mean that politicians also have a vested interest in promoting certain levels of fear about particular (often socio-culturally based) risks in order to be seen to be protective and caring in what might loosely be termed a kind of political 'protection racket' (Douglas 1992; Sunstein 2005).

A complicating feature here and one critical to the connection between risk and regulation is the reality that socio-cultural norms remain based, at least in part, on the legitimacy of the scientific method as central to uncovering 'real' risks and their causes. Socio-cultural risks may then be presented as actuarial risks. 'Evidence-based' or 'evidence-led' policymaking and regulatory reform is a taken-for-granted virtue. An actuarial narrative may well be the 'presentational' form that any risk (whether actuarial, socio-cultural or political) must take in order to be seen as 'real' (see Brunsson 2002). The risk narrative is bound by a need to identify what the precise nature of the harm is, what the cause of that harm is (in the form of linking cause and effect) and the probability of its occurrence. Concerns about political and socio-cultural risks must be presented and debated as if they were an actuarial risk – even if concerns are socio-cultural in their origin and form. Post hoc assessments of how a risk was dealt with, then, must be presented as consistent with actuarial reasoning.

This has particular implications for actuarial risk assessments based on scientific or technical assessments of risk. Whereas, as we saw above, science understands itself as uncertain, such humility and restraint tends to fail in the transition of 'evidence' into policy. Within the political arena 'evidence led' policies understand science as certainty, 'facts' able to bolster and support a particular ideology (Bedsworth and Kastenberg 2002; Beyea and Berger 2001; Gable 1992; Habermas 1989b). This does not always succeed; indeed scientific uncertainty may often form the basis of disputes (Giddens and Pierson 1998) catapulted into the public arena during a debate about regulatory reform. Uncertainty becomes a commodity in a similar fashion to certainty. As Bedsworth and Kastenberg state:

> In a regulatory decisionmaking process, uncertainty can be used to advocate precaution in pursuing potentially harmful environmental choices (the Precautionary Principle), to advocate cost-effectiveness, or to delay regulatory action altogether. Uncertainty serves as an influential rhetorical and strategic device in environmental regulation and decisionmaking. (2001 p.17)

MEETING THE RISK CHALLENGE?

Before turning to the data, there is a need to provide some orientation towards analysing what may be helpful to deal with the complexity of risk and risk management that affects regulation. The argument from this chapter is that analyses of regulatory reform and compliance need to be sensitive to political and socio-cultural as well as actuarial risk. How each form of risk affects what reform takes place and what form compliance takes may help explain where regulation can be effective and where it cannot.

The particular strengths of and challenges to regulation as an instrumental form of government control also needs to be analysed. This instrumental quality has clear benefits in terms of making gains in reducing some forms of actuarial risk explicit. It may also have benefits for reducing socio-cultural and political risk. But this goal-oriented quality may have problematic consequences where the risks and rewards from a given activity are tightly intertwined. Reducing one risk may increase another (Sunstein 2005). Regulatory reform may also deflect attention away from arguably more successful ways of addressing socio-cultural and political risk challenges, partly because it is so immediate and apparently effective in 'doing something'.

The dominant method within the policy literature in terms of dealing with the prioritisation and embeddedness of actuarial risk is some form of cost/benefit analysis predicated on expert assessments of risk. But, there are other possibilities here, arguably better at meeting the complexity of the risk challenge described above such as the need for heightened levels of communication and deliberation around which risks should take priority and how they should be dealt with.

Cost Benefit Analysis

A robust cost benefit analysis (CBA) is often promoted within governments as the optimal method of prioritising risk and assessing which regulatory reform will be most effective and efficient in bringing about the desired reduction in risk (see for example Sunstein 2005; Viscusi 1992). CBA may be undertaken at a number of points in order to inform the necessity for effectiveness and efficiency of regulation. Firstly, a cost benefit analysis can be undertaken to enable placing a priority on one risk as opposed to another, and secondly a cost benefit analysis can be made around the efficiency and effectiveness of the specific regulatory controls proposed.

CBA at the point of prioritisation of the risk often requires a quantitative calculation. This calculation is based on a scientific or technical assessment of the risk in terms of the nature of the hazard, the probability of occurrence and the cause of the risk. A monetary value may then be placed on human life and health, or the environment or both depending on the risk. There are various ways to determine the monetary level including statutory tables which contain the necessary values (for example for a death, injury, and so on), calculation of monetary costs associated with loss of productivity, levels of state services needed, or alternatively quantification may be based on surveys gauging an individual's 'willingness to pay' for one benefit or another (Viscusi 1992).

Once the values are obtained then a calculation can be made as to whether the benefits accrued from managing a risk exceed the costs. One version of this is based on an 'in/out' principle. So, for example where Net Present Value (that is, the level at which the benefits exceed the costs) is calculated at above 0 it should be acted on, but not where the quantified result is below 0 (Environmental Assessment Institute (EAI 2006) hereafter EAI). The rationale here is that the overall project (such as an environmental risk management strategy) adds to overall societal welfare (EAI 2006).

CBA is also used to assess whether a particular regulatory approach is justi-fied, effective and efficient. This form of CBA requires firstly an appraisal of the current level of risk (before any additional risk management measures are put in place).[8] Secondly, the expected reduction that would occur from the new proposed measure (the benefits) is assessed and finally, the costs associated with putting in place the risk reduction measure.

Cost benefit analyses are aimed most explicitly at addressing actuarial risk. Indeed, they may well have a strong role to play here. But, their capacity to do so depends on the quality and quantity of the scientific and/or technical knowl-edge underpinning each analysis. CBA is predicated on the capacity of an actuarial assessment of risk to be able to identify the exact nature of the hazard, to cost that hazard, and to understand the causal mechanisms in order to evaluate whether the controls will address the risk. The levels of uncertainty and ambiguity around particular actuarial risks discussed above are critical considerations in the integrity of any CBA to form the basis for good decision making.

The capacity of a cost benefit analysis, however, to deal with socio-cultural risk concerns or political risk also needs close attention. There are ways that such risks may come into play productively through the process of CBA in a productive way. So, Sunstein (2005) argues that the value of CBA lies in its capacity to generate reflection. The process of developing the knowledge as well as disseminating it creates debate and deliberation about whether deploying the required resources in risk management is warranted. This process can be critically important since risk management is essentially a trade off, as reducing the risk of one kind often creates or increases risk of another kind. Required risk management through regulation, for example, may make one good more expensive and out of reach for the poor as indus-try passes on the cost of the regulatory control. The result can be that the rich become progressively safer and the poor less so (Keeney 1996; Sunstein 2005). Making these costs and benefits explicit and to whom can be a powerful source for reflection.

Further, socio-cultural concerns may well influence debates around how to place monetary values on particular events (such as a death or an injury) and what should be counted as a benefit and what counted as a cost. Essential deliberations may ensue in terms of who bears the cost and who gains the benefits. This process of communication and reflection may well be important in addressing risks of a socio-cultural and hence political nature.

But, there are some particular problems here with CBA that need to be made explicit. The first is the level of transparency and accountability of the scientific or technological knowledge underpinning any calculation of a particular CBA undertaken. For a CBA to generate helpful reflection it would need to engage with a broader audience, beyond those with particular forms of expertise. It needs to be able to communicate the substance of the assessment, not just act to convince through some end figure seen as authoritative in itself. In some situations this may be possible. In others it may not if the particular assessment itself is indeed complex and beyond the reach of many.

This leads to the challenge of dealing with complexity. It may be, for example, that the complexity itself is problematic and obscures more than it elucidates, as is the case with some financial instruments aimed at securitising debt which are later found to rest on a set of false assumptions. However, the complexity might be necessary and valid as the particular actuarial risk of concern may well be complex in either its effects, or its causes, or both. Here, trust in the necessary expertise comes into play (Fischhoff 1996; Leiss 1996). In order for the influence of a CBA to be positive, not only do the actuarial assessments need to be sufficiently accurate but the source of the information would need to be seen as trustworthy.

This returns us to the problem of political risk. The capacity of CBA to be of assistance in reducing political risk is dependent, in part, on how well it can deal with actuarial and socio-culturally based concerns about its validity. But, there are considerable challenges here. Firstly, the taking of actuarial risks seen as necessary from the point of view of maintaining economic investment may well not be provided with the necessary resources for a sufficiently independent scientific or technical analysis to be made. So, determinations by governments regarding the procedure needed to calculate costs and benefits may contain inherent biases, for example to support industry. Or, governments needing to heighten their credentials in terms of providing security may, for example, decide that strong action against a particular form of actuarial risk is politically beneficial, independently from any CBA to the contrary. As Sunstein (2005) has argued, low probability but high impact actuarial risks may be particularly vulnerable to being used for political ends.

Communication: Risk Management as a Social Project

Any rigorous analysis of CBA highlights the reality that risk governance and regulation essentially are social projects (Renn 2008). Simply focussing on the need for an effective process based on CBA can never be sufficient here, since how actuarial risk is communicated can elicit quite different public responses. Actuarial risks can be expressed in many ways (deaths as a percentage of population; deaths per unit of activity, for example) (Kunreuther and Slovic 1996). Manipulation of the presentation of information in order to bring about a particular result may then occur, which can either enhance or detract from making good decisions about regulation. Engaging productively with risk debates, together with the values and interests at play, is critical.

For many, the need for and challenge of communicating around actuarial risk means that public participation in both risk assessment and risk management is essential (Kunreuther and Slovic 1996). Society is beyond the point at which expert views can be accepted uncritically. Risk management is more than 'getting the numbers right' or 'getting the CBA right' or 'treating the public with respect' (Fischhoff 1996). It is progressively seen as a collaborative enterprise, one where 'lay' experiences may be critical in highlighting the causes or impacts of particular actuarial risks (Wynne 1996; cf. Fisher 2007). There are then, good reasons to include more individuals in the risk and regulation debate (Fischhoff 1996; Leiss 1996).

The opening up of assessments of risk to broader and more diverse audiences brings into play a range of possibilities. Clearly those particularly affected by a given actuarial risk may have more access to influence policy-making (Braithwaite and Drahos 2000). There is the possibility of networks of dialogue evolving where normative change can evolve and a consensus around a particular risk develop (Braithwaite and Drahos 2000). It is not hard to imagine how this can be beneficial, both in terms of actuarial and socio-culturally based concerns.

To deal effectively with socio-cultural concerns, however, requires attention being paid to conflicting values and interests. Clearly, there are competing views here in terms of how such conflict is best dealt with. On the one hand are attempts to map the conditions under which an overarching consensus is made possible (Habermas 1996); on the other, are those who would argue that appealing to a diversity of views and values (of multiple publics) is both more realistic and contains greater progressive potential (Fraser 1992). An opposing view argues for an appreciation of the benefits of the flawed reality that is law and politics, benefits that need to be well understood before envisioning some idealistic future (Wickham 2006; 2010).

Arguably, independent assessments of risk and independently generated demands for change based on diverse values may well lead to progressive outcomes. Further, an easy dismissal of the current, albeit imperfect, reality of law and politics for some unrealistic vision would indeed be problematic. But there are problems of juridification where multiple competing demands find their way into law (Teubner 1998). Further, prior demands in terms of earmarked funds and prior budget allocations can significantly limit the capacity of the state to change in light of particular concerns that arise (Cantor 1996). There is no way within a conceptualisation of the notion of multiple publics to assess the problem of how to allocate public resources. From an idealised economic framework the outcome should be determined by the market under some rubric that emphasises 'willingness to pay' as the ultimate arbiter of whose concerns should be met. Others may argue that the value of sheer political power and protest determines allocation of government resources. Neither of these approaches, however, allows for a human connection beyond that based on political muscle or economic wealth. This brings us back to the necessity for some sort of overarching 'we' to be developed. Clearly, there is no need (nor is it in anyway reasonable or desirable) for an entirely consensual society. But, reaching consensus at some level about which are the risks that are most threatening and which are not would seem to be important in the development of good regulation.

This brings us, then, back to the challenge of political risk. Whatever normative settings are proposed to enable decisions to be made about when to allocate resources and to regulate will need to be able to meet the challenge of the potential pitfalls posed by governments' intent on shoring up their political fortunes. This is particularly the case in the context of high profile disasters that form the empirical contribution of this book. Disasters place particular political pressures on governments and political leaders, pressures that they may not be capable of resisting (Boin and t'Hart 2003). There are also opportunities, however, for making progressive steps. Yet to make such steps may well require the particular government in question to be capable of engaging productively with the not inconsiderable challenges to political legitimacy that may arise from a range of different quarters.

CONCLUSIONS

This chapter has covered significant territory in its analysis of risk, from a critical analysis of scientific and technical approaches to risk through to the need for a sociological account of risk and danger as well as an analysis of political risk. The basic argument has been that to understand how risk affects regulation, risk needs to be understood as multiple in form, not singular. Critically, each ideal type of risk has integrity. Yet, our capacity to grasp each may well be limited, and so each is understood as both independent and socially constructed. Our capacity to apprehend actuarial, socio-cultural or political risks may well be incomplete. Each if not attended to may have the potential for surprise. So an actuarial risk not yet visible or wrongly categorised as safe may threaten many; socio-cultural fracture may lead to significant levels of conflict and violence or political risk may rise precipitously so that there is a critical loss of political legitimacy of a particular government or at a deeper level in the legitimacy of government itself. It is in this complex terrain of risk that regulation may be called upon to manage. Regulation, then, may be aimed at resolving not one, but a number of risk challenges variously actuarial, socio-cultural and political in origin. It may be more or less effective in achieving risk reduction ends in these disparate areas.

This discussion of risk has added to the analysis of regulation in Chapter 2 in several ways. The instrumentalism of regulation highlighted in that chapter has been teased apart here through recognising that it has both actuarial and political risk dimensions. So, actuarial risk assessments – for example as operationalised through some cost benefit analysis – may necessarily result in a narrowing of attention bringing greater clarity to a particular issue. At the same time, the political drive to retain legitimacy may also benefit from a narrow framing of regulation, a ready appeal to a 'problem based' approach. The analysis of risk above, however, also suggests reasons to doubt that such an instrumental frame of reference can form a firm foundation for an effective regulatory strategy. Where intent is involved, or the underlying risk is particularly complex, a narrow instrumental framing of actuarial risk may make reform achieve only temporary gains. Further, socio-cultural risk demands may not be so easily assuaged by narrowly based approaches, unless perhaps the regulatory reforms clearly reflect socio-cultural norms in order to reassure the citizenry of their security. With the need to address three – not one – risk demands, the regulatory response to disaster may well be required to construct a narrative around cause and effect that can tame each of these three risks, which then shapes the necessary reforms that such a narrative implies.

Finally, the discussion above has highlighted the way political risk critically involves a concern with the vibrancy of the market and the economy. Here – and perhaps most critically with financial regulation – instrumental framing may be preferred so as not to dampen entrepreneurial vigour. Yet, herein lies an additional paradox. Whilst actuarial calculations seek to dispel ambiguity and uncertainty the analysis above suggests that uncertainty is needed to spur entrepreneurial risk taking. The challenges for effective regulation again loom large.

With a clear focus on the political dynamism of regulation, its dependence on (but ambivalence towards) instrumentalism and finally the complexity of the risk management task it faces, it is time now to turn to the case studies themselves. The three events: an industrial disaster, recent terrorist attacks centred on 11 September 2001 and the collapse of HIH Insurance in 2001 provide a rich opportunity to study the regulatory crises that result from disparate risks. The following chapters will explore each stage of the regulatory journey from the framing of the three events in Chapter 4, the regulatory response to each in Chapter 5 and then a detailed analysis of how these reforms were responded to at the Major Hazard Facilities (Chapter 6) and at air and seaports (Chapter 7). The particular challenge for financial regulation with its ambivalence towards uncertainty forms the basis of Chapter 8.

NOTES

1. 'Risk adversity at the swimming pool', *The Oxford Agenda, the Home of Mordant Causes.* Available at http://oxfordagenda.wordpress.com/2007/08/21/risk-adversity-at-the-swimming-pool/
2. 27 February 2009 'Australia Fire Fear Shuts Schools', BBC News Channel. Available at http://news.bbc.co.uk/1/hi/world/asia-pacific/7914059.stm
3. 'Cheney Says Obama Has Increased Risks', A. G. Sulzberger, *New York Times* 15 March 2009. Available at http://www.nytimes.com/2009/03/16/us/politics/16cheney.html?_r=1
4. I recognize the problem of mixed metaphors here, but the point is well and colourfully made!
5. Whilst such risk is almost always perceived of as bad and dangerous, sociological analyses of socio-cultural risks trace how they (and the individuals associated with them) can act as catalysts for social change. See M. Douglas (1992) *Risk and Blame: Essays in Cultural Theory.* London: Routledge. E. Durkheim (1964) *The Division of Labour in Society.* New York: Free Press.
6. I would challenge those with such a viewpoint to turn the spotlight on themselves and declare that their only concerns are those that affect their own interests in terms of power and material goods.
7. It will be remembered that many countries spent many billions of dollars in 'stimulus packages' from 2008–10 in order to turn various national economies around. These will have to be paid back, and during an upswing in order to prevent over-stimulation. Cutting back spending creates problems for governments and raises political risks.
8. Some CBAs that accompany a regulatory impact statement require that the initial risk be calculated before any controls (even existing ones) are included in any analysis.

4. Making sense of the events

... After returning to the fire shed, Cumming went to the Crude Stabilization Plant intending to shut in the vapours to Gas Plant 1. He found a valve key and started to lever the valve shut. The fire was getting worse. He managed to get the valve within two inches of being closed when the hand wheel fell off making the valve inoperable. At that time the last explosion occurred. Cumming made for the main gate ...[1]

... (in the aftermath of September 11th) we were fielding twenty to thirty phone calls a day from people who were scared of planes flying over their house. Some members of the public when a plane went over their house they were terrified and they were calling us and calling everyone. What Al-Qaida did with that attack, and they didn't intend it, was they found the ideal medium to generate world wide panic.[2]

'Beware the ides of March.' The soothsayer's words have become synonymous with unheeded warnings since they were penned by Shakespeare some 400 years ago. Caesar's response – 'He is a dreamer; let us leave him: pass' – is less well known but equally apposite. These words sum up the life and times of HIH, and they resonated eerily through the inquiries I made.[3]

Disasters loom large in our psyche. The heroism, the fear of what might happen and the search for clues to why the disaster occurred, all are familiar elements of the immediate aftermath of catastrophic events. To varying extents each was evident in the three cases that form the centre of this book. As the first quote above illustrates, the explosions and fire at the Longford gas plant were accompanied by the heroism of those who, in the middle of the mayhem and at risk to their own safety, tried to reduce the impact of the disaster by closing valves to reduce the fuel for the fire. The second quote illustrates what *might* happen next as airport managers across Australia experienced the brunt of public fear in the immediate aftermath of the attacks in the US on September 11. Local residents living in houses under flight paths in Melbourne, Sydney or Darwin suddenly felt themselves vulnerable, not simply from chronic noise or pollution but from deliberate attack. The final quote from the Honourable Justice Owen, Commissioner of the HIH Royal Commission into the collapse of HIH Insurance on 15 March 2001 portrays the search for signs missed and warnings unheeded. This commission, together with that into the Longford incident are emblematic of investigations and commissions set up in the wake of a disaster that interrogate multiple witnesses; sift through voluminous piles of text and unending screens of data to find answers to perennial questions of 'why did this event happen? What can we do to prevent it from happening again?'

The purpose in this chapter is to describe what happened in each of the three events. The subsequent chapters answer the question of measures taken to prevent a repeat incident and the role regulatory reform played in efforts to make Australians more secure. What is important for our purposes here is to highlight aspects of each of the disasters that are necessary to understand from the vantage point of subsequent regulatory reform. In keeping with the analysis in Chapter 3, the description of the events: Longford, September 11 and HIH are shaped in light of not only their physical and financial consequences (that is, an actuarial reading of events), but also the socio-cultural and political threats each laid bare. In two of the cases, Longford and HIH, there is a central focus on the sequence of events that led to the catastrophe. In all three cases, the understanding of what caused the catastrophe was to a greater or lesser extent malleable, so that it was not self-evident which elements need to be included as 'causal' and which excluded, but they were selected from a range of possibilities. In each of the three cases there was not only a narrative developed that made sense of technical or actuarial uncertainty, but also one that made a moral story out of ambiguity. The identification of whom or what caused the disaster, then, generated a moral as well as a technical account.

The substantive realisation of disaster often creates a political dynamic for change, a need for government to act (Hancher and Moran 1998 p.29). In part, this condition arises simply because the human and financial impact of the disaster invalidates the claims of the bureaucratic system to value and protect human life and wellbeing. In short, value and bureaucratic rationality conflict (Gerth and Mills 1991 [1948]; Weber 1964 [1947]). Critically, in each of the cases discussed here the disaster events signalled a failure that included regulatory failure. The regulations and bureaucratic measures in place at that time were unable to prevent the catastrophe. Why they were considered to fail and how they were considered deficient depended on the way the event itself was understood.

THE LONGFORD GAS PLANT EXPLOSION

The Longford Gas plant was operated by Esso Resources Australia (ERA) and owned jointly by Esso (a subsidiary of the US Exxon Corporation) and BHP Petroleum (Bass Strait) (a subsidiary of The Broken Hill Proprietary Company Ltd).[4] The disaster began on 25 September 1998 when a vessel at the gas processing plant ruptured, releasing tonnes of vaporised hydrocarbons into the atmosphere. The vapour subsequently ignited, leading to a series of explosions and fire, which killed two men and injured a further eight. The fire was intense and was unable to be fully extinguished until 27 September over two days later. The state of Victoria was critically dependent on this plant, which supplied most (98 per cent) of Victoria's gas. Gas was also the primary energy source for 80 per cent of homes, 50 per cent of commercial enterprises and 25 per cent of industry, amplifying the overall impact. As a result of the explosion, gas supplies were cut to the state (except for emergency purposes). Final restoration of gas to the state did not occur until 14 October 1998, over two weeks later (Dawson and Brooks 1999; Hopkins 2001).

The financial and physical impacts of the disaster were extensive. It was estimated that 1.4 million households and 89,000 businesses lost gas supply. The loss of supply had a bewildering array of effects from producing cold showers and a loss of cooking facilities at restaurants, to a temporary halting of cremations (Walker, Robinson, Tebbutt, Lin, Bisset, Burns and Schauble 2006). Further, the explosion halted the supply of ethane, a precursor chemical for the plastics industry, which meant the halting of production of some plastics in cases where alternate supplies could not be found. It was estimated that tens of thousands of workers were temporarily stood down (including 7000 in the vehicle industry) with the Federal government losing $300 million in taxes (Walker, et al. 2006).

The explanation for the explosion at Longford rested on a strong technical narrative of physical causes. A Royal Commission, chaired by Sir Daryl Dawson, a retired High Court Judge, and Commissioner Brian Brooks, an engineer and technical expert, was set up in the wake of the disaster to investigate the causes of the disaster and the failure of gas supply from the Longford Plant, the steps Esso should have taken to lessen the risk of disaster and cessation of supply and to make recommendations of necessary changes to legislation or administrative procedures. The report of June 1999 entitled 'The Esso Longford Gas Plant Accident: Report of the Longford Royal Commission' contained a detailed account of the physical causes of the explosions and fire. Essentially, within the report what was described in considerable detail was the way the plant 'acted' in Latour's (2005) terms. The critical problem identified by the commission was the catastrophic failure of a heat exchanger (known as GP905). This failure in turn was caused by what is known as 'cold metal embrittlement', a descriptive name for a property of some metals that become brittle at very low temperatures and can subsequently shatter under thermal shock when heat is applied. In this case, there was a loss of lean oil flowing through the GP905 exchanger, a flow necessary to keep it at the proper temperature. This was combined with a larger than usual quantity of condensate flowing through the exchanger at very low temperatures. Consequently, the temperature of GP905 dropped precipitously. The commission estimated that the temperature of the vessel at the time it fractured was –48 degrees Celsius.

The design specification for the vessel assumed a normal operating temperature of +10 degrees Celsius. When heated lean oil (at approximately 250 degrees Celsius) was reintroduced in order to reheat the vessel it instead fractured and a hydrocarbon mist was released. That mist subsequently ignited (Dawson and Brooks 1999).

These mechanical, physical and chemical reasons for the failure of GP905 were subject to intense scrutiny. However, whilst many of the mechanisms leading to the failure were uncovered, some level of uncertainty remained about the exact causal sequence of physical events even after the Royal Commission. This was uncertainty that Esso sought to exploit at a later stage. The Commission surmised that the loss of lean oil was the combined result of a failure of an automatic valve that controlled temperature and incorrect manual bypass valve operation. This loss of lean oil was combined with an abnormal build-up of condensate at very low temperatures. The Commission argued that it was indeed the subsequent reintroduction of lean oil that was the cause of the fracture. It remained uncertain, however, about other events. One example here was the specific reason for the failure of three warm oil recirculation pumps (known collectively as GP1201) leading to the loss of lean oil. Several hypotheses were followed and tested by the Commission assisted by the necessary engineering expertise, but none proved satisfactory as evident in the text of the final commission report:

> … Some time prior to 7.00pm on 25 September the Rich Oil De-ethaniser (ROD) began to carry over additional material into its vapour line. It is likely that this was entrained liquid. The cause of this carryover has not been identified. It is known that in the past, excessively cold and light feed into the ROD has caused flooding but the mechanism by which this occurs is unclear. … (however) the conditions on the morning of the 25th of September were a long way from the column's flooding limit. (Dawson and Brooks 1999 p.96)

Despite uncertainty over this particular sequence of events the Commission concluded, on the balance of probabilities, that in some way the carryover was 'highly likely' to be the reason for the critical pump to shut down and cut off the lean oil supply. Actuarial uncertainty, however, remained as to why the automatic measures failed that day.

Such uncertainty, however, did not form the basis for disputed narratives about the cause of the disaster during the Royal Commission. The reason for this was that the problem of cold metal embrittlement was well known by engineers generally and by management at Esso headquarters. Whatever the cause for loss of lean oil leading to extreme low temperatures, the last thing to do was to reintroduce hot oil. This was a catastrophic decision.

Initial disputes arose at the Commission hearings about who *should have* known about the problem of cold metal embrittlement. Esso argued vigorously that the operators should have known. Indeed, evidence was tendered that operators were specifically tested on this in order to achieve a 'Tech 1 or 'Tech 2' rating, a rating necessary for a position as an operator. For Esso, the causal narrative was clear: operator error was the reason for the disaster (Hopkins 2001 pp.17–20). The Commission disagreed. It firmly rejected this explanation and in its findings stated that the real causes of the disaster were poor staff training and a lack of proper current operating procedures that would have clearly warned of the dangers of a loss of lean oil for the safety of the vessel in question (Dawson and Brooks 1999 p.234; Hopkins 2001 p.21).

Certainly, the state of knowledge about major hazard safety that existed at the time of the explosion in 1998 went well beyond a reductionist explanation of operator error. As a large multi-national company, Exxon would have been amongst the best placed to have known and understood the lessons learnt from previous industrial disasters, such as those emanating from the Seveso explosion in Italy and the Piper Alpha disaster in the North Sea off the coast of Scotland (De Marchi, Funtowicz and Ravetz 1996; Newman 1999). The approach to safety developed following each of these two previous events understood operator actions to sit within a broader organisational structure and culture of safety (or rather its lack). An error of this magnitude by an operator made no sense as a sufficient explanation. Indeed, the difference between 'active' causes (such as operator error) and 'latent' conditions (such as a lack of proper knowledge, poor equipment design, and so on) was well recognised in occupational health and safety literature before the explosion occurred (Reason 1997). Specifically in terms of previous disaster inquiries, the emphasis on poor operating procedures and problematic maintenance had been highlighted by the Cullen Inquiry into the Piper Alpha explosion ten years before Longford in 1988 (Cullen 1990). The Cullen Inquiry reported in November 1990, eight years before Longford.

At the centre of the professional knowledge on occupational health and safety is recognition of the need to promote a consciousness around safety. 'Safety consciousness' brings into sharp focus the implications for the safety of those on site arising out of day-to-day decisions around production, or simply tasks aimed at 'getting the job done' (Hopkins 2001; 2002b; Weick, Sutcliffe and Obstfeld 1999). That a notion of safety consciousness is considered as 'expert' knowledge appears at first glance somewhat incongruous, rather vague and open-ended. Yet, the evidence of a lack of such mindfulness, particularly at a complex hazardous industrial plant (and specifically at Longford) confirmed the importance of an ongoing awareness of, and attention to, safety. There was a litany of examples to animate accusations of the lack of safety consciousness at the plant. These included a previous near miss around cold metal embrittlement in August 1998, the significance of which was not picked up by ERA headquarters in Australia and no remedial action undertaken. In terms of training there was no method for assessing whether the operators really understood about safe operation of the plant. It was clear from the commission inquiry that their knowledge around critical safety issues was superficial. For example, the meaning of terms such as 'thermal damage' used in operator testing were not clearly understood (Hopkins 2002b), despite thermal damage being exhibited by brittle fracture of a vessel and hence being critical for the integrity of the particular plant, Gas Plant 1, where the explosion occurred. Further, there was a problematic system of alarms with too many demanding attention and little thought given to a design of the alarms indicating which needed to be attended to immediately and which could wait. As a result, critical safety alarms had been systematically ignored. Further, the Longford complex had been redeveloped with two new plants included that required lowering the operating temperature of Gas Plant 1 to below its design (optimal) operating temperature. Each of these individual problems was compounded and allowed to fester with the failure of the company to undertake a systematic hazard analysis (known as a HAZOP) of Gas Plant 1 even though it was the oldest plant on site, was operating outside its design parameters and was most in need of such an assessment. These examples are amongst only a few of the indicators found as a substantive indication that safety was not uppermost in the mind of Esso management (Dawson and Brooks 1999; Hopkins 2001).

What was clear through the Commission investigations was the way mindfulness on site prior to the disaster was directed towards production. Indeed, the only mention of the problem of excessively cold temperatures in Gas Plant 1 in manuals used on site was in relation to how it negatively affected the quality of the product, not the increased risks it posed to the safety of those on site. Further, there was a high degree of connectedness between the three gas plants on site, so that in the event of catastrophic failure of one plant (which was indeed what had occurred) it was difficult if not impossible to isolate a fire from being fed fuel from the other two plants on site. Such interconnectedness, however, was a natural outgrowth of an emphasis on production levels and product quality. Hence, the design of the plants on site, the design of the particular elements of equipment (such as monitoring alarms) and the organisation of production and personnel each signalled that production, not safety was the top priority.

Esso in their response to the disaster not only misread the expectations around adequate safety levels in their explanation for the Longford disaster. By arguing that the operators were to blame, Esso also completely misunderstood the normative expectations of the Victorian public around occupational health and safety and company responsibility. 'Blaming the worker' as a means of explaining death at work was widely understood as an attempt to deflect blame and avoid responsibility (Quinlan and Bohle 1991). Esso as an extremely large and well-known corporation, in particular, was arguably the entity amongst the least likely to find any resonance publically with this approach. Indeed, such an argument was read as arrogance and a blatant disregard of its responsibilities.

The decision of Esso to blame operators for the disaster was met by the Australian media taking Esso and its parent company Exxon to task. The Australian Broadcasting Corporation's (ABC) *7.30 Report*, a nightly current affairs programme, went to air on 3 May 1999 opening with, 'We explore serious allegations about the commitment to safety of Esso's parent company Exxon, and claims that the oil giant operates a world-wide scheme designed to conceal possible evidence of culpability in disasters ...' (Kerry O'Brien, ABC 1999).

The programme interviewed a series of ex-employees who painted a very grim picture of the company, arguing amongst other things that 'Esso's safety record is a sham' and that 'Lost Time Incident (sic) figures were being fudged'. The company was depicted as inhumane and secretive. A former employee interviewed on the programme stated 'ethics, moral obligations, staff, family attitudes or anything, just falls by the wayside with the perspective on profits and just getting the gas and oil flowing'. Jill Singer, the investigating reporter further argued, 'Right across the world, Exxon keeps a vice-like grip on damaging information'. Such a claim was supported by the fact that the Coroner had seized a draft report of the investigation Exxon undertook into Longford before it could be destroyed. This report[5] clearly outlined significant shortcomings by Esso at Longford. The final report of the company was a far more anodyne document (ABC 1999; Hopkins 2001).

Esso realised rather belatedly that it had made a tactical error in blaming the operators during its evidence to the Royal Commission. In the criminal trial that followed the Commission, Esso did not use the defence that operators were to blame. Indeed, it did not even choose to cross-examine the operator it felt was most responsible – a clear indication in an adversarial trial in front of a jury that such a tactic would have been viewed very dimly indeed (Hopkins 2002a).[6] Esso was charged with 11 offences under Occupational Health and Safety legislation, and tried in the Supreme Court of Victoria, the highest court in the state. This was unusual; offences of this nature would normally be heard in the County Court (one level down) or even the Magistrates Court (at the lowest level). But, the prosecution successfully argued that it should be heard in the Supreme Court, based on its legal significance.

Stripped of the possibility of defending itself through blaming the operators, Esso's defence lawyers then needed another rationale for their defence. The first tactic was to reduce the number of charges. It argued prior to the trial that the charge of 'failure to ensure the safety of persons other than employees' should be dismissed on the grounds that it had no control over the emergency workers once on site, and perhaps that the Country Fire Authority might be liable for the safety of their own members rather than Esso. The judge vehemently disagreed stating, 'The submission I have just had the misfortune to hear is both wrong in law and callous in character' (cited in Hopkins 2002a p.21). Again, Esso was judged as heartless.

The second tactic should come as no surprise in light of the discussion of actuarial risk and uncertainty in the previous chapter. Esso fell back on raising technical uncertainty as to the cause of the rupture of the heat exchanger, GP905. It challenged the allegation that the cause of the explosion was cold metal embrittlement brought about through the reintroduction of lean oil. Indeed, it suggested, somewhat surprisingly, that there was no proof that the reintroduction of hot oil had actually occurred. Various strategies were aimed at exploiting the uncertainties that remained in the wake of the Commission. As this was a criminal trial it was not necessary for Esso to explain the cause of the explosions and fire, rather the prosecution needed to prove Esso's culpability beyond reasonable doubt. Hence, if Esso could raise doubts about the prosecution's explanation and suggest possible alternatives then it might avoid liability. This was important not only for the criminal trial, but for subsequent civil cases (Hopkins 2002a). As argued in Chapter 3, scientific uncertainty is a common strategy used to frame responsibility (see above pp. 40–41 and Beyea and Berger 2001). In this trial, then, scientific uncertainty became a commodity.

The final method was to call on fate. If cause could not be established, then this was a plain accident, and accidents happen. Esso counsel lamented 'Why can't it be that you can have an accident in this world of ours? Why can't it be that you do not know how something happened?' (cited in Hopkins 2002a p.29). Again, Esso (in this case Esso's defence) fundamentally misread sociocultural expectations that scientific explanations reveal cause and effect. Whilst uncertainty might exist, it is no longer possible for a company like Esso to blame fate, Allah or God for misfortune (Haines and Sutton 2003), in this case as sufficient explanation of an explosion and fire at one of their gas plants.

Esso was unsuccessful in defending the charges. Indeed, its various strategies had the opposite effect. Some failed spectacularly. In trying to encourage its experts to generate alternative explanations for the explosion, explanations it could use in its defence, it had written a letter to them stating, 'the failure was due to embrittlement following the vessel being subjected to temperatures below those for which its metal was not designed'(cited in Hopkins 2002a p.30). This letter was discovered by the prosecution late in the trial. In trying to exploit uncertainty, Esso had not conceded to that point the most likely cause of the explosion was brittle fracture and had thus made the prosecution go to great lengths to prove the point. Uncertainty as a commodity, however, was proving of little worth. Further, in trying to shed doubt that a HAZOP would have uncovered the problem of cold metal embrittlement, Esso put its own expert witness in the witness box. Cross-examination by the prosecution turned this witness into a star witness *for* the prosecution, stating under the prosecution's questions that the problem of embrittlement would have emerged 'coming at them like a steam train' (cited in Hopkins 2002a p.31).

The jury convicted Esso on all 11 counts. The judge in sentencing was damning, finding that 'The events of 25 September 1998 were the responsibility of Esso: no one else. Their cause was grievous, foreseeable and avoidable. Their consequence was grievous, tragic and avoidable' (cited in Hopkins 2002a p.33). Esso was fined a total of $2 million, the largest fine ever levied to that date under *The Occupational Health and Safety Act 1985* (Vic). It was highly significant that on two of the counts it received the (then) maximum penalty of $250,000 with an additional $50,000 penalty in each case. Previous fines under the Act had been around 7 to 15 per cent of the maximum (Wheelwright 2004).

The narrative generated around the events at Longford by the Royal Commission and confirmed by the trial was significant for what was to follow. The Royal Commission and then the trial had succeeded in placing responsibility for safety at the door of the company. Major Hazard Facilities (MHFs) are highly complex and, when poorly managed, extremely dangerous. Placing responsibility in this way made possible the development of a regulatory regime that required MHFs to design risk management regimes that could engender an ongoing consciousness of safety. The complete misreading by Esso of public expectations also signalled to the Victorian government that their actions in terms of regulatory reforms would be closely watched – and would be heavily criticised if not considered adequate. The deaths at Longford also gave support to an ongoing campaign to introduce industrial manslaughter laws in Victoria. The long-serving Liberal premier of that state, Jeff Kennett, lost the state election on 18 September 1999 in a surprise result that provided government to the Labor Party after a seven-year absence. The introduction of industrial manslaughter had been a prominent part of the ALP's 1999 election campaign. Once in power, the Victorian ALP introduced a bill into the parliament to enact a new crime of industrial manslaughter (in 2001), a bill that had the strong support of the union movement and also considerable public support, in part, by virtue of memory of the Longford explosion. The bill was, however, defeated in the upper house (legislative council) where the conservative parties held sway. Facing a tight election in 2002 and considerable opposition by industry, the then Premier Steve Bracks went into the 2002 election promising not to reintroduce the industrial manslaughter bill.

But, as Hopkins (2002a) eloquently points out, the causal narratives that prevailed around the reasons for the disaster (and hence the solutions) were not complete. Prosecutions and criminal law reform did not consider the role of the government in exacerbating the state-wide impact of the Longford disaster. The dependence of Victoria on a single source of supply was not an issue the Royal Commission was asked to consider, neither was it present in public debates around industrial manslaughter, despite the critical impact this had on the community. Absent, too, was the impact of the privatisation of the gas industry that had been completed just before the explosion in 1997. Despite this, there was much about the post-Longford investigation and subsequent trial that augured well for effective regulatory reform in Victoria. Occupational health and safety, however, was a state not a Commonwealth responsibility in Australia. Given these jurisdictional limits, would such lessons be learnt by other Australian states?

THE TERRORIST ATTACKS OF 11 SEPTEMBER, 2001

At one level, to include the terrorist attacks of September 11 in the United States of America (US) in a study of Australian regulatory response to disasters appears somewhat contradictory. No terrorist attack occurred on Australian soil, no dramatic explosion happened in a local setting akin to the Longford disaster. Neither was there a flurry of newspaper articles speculating about the possibility of attack within Australia before September 11, compared to the rumours in the media around the health of HIH (Insurance) prior to its demise.

Yet, a number of Australians were deeply affected. Indeed, the loss of Australian life was the greatest of the three events in this book, with eleven deaths from the attacks. However, it was still possible that it could have been understood as a death in a foreign land, not as a fundamental threat to Australia. Had the attack occurred in another country, rather than the United States, the perception of threat may have been quite different. But, it did happen in the US. The attack generated iconic images that flashed around the world and Australians, like many others, were transfixed by the spectacle. A year later, an attack on 12 October 2002 in Bali, a popular tourist destination for Australians, led to 202 deaths, 88 of whom were Australian. Other attacks followed: the bombing of the Madrid Train Station on 11 March 2004 that claimed 191 lives; the London bombings on 7 July 2005, claiming 54 lives including one Australian; and then another attack in Bali, on 1 October 2005, claiming 20 lives including four Australians. From these events it appeared that it was simply a matter of time before a terrorist attack occurred on Australian soil. Each of the attacks subsequent to those in the US in 2001, and in particular the 2002 Bali Bombings, gave rise to a sense that Australia was indeed at high risk of attack.

This tension between geography and vulnerability was evident in the response of Australia to the terrorist attack in the United States of 11 September 2001. There could be neither a public inquiry into what happened in the United States nor a Royal Commission or public hearings. In Australia, there were no witnesses called or cross-examined regarding the causes of the terrorist attacks in the US, nor was a rigorous assessment undertaken of threats of an attack within Australia prior to legislation being introduced into the parliament.[7] There was no jurisdictional control over this attack that would provide the impetus for such an investigation to occur prior to the development of a legislative response. Hence, processes and sources of accountability for government action (or inaction) based on an analysis of the critical event itself, processes familiar in the other two disasters (Longford and HIH) simply were not present in this case. Inquiries that did occur, did so in the wake of presentation of bills into the parliament (see for example Senate Legal and Constitutional Legislation Committee 2002).

A sense of vulnerability within Australia after September 11, however, demanded a response. There were a variety of investigations and assessments of the threat these attacks posed to Australia that purported to underpin this response. Public documents included a defence update entitled, *Australia's National Security: A Defence Update* (hereafter Department of Defence 2003) and a Department of Foreign Affairs and Trade (DFAT) White Paper entitled, *Advancing the National Interest: Australia's Foreign and Trade Policy White Paper* (Hereafter DFAT 2003) and a further DFAT White Paper in 2004 entitled, *Transnational Terrorism: The Threat to Australia* (Hereafter DFAT 2004). There was also the setting up of the National Counter-terrorism Committee (NCTC) (which first met in November 2002 under the auspices of the Intergovernmental Agreement on Australia's National Counter-terrorism Arrangements of 24 October 2002). The NCTC's task amongst others was the development of a National Counter-terrorism Plan, together with various reports from the Departments of Foreign Affairs and Trade and from Defence.

The content of the documents and committee deliberations into the causes of terrorism and the threats posed to Australia that are publicly available stand in stark contrast to both the Longford and HIH Royal Commissions, discussed above and below respectively. These counter-terrorism assessments and investigations contained none of the detail and dense analysis that was present in the Royal Commission reports into the Longford and HIH disasters. Further, these assessments were produced by public servants at the behest of politicians and so lacked the visible independence of a Royal Commission. The various reports were overseen by government ministers and public servants rather than commissions chaired by retired eminent judges or engineers.

The assessment of actuarial risk available to the public setting out the potential impact, likelihood of and vulnerability to future terrorist attack lacked a solid and grounded analysis. Such an actuarial narrative was essential for providing substance behind a resulting regulatory response. In part, this jurisdictional anomaly of where the attacks occurred and level of political control over the assessments that did occur partly explains a lack of such a narrative pertinent to Australia. A second reason lay in the nature of the particular actuarial risk itself where levels of uncertainty and ambiguity were high. Thirdly, even if there had existed sound evidence of an imminent threat, the results would not necessarily have been made public since the risk would have been driven by intelligence material. Overall, then attempts that were made to construct a defensible and public actuarial narrative were much more challenging and problematic.

The high levels of uncertainty acknowledged in the analysis of actuarial risk in these documents, however, did not result in a call for caution and the need for a more detailed analysis. Rather uncertainty was combined with exhortations for action. The relevant papers and documents that provided the ostensible assessment of actuarial risk contain vivid illustrations of the slippage between acknowledgement of uncertainty and the presence of a palpable threat. So the 2004 DFAT White Paper stated that 'Australia must also now face the threats of ambiguity and the unknown' (DFAT 2004 p.vii) whilst also stating 'the demands of these terrorists are absolute'. In taking this position it reiterated the 2003 argument that, 'Unlike traditional forms of terrorism, the terrorist threat from Islamic extremism is not limited by geography and not amenable to negotiation. It has a particular edge for Australia in South-East Asia' (DFAT 2003 p.x).

Uncertainty was dispelled through calling for action. Narrowing either impact or especially probability was considered impossible, so uncertainty was a situation that Australia just had to deal with. The 2004 White Paper stated: 'We have to adjust to a threat that is not only alien, but unconventional and unpredictable. Its presence is largely unseen and unknown' (DFAT 2004 p.4). To 'adjust' was to act decisively in the face of uncertainty.

The level of the response considered appropriate was then shaped by the potential impact. The conclusions reached by each of these papers were that the potential for destruction was extreme. The DFAT 2003 paper stated: 'Our ultimate fear is the possibility of international terrorists acquiring weapons of mass destruction and, through them, the capacity to kill tens or hundreds of thousands of innocent people' (2003 p.xi). Hence each of the three documents emphasised the serious nature of the threat posed by what was termed 'Transnational Terrorism' (Department of Defence 2003; DFAT 2003; 2004). The potential for an attack was heightened since the 'grave threat' (DFAT 2004 p.v) was underpinned by a new Muslim extremist ideology motivating indiscriminate acts of violence undeterred by geography. Further, Australia was specifically noted as a target (DFAT 2004 p.66). Globalisation made Australia more vulnerable through the ease of travel and communication and this was combined with arguments that the world was a more dangerous place with a proliferation of both the number of weapons and objects that could be used as weapons (DFAT 2004 p.4).

In the face of such an assessment the documents exhorted the public to get behind the government. They contained an explicit demand for all Australians to recognise the 'unseen and unknown' (DFAT 2004 p.4) threat and acknowledge the need for a strong response. This was achieved not by the production of clear evidence to convince citizens of the level of threat, but by force of phrase. Perhaps pushing the limits a little, the contents here were at times reminiscent of arguments made about the existence of witches existing in the witch-hunts of the 15th century where denial of the possibility of witchcraft was proof of heresy and gave rise to accusations that the denier themselves must be a witch (Kramer and Sprenger 1486). In the case of terrorism, suggestions that some might have been tempted to make in the wake of September 11 that the terrorist threat may be overblown would be considered dangerous. Such views, the documents considered, would make Australia and Australians a greater target for attack. As the government White Paper on transnational terrorism stated:

> The extent of the terrorist threat to Australian interests abroad is only mitigated by the level of international co-operation to fight it. *Complacency, denial or delusions of immunity do not only reduce international co-operation to a dangerously low common denominator: they draw the danger to the areas where resistance is weakest* (emphasis added). (DFAT 2004 p.xii)

Ultimately, the assessment of actuarial risk that emerges from the documentation is that the threat was immense. It was everywhere and required a level of resources and management that was unheard of in the years before September 11. At a very real level, Australian government attempts to assess the actuarial risk set up a scenario which was simply impossible to risk manage in a systematic fashion.

The actuarial risk assessment was also limited in particular ways. It was reminiscent of Renn's (2008) notion of risk class 'Cyclops' where the understanding developed of the causes that lead to a heightening of a particular risk (in this case of a terrorist attack) are one-dimensional. For example, the possibility that the response to terrorism could engender the motivation for fresh recruits to a terrorist's cause was almost entirely absent from the assessment of risk. There was a particular reason for this, namely that such a view would threaten Australia's support for US military action. The possibility that participation in the 'War on Terror' might generate ongoing problems – including exacerbating the problem of extremist violence – was not considered. Rather, a strong (that is, good) response meant a military response. The 2003 Defence update stated, 'Our participation as a US ally in the War on Terror might attract some criticism. But a weaker or equivocal response to this threat would not serve Australia well or decrease our vulnerability' (Department of Defence 2003 p.13). The government view was that military responses and strategic military and intelligence partnerships would protect Australia best.

Clearly, then, this documentation produced in the aftermath of September 11 must be read in light of the decision by the Australian Government to join the United States' formed 'Coalition of the Willing' and assist in the invasion of Iraq. The emphasis on weapons of mass destruction within the text only makes complete sense in this light. The 2004 White Paper stated:

> Iraq represents a major challenge to international security. The Iraqi regime has used chemical weapons against Iranian soldiers and its own people. Since its unconditional agreement in 1991 to give up weapons of mass destruction, Iraq has continued its efforts to procure equipment, material and technology that could assist its weapons of mass destruction program. Saddam Hussein's desire for weapons of mass destruction remains undiminished. Iraq's flouting of international norms and persistent defiance of the United Nations Security Council call into question the authority of the United Nations and the effectiveness of international law. Saddam Hussein's virulent anti-Western stance and his support for terrorism raise the possibility of his making available weapons of mass destruction to al-Qaida or other terrorist groups. The Australian Government considers continuation of the status quo with regard to Iraq to be unacceptable. (DFAT 2004 p.44)

The metaphor of Cyclops as a way to encapsulate the risk-assessment process undertaken here in terms of the risk of a future terrorist attack also can be usefully extended to consider the historic orientation of both Australia and the United States to define state strength by military capability. The political dominance of this view was clearly evident during the Cold War (Carroll 2006). Within the documentation produced by the Australian Government in response to September 11 the role the Cold War played in the dissemination and proliferation of weapons across the world and the support of the United States of the Mujahedeen in the war against the Soviet presence in Afghanistan (Carroll 2006) were entirely absent.

Solutions to extremist violence that are based on a one-dimensional assessment of actuarial risk are problematic (Krueger 2007). This is irrespective of content, since any assessments based on too narrow an appreciation of cause all fall within Renn's Cyclops risk class. In doing so, they have the potential to generate seriously limited methods of risk management and control.

It is not my intention to oversimplify the very complex and challenging dynamics that lay behind the terrorist attacks of September 11 and subsequent incidents. It is well beyond the scope of this book to undertake a critical analysis of the reasons behind the generation of the most recent manifestation of terrorism. However, the elements of a risk assessment: consequence and probability based on a rigorous examination of cause and vulnerability require a detached and open-minded stance. Hence, from an actuarial vantage point, the impact on Australia to date from terrorist attacks remains significantly lower than the yearly toll from road trauma. Indeed, historically the deaths from terrorism within Australia remain very low, arguably at two. Further, reaching an objective assessment of probability, one based on an open-minded appraisal of cause in the context of preventing a terrorist attack, remains in its infancy. In terms of the proliferation of weapons that materially affect vulnerability (as they might be brought into the country) as well as impact, the role played by the Cold War including by the United States and other Western nations (as well as the former Soviet Union) clearly are important to understand (Carroll 2006).

The impact of the terrorist attacks in the United States on Australia, however, went well beyond actuarial concerns. Despite the loss of Australian life as a tangible indicator of actuarial risk impact, what emerges from the historical record of Australian experiences from September 11 is a sense of these attacks as a threat to humanity and to Western civilisation. The documents produced in the wake of 11 September 2001 make more sense if they are understood not as attempting a rigorous actuarial risk assessment, but responding to threats that were predominantly socio-cultural and political.

It is important to remember in light of the arguments of Chapter 3 that such risks are real. Hence they generate the need for individuals and groups to undertake socio-cultural and political 'risk assessments', in order to know what threats are faced by both the individual and the collective. Socio-cultural and political risks rest on a very tangible core: namely the potential for a catastrophic loss of social integration in the case of the former risk and a loss of political legitimacy in the latter. As Chapter 3 highlighted, however, both of these risks are subjected to 'risk assessments' that may be more or less accurate.

A useful method of exploring these socio-cultural and political 'risk assessments' in the aftermath of September 11 within Australia is to examine the condolence motion presented by the Liberal/National Coalition government to Parliament on 17 September 2001. This motion gives a vivid sense of how the attacks of the week before were understood by the government and what threats they were considered to pose to Australian society. Appraisals made at the time of levels of both socio-cultural and political risk in large part presaged what was to follow.

The narrative frame of the condolence motion is important to understand. It began and ended with an expression of humanity. This beginning and end, however, was joined by defining the attacks as a new war. Who this enemy was, however, remained unstated. The motion opened with an expression of horror at the attacks and empathy for the people of the United States. It was seen as a threat to all 'free people', to which the United States responded by acts of heroism. It continued by stating that such an attack needed to be understood in military terms and as such required the invocation of the ANZUS treaty, the security treaty between Australia, New Zealand and the United States. Australia, then, it maintained must stand firm with the United States and to join with it in necessary 'action'. Finally, in Part 8 there was a statement on the need for tolerance and inclusion, a tentative reconnection in the narrative structure back to a common humanity.

> The Condolence Motion as it was presented to the Australian Parliament on September 17th 2001. The motion:
> (1) expresses its horror at the terrorist attacks which have claimed so many lives in the United States of America;
> (2) conveys to the Government and people of the United States of America the deepest sympathy and sense of shared loss felt by the Government and people of Australia;
> (3) extends condolences to the families and other loved ones of those Australians killed or missing as a result of the attacks;
> (4) declares that such attacks represent an assault, not only on the people and the values of the United States of America, but of free societies everywhere;
> (5) praises the courageous efforts of those engaged in the dangerous rescue operation still underway;
> (6) believes that the terrorist actions in New York City and Washington DC constitute an attack upon the United States of America within the meaning of Articles IV and V of the ANZUS Treaty;
> (7) fully endorses the commitment of the Australian Government to support within Australia's capabilities United States-led action against those responsible for these tragic attacks;
> and
> (8) encourages all Australians in the wake of these appalling events to display those very qualities of tolerance and inclusion which the terrorists themselves have assaulted with such awful consequences (Hansard 2001a p.30739).

The speeches in response to this condolence motion presented both in the House of Representatives and the Senate on 17 September, the first sitting day after the September 11 attacks, animated these themes and the tensions within their narrative structure. Horror was expressed at the inhumanity evident in the attacks. Peter Costello, the Australian Treasurer at the time stated:

> Our hearts are heavy as we think of those that have died and of the families who have lost loved ones. There is indescribable sadness at the waste of life that arose out of these incidents. The thing about evil is that it is indiscriminate. Those who kill based on hate or fanaticism do not have any regard for the people who are their victims. They do not have any regard for those that are living their everyday lives. It has been said that this is an attack on civilisation because it is an attack on the right of people to go about their ordinary lives without being killed. (The Hon. Peter Costello, Hansard 2001a p.30758)

There was unequivocal bi-partisan support for the condolence motion. Senator Cook, Opposition Leader in the Senate saw the attack as a manifestation of 'pure evil', picking up on a headline in an Australian newspaper, the *Herald Sun,* in his speech, stating that 'This fearful image (of a Boeing 737 in the shadows of the World Trade Center moments before impact) had the simple and accurate headline 'Pure evil' (Hansard 2001b p.27168). Put simply, the attack was, '... an attack on all decent people of all races and all religions' (Daryl Williams, Attorney General, Hansard 2001a p.30760).

There were a variety of ways in which the bond between Australia and the United States was expressed. The Prime Minister John Howard[8] had been in Washington on the day of the attacks, which led to an emotional closeness with the events. Howard described the day of the attacks in Washington: 'It was a beautiful Washington morning – with just a touch of Autumn ...' (Hansard 2001a p. 30739) and went on to state '... I felt an enormous sense of empathy towards the American people who had suffered this awful deed' (p.30740), later on describing how he had the opportunity to extend his condolences to Senators Clinton and Schumer (representatives of the state of New York) and concluding that 'the bonds between our two nations run very deep' (p.30741). The (then) Opposition Leader, Kim Beazely responded, concurring with this assessment of kinship between the two countries drawing, on the actions of the United States in World War II, 'We in Australia owe our freedom to the United States. In our darkest hour in 1941 our wartime Prime Minister called on the Americans, and they did not let us down' (Hansard 2001a p.30745). Others were more prosaic in their assessment with Laurie Brereton, an ALP member of the House of Representatives, commenting that 'Australia stands foursquare with the United States' (Hansard 2001a p.30752). Others were poetic, Christopher Pyne a Liberal member of the House of Representatives, drew on the Book of Ruth in the Old Testament in his speech to illustrate his sense of the connection between the two countries:

> ... I will go where you go. I will live where you live. Your people are my people. Your God will be my God. The words of Ruth say much more eloquently than I could how we feel as Australians about our kinship with the people of the United States. We feel complete solidarity with them in everyway. There is no daylight between us and the people of the United States, not a fraction. (Hansard 2001a p.30773)

Speeches in both houses of parliament on that day are well understood as expressing a sense of ontological threat, a socio-cultural rather than an actuarial risk, arising from the September 11 attacks. The response to such a threat was, as the condolence motion stated, to join with the United States in their military response to the attack. No person was safe. Peter Reith, the Minister for Defence argued '... no-one is immune from this sort of behaviour' (Hansard

2001a p.30755). The Attorney General Darryl Williams mirrored this sentiment arguing '… what has happened demonstrates that terrorism of any manifestation represents a threat that knows no borders' (Hansard 2001a p.30760).

There was some equivocation at this point and differences in emphasis arose. A number of the Members understood that this was a decisive point in history that would determine the future course of events. Wayne Swan (ALP) reflected:

> Citizens around the world are now rightly asking questions about their own nation, about their world and about the direction in which the world should now move. As we look to the future, I sincerely hope that the terrible events of the last week do not trigger a vicious cycle of hate and war. (Hansard 2001a p.30784)

Others saw the choice as simple. The United States was attacked and had the right of self-defence. Kathy Sullivan, Liberal Member for Moncrieff argued: 'There has been a constant reference over the past week to America's 'just right of retaliation' under these particular circumstances. Frankly, I do not see an American military response as retaliation; I see it as an act of self-defence' (Hansard 2001a p.30785).

This tension between views erupted within the Senate into open disagreement. The emphasis on a military response was the area that was most visibly and pointedly contested not predominantly by the opposition, however, but by the minor parties (the Greens and the Democrats) in the Senate. Together, they expressed strong concern with the invocation of the ANZUS treaty and the apparent open-ended nature of the support for United States action in response to the attacks.

The concerns of the minor parties met with rebuke by government senators. Opposition by one Senator, Natasha Stott Despoja, the Leader of the Australian Democrats to sections 6 and 7 of the condolence motion (invocation of ANZUS and support for US-led action) led to an outburst by Government Senator Amanda Vanstone, 'Don't you know the difference between a condolence motion and a debate?' (Hansard 2001b p.27166) she decried.

This interjection is significant. Within the context of a condolence motion in the parliament, the classic socio-cultural risk parameters are at play where emotions and values are foremost and loyalties on display. Debate in response to a condolence motion then, can be considered 'matter out of place' (Douglas 1966 p.36). Socio-cultural norms here rested on a substantive and emotional core where analysis was abhorrent. Exhibited here is a classic conflict of rationalities (Gerth and Mills 1991 [1948]; Weber 1964 [1947]) where analysis is foreign to an expression of empathy and solidarity. As such it brought condemnation.

But, of course this expression of socio-cultural normative solidarity in the condolence motion was taking place within the quintessential house of politics, the Australian Parliament. In this setting an appeal to norms irretrievably was embedded within political strategy. The strategy used by Senator Vanstone was to disparage the Democrats for their insensitivity (drawing on value rationality), yet for the Greens and Australian Democrats to accept that the motion meant accepting the normative narrative of that condolence motion (humanity-war-humanity).

Socio-cultural norms are contested. And these contests are, as Mary Douglas reminds us, political (Douglas 1992). In the face of a perceived ontological threat, these contests took on a heightened significance. Senator Vanstone expressed in the parliament the same exhortations evident in the defence and foreign affairs documentation: if you are not with us, you must be against us.

Others, however, moved away from such brinksmanship. Evident in some speeches on that day were the concerns expressed of the need for composure. Care and reflection in Australia's response were required in order to preserve an open and tolerant society. Anna Bourke, the Member for Chisholm urged for, '... calm in the wake of this tragedy. To do anything less would be to dishonour those whose lives have been so irreversibly changed. Whilst it would be understandable, we must not approach this with an uncontrolled sense of revenge and anger' (Hansard 2001a p.30759).

Others called for a reflection of the economic cost that would be involved. There was recognition that significant resources might be diverted to security, scarce resources that had the capacity for sustained benefits in other areas. Such a diversion, some argued, would be for little gain. Julia Irwin, Member for Fowler argued:

> In the coming years our banks will probably spend more on security than it would cost to relieve Third World debt. Our security services will intrude more and more into our privacy, but we will still be vulnerable until we come to terms with the causes of terrorism, until we learn that from those who preach hatred do so not only from minarets but from our radio stations. Until we condemn hatred in all its forms, we can only expect terrorism to continue, and the thousands who died in the United States last week will have died in vain. (Hansard 2001a p.30793)

The narrative of the condolence motion, however, itself was influenced by a number of other contemporaneous events. The attacks of September 11 occurred within a highly charged atmosphere within Australia. There were critical occurrences, some of the government's own making and some beyond their control, both of which pre-figured and shaped the debate in the early weeks and months after the attack. The element most clearly influential here was the government's blurring of the boundaries between terrorists and asylum seekers. The Liberal/National Coalition government had been trailing in opinion polls and had used the arrival of asylum seekers by boat as a means to increase their popularity. This culminated in the Tampa crisis in August 2001, where a wooden vessel filled with asylum seekers became stranded in International waters. They were picked up by a Norwegian cargo vessel the MV *Tampa* which requested permission to land at Christmas Island, an Australian outpost close to Indonesia. However, the Australian government denied access to the ship. The result of the debacle was that Australia was reported by Norway to the United Nations, the United Nations High Commissioner for Refugees and the International Maritime Organisation. Within Australia, however, it also led to what was known as the Pacific Solution, the processing of refugees on the island of Nauru.

The Australian government's response to the *Tampa* was popular, but divisive. It led to a significant improvement in the Liberal/National Coalition government's political fortune. This in turn meant that a reversal of the strategy of gaining strength through division in the wake of the terrorist attacks in the United States would threaten this new found popularity and risked the government losing face with what it saw as key sections of the electorate.

Asylum seekers thus became connected irreparably with terrorists. As such, they could be described as less than human. Following September 11, on 6 October 2001 the government claimed that parents on another vessel of asylum seekers, dubbed the SIEV 4 had 'thrown their children overboard.' Subject to a comprehensive senate inquiry this claim was later found to be false (Senate Select Committee 2002). Despite this finding, the political wind moved further in the direction of the Liberal/National Coalition. An election was called for 10 November 2001.

It is significant, then, in the context of heightened emotion that there was a plea not to use the election to divide an anxious community. Bob McMullan (ALP) appealed, 'It is very important that all of us, here as members of parliament and throughout the community in the lead-up to this election do not do or say anything that would divide rather than unite our nation' (Hansard 2001a p. 30761).

Such pleas, however, were to little avail. The Coalition strategy worked and their legitimacy to govern was confirmed. The Liberal/National Coalition with John Howard as Prime Minister won convincingly in the 10 November election. The Coalition's sense of the dominant public appraisal of socio-cultural risk, together with their assessment of their own political risk, set the scene for the particular framing of actuarial risk discussed above.

The implications this held for the regulatory response to September 11 will be closely analysed in the ensuing chapters. However, there were two events of critical import for the airline industry that occurred around the same time as the terrorist attacks in the United States. The first was the continuing privatisation of airports across the country. The privatisation of Sydney Airport, the largest and the last airport to be privatised, hung in the balance at the time the terrorist attacks occurred. The second event was the collapse of Ansett Airlines on Friday 14 September, stranding hundreds of passengers across Australia. Any response, then, would need to be cognisant of the economic travails of the airline industry.

In conclusion, the terrorist attacks of September 11 revealed a distinct patterning of the three risks discussed in Chapter 3. The actuarial risk was assessed by the government of the day as extreme and pervasive. Such an assessment led predominantly to a government call for military and intelligence response as central to reduce the threat of future attack. However, the construction of actuarial risk as posing this level of threat necessarily spilled over into a demand that regulatory initiatives cover all possible bases for an attack – clearly an impossible task.

This actuarial risk assessment rested on a tenuous base. There was little rigorous assessment publicly available of vulnerability, let alone probability. Uncertainty was not (and possibly could not) be dispelled through an actuarial analysis. To understand why the actuarial response was skewed towards a military and intelligence response requires understanding that the predominant risk at play here was not actuarial, but rather socio-cultural (that is an ontological threat to the existence of 'who we are') and political. The threat to the legitimacy of the Liberal/National government was evident in the early months of 2001. Their response to this heightened risk of their demise prefigured and to a certain extent determined the response to the political risk posed by the terrorist attacks. The regulatory implications, then, were clear. The regulatory response necessarily would be shaped by a political and socio-cultural orientation that set regulators and regulated sites an impossible actuarial task.

THE COLLAPSE OF HIH INSURANCE

The central challenge in dissecting cases of corporate collapse lies in paring risk-taking that is beneficial to the economy and hence the broader community from that which brings about suffering and hardship to that same community. This is not an easy process as definitions of 'acceptable risk-taking' shift. Indeed, the history of HIH Insurance Ltd reveals an entrepreneurial founding, of individuals chasing business opportunities as they arose and which, on the face of it, appeared to be advantageous to the community through the provision of low-cost insurance and welcome investment returns. However, the heyday of HIH in the mid-1990s was followed by the company's demise. Entrepreneurial risk-taking by the company was redefined as evidence of poor management that, when combined with a market downturn, led to a downward spiral. The final stages of HIH included an unseemly 'dash for cash' by insiders when the end of the company appeared imminent, (a practice common in cases of corporate failure), behaviour that accompanied the company's final collapse in a mass of debt.

The history of HIH Insurance, as outlined in the HIH Royal Commission (Owen 2003, Vol I Chapter 3) describes how the company began trading as MW Payne Liability Agencies Pty Ltd when the two founders, Ray Williams and Michael Payne saw a profitable opening in the insurance industry through the Lloyds of London franchise. The two men worked as agents in Australia for two Lloyds of London syndicates mainly in workers' compensation insurance, first in Victoria, then Tasmania and other states. Three years later, the success of the business attracted CE Heath, a major UK insurance company, and in 1971 the company was acquired by CE Heath, and in the process changed its name to CE Heath (Underwriting). It continued successfully in the workers compensation insurance market until legislative changes in Australia in the mid-1980s required a change in direction. The nationalisation of workers' compensation insurance in key states saw CE Heath diversify into different insurance classes (property, commercial and professional liability). The company was restructured and became known as CE Heath International Holdings. The company continued to expand internationally, acquiring businesses in Hong Kong and California and, notably, in 1995 it acquired CIC a large general insurer. CIC was controlled by Winterthur a large Swiss insurer and as a result of the deal Winterthur became a significant shareholder in a renamed entity HIH Winterthur International Holdings Limited. Over time, though, differences of business strategy saw Winterthur sell its shares in 1998 by way of a fully subscribed float that demonstrated confidence by the Australian public in the (now renamed) HIH Insurance Ltd (hereafter HIH).

HIH encountered progressive problems particularly after the exit of Winterthur. Its ambitious growth through acquisition was creating difficulties as overseas operations, both in the UK and California, lost money. These losses were compounded by a business strategy adopted by HIH of aggressive selling of budget-priced insurance combined with optimistic costing of long-tailed liabilities. The failed realisation of a profit on key investments coupled with this business strategy was critical in its eventual demise. The acquisition of FAI insurance in 1999, replete with its own problems of significant debt, compounded HIH's difficulties. Despite various attempts to save the company, provisional liquidators were appointed on 15 March 2001 and on 27 August of that year the HIH group (of 30 companies) was placed into official liquidation.

The Royal Commission chaired by the Hon. Justice Neville Owen began hearings into the collapse on 19 September 2001 and reported in April of 2003 in a three-volumed report entitled 'The Failure of HIH Insurance' (Owen 2003). The report reveals how for much of its 33 years the fortunes of the company were driven by Ray Williams who essentially acted as chief executive of the business from 1968 until he stepped aside in October 2000. The Commission report stated that the main reason for the collapse of the company was, on one level, quite simple: there was insufficient provision made to service the ongoing liabilities of the company, hence in March 2001 there was no money to service the company's debt obligations as they became due. The analysis of why this crisis eventuated, however, reveals a much more complex picture since grasping the underlying financial health of a group as large and diverse as HIH[9] was (and remains) a challenging task.

The assessment of the failure of HIH made by the Commission follows a process familiar to actuarial assessments identifying impact and cause. The spread of the impact from the collapse revealed by the commission was considerable. The report estimated that the losses from HIH were between $3.6 and $5.3 billion, making it the largest corporate collapse in Australia's history. To bring this sum to life, Justice Owen described in his report some of the detail of the harm to individuals and communities wrought by the collapse. He pointed to the approximately 200 permanently disabled people who were no longer receiving their regular payments from HIH by virtue of their disability insurance policies, the school teacher diagnosed with a brain tumour who no longer had access to an income from his income protection insurance policy, of retirees who had lost superannuation savings invested with HIH and thousands more who had lost insurance coverage. It was this loss of insurance coverage that then rippled throughout the Australian community in not such a dissimilar fashion to the loss of gas that affected the whole Victorian community in the wake of the Longford explosion. As public liability insurance vanished for HIH policyholders, local community events were hard hit: fetes were no longer able to be run; parades were cancelled; and individuals in both their private and working lives together with organisations suddenly found themselves liable for losses they assumed they had had covered through insurance contracts with HIH. Added to this, of course, was the loss of over 1000 jobs for the employees of the HIH group of companies (Owen 2003, Vol I pp.xiv–xvi).

The analysis of why the HIH group failed contained within the Royal Commission Report is intriguing. What is evident in the financial arena is that the connection between the assessment of financial risk and the essential underlying reality of insolvency is constantly shifting. Essentially, when an assessment of worth is made, circumstances may change or different assumptions may be introduced into financial models that can transform what once appeared as a bold, creative but sound business strategy into a highly dubious commercial venture.

Hence assessing the actuarial risk of a company's demise before such an event takes place is a challenging task. There are multiple considerations including the state of a particular market and the accuracy of assumptions about future liabilities. The starting point for analysis by the Royal Commission into the demise of HIH was to review the state of the market or what is termed the 'insurance cycle'. In order to understand the reasons behind the collapse, the Commission described the process of the rise of insurance company profits over a period (which peaked in this case in the mid-1990s), which was followed by a precipitous decline through the late 1990s and into the 2000s. In the case of insurance in Australia, the industry as a whole reported its highest ever underwriting loss (that is, the difference between premium paid and moneys paid out in insurance claims) in December 1998, some 40 per cent higher than any underwriting loss in the previous 20 years (Owen 2003, Vol I p.66).

The dynamic of this insurance cycle was affected by its interconnectedness with the investment market and with banking. During the boom years of HIH Insurance in the mid-1990s and until its demise, companies generally did not make a profit on insurance premiums. The money gained from premiums was habitually lower than that paid out to the insured. Losses from underwriting were the norm. Premium payments brought in money and time with income and profit generated through returns on investment. Secondly, boundaries between insurance and banking sectors were disappearing. Banks could compete with insurance companies for business that, in a tight market, drove prices down. The effect of this reliance on investments and competition from the banking sector increased the interconnectedness between various financial markets. Stress in one arena translated to stress in another. So, if returns on investments declined (for example lower than expected returns on property investments) then the financial viability of the insurance market also declined. HIH in particular was well known for its low premiums. Indeed, some saw it as responsible for keeping insurance premium prices low during the insurance market boom years in the mid-1990s. However, when the market turned so did the fortunes of HIH. The downturn of the insurance cycle did not only affect HIH. Three Australian reinsurers also experienced difficulty and two – New Cap re and REAC – collapsed in 1999 and 2000 respectively (Owen 2003, Vol I p.66).

However, the Royal Commission was not about to blame the insurance cycle for the collapse of the company. It stated bluntly '… market conditions provide neither an excuse nor an explanation for HIH's predicament: most insurers weather the storm' (Owen 2003, Vol I p.xvi). Since other insurers survived, then, the reasons for the collapse could not be placed at the feet of market fate.

But in the Commission's view the demise of HIH did not involve whole-sale criminality of individuals, either alone or in concert, intent on stripping the company of its assets. The goal of the directors, it argued, was to run a successful business, not to steal money. Misleading statements about the company's financial health made by senior management were seen as misguided attempts to keep the HIH group alive – at least for just a bit longer. Justice Owen wrote: 'HIH is not a case where wholesale fraud or embezzlement abounded. Most of the instances of possible malfeasance were borne of a misconceived desire to paper over the ever-widening cracks that were appearing in the edifice that was HIH' (Owen 2003, Vol I p.xvi).

The substance of the Commission's analysis of the cause of the collapse was that HIH failed to set aside sufficient reserves to cover claims on insurance policies.[10] HIH consistently held insufficient reserves, whether from premium money or returns on investments, to cover claims. The reasons for this under-reserving related in part to how necessary reserves were calculated (the letter of the law if you will) which contained inherent uncertainties together with the spirit with which these various calculations were made and uncertainties resolved.

The resolution of uncertainties was largely influenced by HIH's corporate culture, about which the Commission was particularly critical. It was, in the Commission's view, a culture dominated by poor leadership:

> By corporate culture I mean the charism (sic) or personality – sometimes overt but often unstated – that guides the decision-making process at all levels of an organisation. In the case of HIH, the culture that developed was inimical to sound management practices. It resulted in decision making that fell well short of the required standards. (Owen 2003, Vol I p.xvii)

The report argued that the directors of HIH (and in particular Ray Williams) used various risk-management strategies not to manage risk but to make a favourable impression on the bottom line. Poor management, one focussed on creating an optimistic gloss on accounts rather than one diligently managing financial risk, meant that uncertainty was always resolved in the most optimistic of fashions. The costs would be lower and incomes higher than a more sceptical mind would assume.

The Commission also was critical of both the board and management, which it felt was overly deferential to the leadership, and in particular to Ray Williams. For the Commission, this blind faith (Owen 2003, Vol I p.xvii) in the leadership was ill placed since the leadership generated poor business strategy. One example explained how HIH was successful in exiting the California insurance market in 1994, just as that market was encountering problems only to re-enter the same market in 1996 incurring significant losses. The report was also critical of the way HIH bought businesses in insurance markets, particularly in the UK, where it had little experience or expertise. Further, many of its businesses were chronically under-reserved, particularly FAI, which HIH acquired in 1998. HIH also made an ill-fated decision to sell most of its profitable lines of insurance to Alliance Australia Ltd (in part to meet new prudential requirements), a decision that hastened its demise.

The Commission found oversight by the board to be insufficient. The board was considered not to have taken a sufficiently sceptical stance on the decisions made by management and the executives. Justice Owen stated 'I formed the view that the board had such a degree of respect for management that the recommendations of management were assumed to have been carefully thought out and therefore to be correct' (Owen 2003, Vol I p.xxxv). There was no systematic method for assessing the performance of either the senior management or the CEO Ray Williams. Further, senior management was never questioned rigorously regarding, for example, what was appropriate remuneration for them, or whether Williams's generous use of HIH resources to make charitable donations was appropriate. More critically, perhaps, the board never systematically interrogated the material they were provided with from subsidiary companies within the HIH group to ensure that the accounts were an accurate view of that subsidiary's financial standing. In this regard, however, the board was hampered by the fact that critical pieces of information, such as the details of the suspect reinsurance contracts and doubtful underwriting practices (for example in film financing) never reached them (Owen 2003, Vol I pp.xxxix–xl).

There is a striking commonality here between Esso Longford and HIH. The lack of a safety consciousness at Esso was in evidence through a litany of problems where critical safety problems were ignored. In the case of HIH, the Commission raised significant concerns with corporate culture, where an ethos was established that singularly focussed on creating a favourable impression of the bottom line and so pushed the letter of the law, occasionally to breaking point, in a manner contrary to prudent fiscal management. Culture was made visible through behaviour. The Commission observed that the focus of HIH was always on the short term. There was, in the Commission's view, a lack of attention to detail and an absence of a business strategy that would ensure the long-term viability of the company. Various methods designed to spread risk (such as reinsurance), or calculate funds that needed to be set aside to cover outstanding claims, (both essential to long-term viability), were subverted and used to craft a set of accounts to convince investors that all was well. Overall, the actuarial risk assessments made by HIH management about the underlying financial strength of the HIH group were in the view of the Commission report, wildly optimistic.

This optimism, however, was encouraged by the inherent uncertainties in the calculations necessary to determine the financial health of the company. Financial risk assessment is, at best, an inexact science. The problem of under-reserving gets to the heart of an actuarial analysis of financial risk in the case of insurance companies. Calculations of what amounts of money were required to cover future claims needed to be made with some accuracy. These calculations were made by two interrelated professions: actuaries and accountants. The calculation of the level of provisioning HIH needed to make rested, in the first instance, on the work of the actuary. Actuaries were employed to calculate what was necessary to set aside to cover insurance liabilities. Their calculations determined what proportion of incoming funds needed to be set aside and hence what funds could be used as part of the overall calculation of profit. Once their work was done, financial managers could prepare company financial statements which would then be audited by the firm's accountant, in this case Arthur Anderson. Critically, money set aside for provisioning could not then be used in the overall calculation of profit.

The assessment made by the actuary, then, is a critical component to the overall calculation of the financial risk carried by an insurance company. The financial health of an insurance company rests as much on an assessment of future liabilities (for example, what future events (disasters, cyclones, and so on) might occur and what needs to be set aside to cover such possibilities) as it does on an assessment of the costs incurred and profits made in the past. Assessing the financial health of an insurance company, then, can prove particularly challenging because of this need to divine what the future holds.

Outstanding Claims Provisions (OCP) provides a useful example of the importance of the calculation of the actuary to the health of an insurance company (Owen 2003, Vol I pp.79–89). OCP are the funds set aside to meet outstanding claims, those claims that are not finalised by the time a financial report needs to be made. Calculation of the amount of funds required to meet outstanding claims (outstanding claims liabilities or OCL) requires that an assessment be made of outstanding liabilities (Owen 2003, Vol I pp.79–89). Such an assessment contains inevitable uncertainty. For example, a claim may have been made to the insurer, but not been finalised (that is, the decision to either refuse the claim or to pay money out has not been taken). Then, there may be the possibility of litigation about recovery from a third party or a range of other potential costs that means a calculation of OCP is always an estimate and never an exact figure. The calculation of OCP rests on past experience of the company and on the professional judgement of the actuary. The Commission stated that, '… the total OCP figure can only be an estimate. It is not a hard figure and so is essentially a matter of judgement' (Owen 2003, Vol I p.81). Further on the report continued in like vein:

> Actuarial methods do not guarantee a correct estimate of the outstanding claims liability. The results are dependent on the actuary's interpretation of the trends evident in past experience and assumptions made about future experience. Past consistency in claims trends can be abruptly disturbed and the actual outcome of the outstanding claims liability will reflect any changes in trends. (Owen 2003, Vol I p.83)

The actuary's calculations were necessarily based on a number of assumptions about likely future costs. However, the Commission explained that even small shifts in assumptions can have significant consequences:

> People with responsibility for estimating the OCP must make assumptions or judgements about individual items: the inflation rate, the discount rate and future claims handling costs are three such instances. Because the OCP is usually such a large figure, small variations in the assumptions can have a significant impact on the end result. (Owen 2003, Vol I p.89)

Overall, an actuary's calculation, then, is (and was in the case of HIH) necessarily somewhat tentative and rests on their professional judgement. Whilst there were and are a set of actuarial standards which guide their work, these were and remain only ever able to act as guides.

Even with reasonably accurate information, a successful insurer must be able to deal with unpredictability. This unpredictability rests on the dynamic nature of the insurance market and the unpredictability of future events. It was clear that HIH was gambling on an upswing in the insurance cycle in order to allow it to continue trading. In order to keep trading, it pushed its actuary to make calculations that were the most optimistic in terms of what outstanding claims it would actually need to cover and hence what it needed to set aside. The calculation of what provisions needed to be set aside (that is, OCP) in the case of HIH critically did not include what is known as a 'prudential margin', essentially a margin for error.

There are methods, however, to help insurers reduce the level of unpredictability they face in terms of the insurance market and unforseen events. Insurers look to other insurers, namely reinsurers, to spread some of their risk and reduce the level of uncertainty they face. Through a reinsurance contract, the insurer transfers risk to the reinsurer, for which it pays a premium.

On the face of it, a reinsurance contract would seem to entail a cost to the insurer's balance sheet, albeit one that would make the future a little more predictable and avert potentially catastrophic calls on company reserves. Yet a reinsurance contract can increase profit in the short term as well as decrease uncertainty. In entering into a reinsurance contract the insurer can reduce provisions it has set aside because it has transferred risk to the reinsurer and so reduced its liabilities. Hence it can reduce the money needed to address those liabilities, namely by drawing down on its OCP. The unnecessary resources within an OCP can now be booked as profit with the result that its balance sheet may improve overall. Again, the work of the actuaries and financial managers is essential in estimating the actual amount of risk that has been transferred to the reinsurer and hence how much it can reduce its OCP and so increase its profitability. One particular type of reinsurance, financial reinsurance takes this one step further; here the insurance company receives the payout on a class of risk *before* it pays the premium price. The premium is then paid over an extended period of time. This latter form of reinsurance, usually reserved for smaller arguably more vulnerable insurance companies, was a particular favourite with HIH.

The ethos underlying financial calculations such as OCP and reinsurance contracts becomes critical. The challenge for regulators is how to engender an orientation towards prudent risk management and away from the misuse of OCP rules and reinsurance contracts as a device simply to improve the look of the accounts. An actuary determined to ensure sufficient OCP, or one clearly cognizant of the need to transfer some risk to a reinsurance contract because of a troubling level of exposure to some particular risk will be focussed on the need to make as accurate assessment of risk as possible. However, when the actuary's focus is on creating a particular impression about the overall profitability of the company, this can become simply another strategy to create a favourable impression of a company.

The ethos of the HIH group was not conducive to sober assessments of its underlying financial integrity. The Commission report turned a critical eye to HIH's accounting practices in the years leading up to the collapse. HIH had a widening gap on losses on underwriting. Between 1997 and 2000 income from premiums increased by 60 per cent but the underwriting loss increased by 300 per cent. As the gap between liabilities and reserves widened the company looked to reinsurance contracts and intangibles, such as goodwill, to make up the shortfall and turn a loss into a profit. The problematic reinsurance contracts became a focus of the Commission's deliberations and it became clear that such contracts were, in fact, little more than loans to keep the company afloat. In relation to one of the FAI reinsurance contracts, designed to give the semblance of a transfer of risk when there was none, Justice Owen stated:

> A wide array of practices was employed to achieve these ends, amongst them the use of side letters setting out arrangements that negated the transfer of risk, the backdating of documents, the inclusion of sections of cover not intended to be called upon, and the use of 'triggers' for additional cover that was unrealistic. The word 'audacious' springs to mind. (Owen 2003, Vol I p.xxxi)

Added to this problematic use of reinsurance was an increased reliance on intangibles on HIH's balance sheet. Intangibles formed 23 per cent of shareholders equity in the company in 1997 rising to 60 per cent in 1999 and 75 per cent in June 2000 before declining to 50 per cent in December of that year. By contrast the Commission noted two comparable insurance companies NRMA and QBE had 0.4 and 4.9 per cent of shareholder equity bound up on intangibles.

These problems with the accounts, however, would seem to be exactly the kinds of issues that a diligent company board (in particular the audit committee) and the company auditor should have highlighted. To the lay person's view, it would seem that these two levels of oversight, watchdogs of the company accounts if you will, should provide the investing public with some level of confidence in the company accounts.

Oversight, however, depends on the accuracy of the information the overseers receive. In order to understand the role of the audit committee and the auditors, Arthur Andersen (hereafter Andersen), in the case of HIH it is necessary to understand the way HIH accounts were prepared. Audit committees and, to a greater extent, auditors rely on the quality of the information provided by the executive management. The Commissioner had considerable misgivings about the integrity of the information sources about company finances stating, 'I doubt the accuracy of much of HIH's accounting and other records' (Owen 2003, Vol I p.xlii).

Overall the Commission argued that the budget systems were sloppy. There were problems with new software (GEN+) used to generate accounts. Reconciliations were not made over extended periods of time, so it was not clear whether future budget projections were, or were not, accurate in the light of history. HIH's accounting practices were complicated by the fact of being a large and complex group rather than a single entity. Accounts were prepared in terms of the various lines of business and not in terms of each entity as an individual company in its own right. This meant that disaggregating to assess the viability of individual businesses in the group in order to assess their individual solvency was made difficult.

This was compounded by the fact that the accounting practices employed by HIH were considered 'aggressive'. Aggressive accounting practices were those that, according to the Commission, '… strains the letter of an accounting standard as far as possible (so) that (it) may or may not comply with the policy underlying that standard' (Owen 2003, Vol I p.xlvi). One example of such practices was the way that income tax losses incurred were then used to generate future income tax benefits associated with those losses. The relevant accounting standard at the time (AASB 1020) stated that determining a future income benefit in this way could only be stated if such an outcome was a 'near certainty.' It was considered a rare and unusual method of accounting only to be used in exceptional circumstances (Owen 2003, Vol I p.xlvii).

What of the first level of oversight by the audit committee of the company board? The Commission found that the audit committee was not sufficiently independent of the directors. Further, the report stated that the focus of this committee was on the figures it was presented with. Yet even here, it did not appear to question the accuracy of those figures and because bad information did not tend to rise to board level, the problem with the accounts and their inaccuracy remained hidden. Their purview was also narrow and did not delve in to the likely financial outcome that would arise from the directors' business strategy.

Finally, then, what did the auditors, Andersen, make of all this? How rigorously did they enquire into HIH's financial affairs? Clearly, the auditors would not necessarily pick up the problem with the underlying integrity of the way the accounts were compiled (although it may have come to light at certain times). However, the Commission was highly critical of the conduct of the auditors. It argued that on many occasions, the auditors had not been sufficiently rigorous in their investigation into HIH accounts. Andersen was criticised by Justice Owen for not interrogating the assessments of the actuary, who was employed as a consultant by HIH to make the necessary calculations of the all-important OCP. The Commission found Andersen was not critical enough in its assessments of HIH accounts with respect to issues such as the use of future income tax benefits (FITB), deferred information technology costs, the level of goodwill that HIH booked to cover its growing losses nor, finally, the appropriateness of not inquiring sufficiently into HIH's capacity to act as an ongoing concern. Andersen did, on occasion, raise issues with HIH in particular with relation to some of the reinsurance contracts of HIH. However, it ran into difficulty since it had approved some similar contracts whilst auditing FAI. When the auditors challenged HIH, HIH executives responded by asking why they did not do so with FAI, which had a similar reinsurance arrangement, in earlier years. In this way, the accountants could be silenced.

What is particularly striking here is that Andersen had undertaken its own assessment of the risk to itself of continuing as HIH's auditor. It concluded that HIH was a 'maximum risk client' and as such required a particularly high level of scrutiny. In undertaking its own risk assessment in terms of its own risk of keeping HIH as a client the auditor identified many of the same concerns as the Royal Commission. It clearly identified the aggressive accounting practices and the problem of HIH consistently not achieving its budget.

There was the possibility that events may have taken a different turn if Andersen had met with the audit committee in the absence of executive management. But, on the one occasion this did occur it generated the extreme ire of the directors, in particular Ray Williams, who labelled the meeting 'unprofessional'.

The question then was, if Andersen understood that HIH was such a high risk, why did it continue to provide HIH with a clean audit? The untangling of this issue revolved around interrogating the issue of audit independence. There were reasons to doubt Andersen's independence from HIH. Andersen had been HIH's auditor for most of its existence (since 1971). Further, there were strong and ongoing links between the two firms and three on the HIH board had previously worked for Andersen. Finally, Andersen provided HIH with a range of non-audit services from which it received a substantial income. So, an obvious conclusion was that there was a lack of independence between the auditor and HIH.

Surprisingly, however, whilst Owen found there was a perception of a lack of independence he did not conclude that there was a substantive lack of independence. He argued that there was insufficient evidence to suggest that Andersen poor-quality audits were a result of a lack of independence (Owen 2003, Vol III pp.166–9). A lack of independence, at least as it related to the provision of non-audit services and rotation of audit partner did not, in the Commission's view, lie at the heart of the problem of a poor audit. Indeed, the report shows that a rotation of audit partner had indeed occurred at HIH. The reason for this, however, related to the demand by Ray Williams that the current partner had acted unprofessionally in meeting with non-executive members of the audit committee without Williams's knowledge as described above. The Commission was critical of Williams at this point and adamant that the audit committee should meet separately with auditors. But it demonstrates the problem with superficial responses to independence, like mandating the rotation of audit partner. The reasons behind the rotation of audit partner that occurred at HIH before it collapsed raises the possibility that rotation of audit partner may do little to increase independence, particularly if a strong financial relationship between company and auditor remains.

Ultimately, the failure of the auditor to inform the market of the parlous state of HIH finances remained somewhat of a mystery in the Royal Commission report. The Commission did not reach any conclusion regarding why the auditor failed to provide a qualified audit when it should have done. In coming to a decision about HIH as a worthwhile investment, however, investors were ill advised to rely on the audit reports.

In terms of the actuarial risk of financial collapse, the demise of HIH demonstrates issues central to the management of this actuarial risk. Firstly, the underlying risk itself is difficult to ascertain. Despite the simplicity of analogies of undertaking a family budget, assessing the viability of a company such as HIH is accompanied by inherent levels of uncertainties, where small changes in underlying assumptions can have significant effects. Secondly, financial instruments set up to spread risk, such as reinsurance arrangements, are useful tools particularly because of this intrinsic uncertainty in assessing financial risk. Thirdly, however, the account demonstrates the critical importance of how this uncertainty is dealt with. If it is used in the pursuit of short-term profit then useful vehicles such as reinsurance become financial wrecking balls ready to wreak havoc when a market downturn arrives, as it undoubtedly will. Finally, then, given the capacity for both productive use and abuse of financial vehicles, company ethos came to centre stage as the determining factor motivating the use of financial instruments and the exploitation of uncertainty for short-term benefit.

Company ethos, however, cannot be divorced either from the nature of commerce and the capitalist market or from broader socio-cultural norms about 'good business practice'. As such, this means there is a need to reflect on the commercial and socio-cultural logic in Australia around the time of HIH's collapse. Commercial norms around good business practice can be seen as a factor that financial analysts take into account when assessing whether a particular company should, or should not attract investment. It is part of their overall actuarial risk assessment of a company, but the lines between actuarial and socio-cultural risk assessment at this point in the HIH story become blurred. Socio-cultural norms relate less to figures and more to people and institutions with questions such as: are they trustworthy? Are they one of us?

Before delving into the socio-cultural risk narrative around HIH, it is worth noting the increasing dependence of the Australian population at large on the share market. Whether as direct investors or through their superannuation fund approximately 54 per cent of all Australians aged over 18 years owned shares in 2000. The figure in 2006 was 46 per cent (ASX 2007). Because of this, there was at the time HIH collapsed and there remains still a significant pressure on companies to produce consistently high financial returns. As governments pull back from pensions, what the stock market does and what individual companies do then becomes much more important. The importance of this pressure from the public to perform was noted by John Palmer, the former head of the prudential regulator in Canada (OFSI). Palmer was commissioned to undertake a report into the activities of APRA, the prudential regulator in Australia around the time of the HIH collapse. Palmer (2002) commented:

> It is important to recognize that financial institutions today face many pressures, of which pressure from the Regulator is but one. Most important by far are pressures from shareholders and financial markets for performance, including historically (and some, including the writer, believe unsustainably) high returns on equity and growth in these returns. These pressures are overwhelmingly strong ... (p.140)

The effect of this, then, is to push an interpretation of uncertainty around financial risk in the most optimistic of directions in order to maintain public confidence and investment – as was evident in HIH's statement of accounts.

The risk assessment made of HIH's worth as an investment, however, clearly rested on more than the accounts. There is an intriguing section entitled 'Market Sentiment' in the Royal Commission report that provides insight into views of the company before its collapse (Owen 2003, Vol I pp.66–73). What this section demonstrates is that for considerable periods of its existence HIH was viewed positively with more than a trebling of the share price from mid-1994 until July 1997 from around $1 to around $3.70. This was a period of significant acquisitions by the HIH group, acquisitions that the Commission (with the wisdom of hindsight) was most critical. In 1997 Standard and Poor's credit rating for HIH was AA-. Market sentiment, then, would seem to be influenced by acquisitions – a 'growth is good' mentality. The view of HIH changed after the sale by Winterthur in 1998. From this point, the market analysts and financial media became divided amongst themselves, a division that led *The Age* newspaper to comment, 'Rarely do you get such a dichotomy of opinion on a stock between analysts. It makes it really hard for the fund managers to decide what to do' (Owen 2003, Vol I p.68). What emerges from the section in the Commission's report is that the primary emphasis of analysts was on company profits and returns to shareholders. The release of company accounts then was accompanied by interpretation of how to view the profit results, analysis that varied from praise for HIHs dealing with the debts from FAI, to argued efficiencies that would come from acquisitions to condemnation for the purchase of FAI and the need for HIH to set aside more money for claims reserve strengthening. As late as July 2000, Credit Suisse First Boston argued, 'We believe management's transparent approach to cleaning up the FAI book is positive and it appears that the company is ready to enter a new phase of organically driven growth' (Owen 2003, Vol I p.72). Such assessments appealed to a sense of trustworthiness in HIH that management were 'transparent', not hiding key bits of information and so worthy of investors' support. At the other extreme were the comments of an unnamed analyst quoted in the *Australian Financial Review* in September 2000 saying 'This is the tip of the iceberg. This business is haemorrhaging' (Owen 2003, Vol I p.72).

Mixed in with these assessments attempting to divine a financial rationale and hence trajectory of the company, then, were those looking to the human dimension in order to understand whether HIH was worthy of support or deserved condemnation. Here, the analysis of risk slips from the actuarial to the socio-cultural. Clearly, it is hard to demonstrate clear lines that distinguish the one from the other. However, the human element of the drama was evident. For example, it is important to remember that the sale by Winterthur took place via a public float. The float was successful and fully subscribed – largely due to support from small investors. After the float the shareholder base of the company increased dramatically from 5265 shareholders before the sale to 29,973 after the float with 60 per cent of shareholders holding less than 5000 shares (Owen 2003, Vol I p.55). Irrespective of the public views of the financial analysts, HIH was seen as worthy of support by small investors.

It is important to try to put together some of the elements of the public perception of HIH before the collapse. Within Australia, at least, HIH was the insurer of choice for small business, particularly contractors in the building industry. The reason for this was most probably the low premium price since HIH fought hard against paying out on claims. HIH was viewed as a dynamic company, a sign of Australia making it on the global stage. Ray Williams was seen as a generous philanthropist, one who was willing to support the company he founded. At times when the company issued shares Williams was often amongst the strongest backers, using his own money to support the company. Rodney Adler also gained the support of both the (then) Prime Minister and the public. Adler was known as a bold entrepreneur whose father had risen from being a near penniless refugee from Hungary after World War II to a wealthy businessman and founder of FAI insurance. The method of business, one at which Adler was argued to excel was in pushing the limits and taking risks. When HIH bought FAI it was suggested that Ray Williams had his eye firmly set on being the largest insurer in Australia (Main 2003) and repeating his success in the CIC venture and that Adler was keen to sell a failing business at the highest price he could get and had plenty of front to do so.

Public (including some financial analysts') perception of HIH and the key players, arguably, focussed to a considerable degree on personalities and sentiment. This is the core of socio-cultural logic, where the concern is with what people and situations symbolise. Dynamic business decisions spill over into public perceptions of the worth of their country or place. As the economic fortunes of a particular company rise, a strong perception is that *our* entrepreneurs are as good as any. Even better when Rodney Adler thumbed his nose at establishment methods of doing business or when Ray Williams demonstrated a genuine affection and concern for those less fortunate and showed that affection through charitable donations. Indeed, both men were awarded the Order of Australia, Adler for services to the Insurance Industry and philanthropy and Williams for his philanthropy in particular to medicine.

After the collapse, however, perceptions of trustworthiness of those most intimately involved changed dramatically. The emphasis immediately turned to the impact of the collapse. The sheer size of the losses involved in HIH suggested that there must have been something criminal going on. Impact clearly has a socio-cultural as well as an actuarial dimension. The harm wrought by HIH generated the perception that criminality must be involved (Haines 2007). From this juncture, then, stories and anecdotes arose of abhorrent actions and venial motivations. What emerged from the various descriptions of the collapse is the way those at HIH were different from 'us'. They were profligate high fliers and so a threat to the social good. Andrew Main in his book on the collapse described how:

> Despite having a budget of $9 million for the 2000 calendar year, the office had spent $32 million on a huge number of items that might have merited an embarrassed smile in a company doing well, but looked like crass waste in a company that was close to insolvency. There had been $1500 worth of jellybeans, for instance, or thirty four gold watches, plus four nights accommodation at the Intercontinental Hotel in Sydney. ... On 9 January 2001 the day the staff were told to stop processing claims, jeweller Percy Marks sent HIH an invoice for thirty eight Berme & Mercier watches at $8000 each. (Main 2003 p.6)

What is important here is not to tease apart whether one individual or another was, or was not, ethical or venial in their motives. Rather, it is to turn the spotlight on the process of condemnation or valorisation itself. It is to understand how the 'condemners' or 'acolytes' are drawing on and exploiting socio-cultural risk narratives making statements about 'who we are' and what place Australia 'should be' and 'where I belong' in that society. Not surprisingly, in the aftermath public commentators most often side with the victims. *The Daily Telegraph*, a Sydney tabloid remarked after Williams had been released from jail 'What about the thousands of people who lost their homes, their income, their superannuation, their businesses, their jobs when the insurance giant HIH fell into a \$5.3billion hole because of Williams' indifference and mismanagement?' (Fife-Yeomans 2008).

The focus of socio-cultural risk assessments is on the impact, the waste of money and the need for retribution. The final 'dash for cash' as the demise of the company seemed inevitable (Owen 2003, Vol I p. xlii) then was retold as an indication that those involved must be criminalised, their activities simply not those that should be countenanced in a decent country. The focus here, not surprisingly was, on blame. The release of the Royal Commission report, for example, was accompanied by media concerns with who would be prosecuted, who would be held to account. The Australian Broadcasting Corporation (ABC) reporter Eleanor Hall asked Stephen Long the Finance Correspondent in their midday news show *The World Today*:

> Now over the last year we've been hearing from some of the key players in this disaster as they have been giving their evidence, very colourful evidence some of it has been too. So, who is being fingered? (Who) is facing charges arising from this report? (Long 2003)

The criminal prosecutions brought by the Commonwealth Director of Public Prosecutions referred by ASIC, then need to be clearly understood in light of socio-cultural practices of condemnation and retribution. The prosecutions, and later convictions in the courts, were a signal that the actions of nine of the senior managers and directors of HIH and associated companies were criminal and as such clearly outside of acceptable conduct. Terms of imprisonment were handed down that ranged from eight years for Bradley Cooper, former chairman of FAI Home Security Group to Ray Williams and Rodney Adler (four and a half years) to Robert Kelly former assistant company secretary to 500 hours of community service.

Finally, then, what was the political response in the immediate aftermath of HIH? Clearly, the setting up of the Royal Commission must be understood as part of that political response. A Royal Commission was seen as independent and hence able to uncover what led to the collapse. The government also needed to be responsive to those who had lost their insurance cover. Julie

Bishop, a government MP speaking to the House of Representatives in a speech on HIH stated:

> ... the government's response to the HIH collapse (is) that our priority was to those left destitute by the HIH collapse. We are a responsive government. We could not, would not and will not abandon those most affected by this event. ... It is easy, perhaps, for some to regard this as a private sector issue and one where government has no role to play. I must say I sympathise with that view. It does resonate with me ... You cannot just shrug your shoulders and say, 'Oh well, bad things happen to good people.' This government says, 'No there are people suffering hardship. We cannot stand by and we won't.' (Bishop 2001 p.1)

The Federal government put in place a $500 million compensation package. The package paid claims of those who were dependent on income protection policies, personal injury claims, claims for a loss of family home and claims of non-profit organisations. Other claims were paid subject to certain criteria and related to personal claims to those with incomes below a certain threshold and claims of small business (less than 50 employees).

Another significant political response was prompted by HIH but connected more broadly with concerns the government had with the health of the Insurance Industry, together with concerns the industry had about public liability insurance claims. This response to the concerns of the insurance industry can be seen in light of both the events of September 11 and the collapse of HIH. As we have seen HIH was an aggressive marketer of low-cost insurance and kept insurance premiums down. Without HIH, insurance premiums rose. The general community, in particular community associations, were left without public liability insurance and the insurance industry was keen to rehabilitate the profitability of their industry in a post-HIH world. The result of this was that government stepped in by constituting a review, 'The Review of the Law of Negligence' chaired by the Honourable Justice David Ipp (known as the Ipp review (Ipp 2002)), which aimed to encourage the states to enact legislative amendments to reduce the industry's liability for public liability negligence claims. These claims were just the sort of long-tailed claims that had led to HIH's demise. In reducing these long-tailed claims, the government stepped into the role of reinsurer by cutting the capacity for public injury claims against insurers and meeting the costs of injuries incurred through the public health system.

Hence, the response of the government to the HIH collapse reflected the broad contours of political risk: reassurance through the compensation scheme following the collapse, then reform of the laws of negligence to assist the profitability of the insurance industry. There were also swift regulatory reforms, ones that preceded the tabling of the Royal Commission's Report. These, however, are best discussed in the following chapter reviewing the regulatory response to each of the disasters described here.

CONCLUSION

Each of the disasters that form the centrepiece of the analysis in this book had a significant impact on the Australian community. Nonetheless, the nature of that impact and the risk each posed differed. In the case of both Longford and HIH there was a strong actuarial narrative to each disaster; however, the capacity to assess this actuarial risk differed between the two cases. Both events revealed levels of uncertainty, but the uncertainty evident in the Longford collapse did not preclude a clear assessment of the causes behind the disaster through the Longford Royal Commission. Esso found this out to its chagrin. HIH, on the other hand, posed a more complex challenge since the assessment of financial risk rested (and continues to rest) on a somewhat more tentative base. In contrast to these two disasters the actuarial assessment of the risk of a terrorist attack within a port or airport in Australia, post-September 11, appeared very slim indeed.

Each of the three disasters also posed a socio-cultural threat. The physicality of the Longford disaster and in particular the terrorist attacks of September 11 generated concerns with what the event signified in terms of 'decent' human behaviour. Esso completely misread the socio-cultural norms surrounding the event and was punished in the courts because it tried to blame a worker. A large corporation does not fare well when it tries overtly to shift blame. In the case of September 11 there was neither a corporation to blame, nor any high-flying individuals. Rather, blame rested on 'foreigners' and in particular asylum seekers. The praise for, and then condemnation of, the main actors in the HIH saga also point to a socio-cultural risk dimension to this event.

The resolution of socio-cultural threats occurred in large part through the actions of a government that needed to demonstrate its concern with the anxieties of the community. In each case, governments sought to reassure: in the case of Longford through industrial manslaughter legislation (which failed), in the case of September 11 through aligning Australia with the US War on Terror and, in the case of HIH, through the compensation scheme aimed at the most vulnerable victims of the HIH collapse.

Political risk, however, also must be concerned with economic investment. Here the response to HIH was most evident in the reforms to negligence law and the concern with maintaining the profitability of the insurance industry. In doing so, arguably government accepted the role of 'reinsurer' (through dealing with injuries through the public health system) whilst also shifting the risk of injury back on to the individual. In responding in this way, the possibility arose that the regulatory reforms to prudential regulation, then, could sidestep concerns about industry health that would be expected to be an ongoing concern for government. Further, it would be expected that in the case of both

Longford and September 11, regulatory reforms would also be shaped by the demands of industry. It is to those reforms that we now turn.

NOTES

1. Account to the 'The Esso Longford Gas Plant Accident Report of the Longford Royal Commission' 1999, p.64.
2. Airport Manager, in interview August 2007.
3. Hon Justice Owen, Commissioner HIH Royal Commission Report 'The Failure of HIH Insurance' Vol. I A corporate collapse and its lessons p. xiii.
4. BHP took no part in the operation of the plant.
5. Esso argued that it was not a draft report, rather some notes on a sheet of paper written by the internal investigator.
6. The narrative of the trial below draws heavily on Hopkins's (2002) excellent work.
7. There was a Senate Committee Hearing into the legislation passed in response to the attacks. There were five bills that were subject to this inquiry related to new security legislation that expanded the definition of treason, created new terrorism offences and gave powers to the Attorney General to prohibit certain organisations as well as legislation into suppressing the financing of terrorism, creating new enforcement powers, tightening border security and allowing broader access to intercept telecommunications. What is unique here is that the inquiry was instigated after a major tranche of the legislative response to September 11 had been developed, not before.
8. It should be remembered that politicians may well have changed roles within the Australian Parliament and a number will have since left the Parliament altogether.
9. It is important to remember that HIH Insurance Limited was in essence a group of 30 companies. The name HIH will be used to refer to the group as a whole and when referring to 'the company' what is being referred to is the group unless it is specified otherwise.
10. It is revealing to note that Owen did not recommend charges under section 588g of the Corporations Act of trading whilst insolvent. The reason stated was that it would be too onerous to prove that the company was trading whilst insolvent given the difficulties of calculating insolvency with a company such as HIH with long tailed liabilities. Owen 2003, Vol III pp.44, 61–2.

5. Regulatory reform in the shadow of disaster

This chapter assesses the regulatory response to each of the disasters. It reveals how regulatory reform was simultaneously propelled by the crisis event (described in Chapter 4), yet also shaped by political risk management aimed at protecting industrial investment whilst reassuring the citizenry that their safety and security needs were paramount. The strategies employed by governments in managing their political risk variously proved a key stumbling block or facilitator of effective reform dependent, in particular, on whether their management of political risk included strong support of the relevant regulators. This support, combined with sufficient technical expertise within, or able to be accessed by, the regulatory authority was the critical combination for effective reform.

Both the geographical location of each disaster and the type of actuarial risk in question also affected regulatory reform. Common themes were apparent across the various regimes: the challenges of sustaining the reform effort and of retaining good people with both technical knowledge and political acumen. Yet there were key differences. Some of these could be explained not by the type of actuarial risk (major hazard or financial risk, for example) but by the level of political risk the disaster posed to the particular government. But the type of actuarial risk also could have a distinctive effect on reform. There were particular challenges for effective financial regulatory reform and it was this area that was most affected by the economic cycle and government pursuit of 'good economic times.' Financial disaster management, in terms of setting up a fund to compensate those most affected or of responding to industry demands for greater protection, could relieve pressure for radical reforms to the regulatory apparatus. Yet relieving pressure in this way threatened to engulf government in ever-increasing financial demands on the public purse. Regulatory reform then was crafted with a keen eye to long-term political financial liabilities.

REGULATORY REFORMS IN THE WAKE OF THE LONGFORD INDUSTRIAL DISASTER

Victoria

The Victorian response to the Longford disaster was the clearest example in this study of regulatory reform able to address the causes of the disaster and which had the greatest likelihood, provided reform momentum was sustained, of preventing a repeat event. The reforms following this disaster drew on the best that international experience had to offer. Clearly, industrial disasters are not peculiar to Australia and there was a wealth of experience in prevention from which Victoria could draw. Responses to the Seveso disaster in Italy in 1976 (De Marchi, et al. 1996) and in particular the Piper Alpha disaster in the United Kingdom in 1988 (Paterson 2000) had resulted in the development of a 'safety case' approach to major hazard facilities (MHFs). This was the model of control around which Victoria designed its regime.

A safety case model is a co-regulatory or perhaps more accurately an enforced self-regulatory (Ayres and Braithwaite 1992) approach. Essentially, what is required is for a MHF to undertake a rigorous analysis of all possible scenarios under which a catastrophic fire or explosion might take place. The site then must put in place controls to eliminate, or at least reduce to an acceptable level, the risk of such an occurrence. The philosophy underpinning the safety case approach taken in Victoria combined strict regulatory oversight with an understanding that each site required a specifically tailored risk-management regime. In a very real sense, the site developed its own regulations under which it became legally accountable.

There were particular noteworthy elements to the Victorian safety case approach as set out in the Occupational Health and Safety (Major Hazard) Regulations (Vic) (2000). Firstly, the safety case needed to be undertaken both with sufficient levels of technical engineering expertise and with 'shop floor' input. It needed to be both technically and socially competent. Workshopping the various hazard and control scenarios with those charged with operating machinery and working on the production line was a key component of the regime. In this respect, the safety case regime had the capacity to increase the levels of communication between various levels of personnel within the plant. Secondly, the regime had a demonstration component. It was not sufficient for a site to say that they had reduced the risk of disaster rather they needed to be able to demonstrate to the satisfaction of the regulator that the risk had been controlled. This central core of communication and demonstration was embedded within a framework that secured, or made a 'case for safety' for the particular site. The safety case also contained an appropriate safety management system that was able to deal with the everyday health and safety needs of all on site. Further, it was an emergency planning document as well as a prevention document. The safety case required an emergency management plan be put in place in collaboration with local emergency services. Finally, the regime had to be transparent and communicated to the local residential community with a copy of the final document placed in the local library. The description of a safety case on the WorkSafe Victoria website labelled 'What is a Safety Case' gives a succinct description here:

- MHFs have to demonstrate their operational safety through a Safety Case developed specifically for their unique operations and situation.
- The Safety Case sets out the **adequacy of the site's safety management system** by specifying **prevention measures** as well as **strategies** for reducing the effects of a major incident if one does occur.
- It can only be prepared following a full examination of a site's activities to **identify hazards and all potential major incidents,** and to determine the **necessary control measures**.
- The safety case must be prepared with the full **involvement of employees and their health and safety representatives** from all of the different workgroups and functional areas at the site.
- The relevant **emergency services** should be consulted on emergency plan preparation, and the **local municipal council** (or councils) should be consulted on actions required for the safety of **local community members** in the event of a major incident (emphasis in original) (WorkSafe 2009).

What were the conditions, then, that made these reforms possible? From the research it was clear that the reforms that followed Longford were enabled by considerable political will and the support of the regulator. The nature of the disaster itself (as described in Chapter 4) suggests some of the reasons why there was such a strong political incentive for effective reform. Firstly, the loss of gas to the state rather than the loss of life was a crucial factor in creating momentum for reform. As one regulator commented, 'There is nothing more political than energy prices or blackouts' (10, p.23).[1] Government simply could not afford a repeat of such a catastrophic loss of supply. Esso's response to the Royal Commission in blaming a worker also galvanised public pressure for change. Yet, political ambitions for enhanced safety to be achieved through criminalisation and deterrence had been thwarted – mainly because the opposition parties sided with industry against the government in their attempts to introduce an offence of industrial manslaughter. This failure meant there remained considerable public pressure focussed on legal and policy reform. Government was pushed to act decisively, but not through denunciatory methods. Instead it chose to address the actuarial risk, drawing on significant technical expertise in order to convince the Victorian public that they had reduced the risk of 'another Longford.'

This then provided the regulator with considerable latitude, which it used to good policy effect. A strong operations manager for major hazards was brought in, assisted by a well-respected Chief Technical Advisor. Critically, when the new unit, the Major Hazards Unit (MHU), was set up it had considerable independence and reported directly to the CEO of Worksafe (the Health and Safety regulator). This gave the MHU considerable budget autonomy and discretion over their activities. Discretion was given to those who could put it to best use by virtue of their specific and necessary technical expertise.

In the first blush of reform the new unit asserted its authority and demonstrated a willingness to shut down sites that were not able to meet the enhanced standards. Indeed, a number of sites decided that the new regime was too onerous and reduced the hazards at their sites so they fell outside of the regime and, whilst still covered by dangerous goods legislation, were not required to go through the safety case process. Safety case requirements only applied to industrial sites (such as chemical plants, oil refineries and storage facilities) that held, handled or processed large quantities of hazardous chemicals and dangerous goods, so called Major Hazard Facilities (MHFs). Reducing inventory, then, could satisfy the regulator's desire to reduce risk whilst allowing sites to reduce their regulatory burden.

What was notable was the fact that the Victorian major hazards regime was not a direct copy of existing safety case models. Much was made of the fact it was a licensing regime and as such allowed the regulator a range of tools with which to control site activities. It also had a much stronger emphasis on demonstration of risk reduction and adequate communication with shop floor operators when compared with similar regimes. This tailoring performed important political and symbolic purposes. It allowed the government to promote its system as world class, important for the government in retaining legitimacy. Further, it signalled to the MHFs in the state that they could not afford to simply pick an 'off the shelf' solution to their safety case regulatory responsibilities. Companies were put on notice. One consultant commented:

> There were quite a few companies who hired consultants that knew how to do offshore safety cases – especially consultants from other states who obviously never read the Victorian regulations. There were a couple of operators that got themselves into really serious difficulties by taking documentation that had been prepared for someone who was aiming to meet a different regulatory regime and then submitting it to the Victorian regulator who then told them that was crap and they had to do it again. (34, p.2)

The development of the regime and its vigorous implementation galvanised the attention of industry onto what was happening at their plant in terms of disaster prevention. Simply going through the motions was not considered sufficient. What was notable here was that the government allowed the MHU significant discretion in the design of the new regulatory framework. Political control of the specific content of the regime was minimal. Such discretion could be used to considerable effect. This unit had the necessary expertise to develop a regime that could succeed in its aim of significantly reducing the likelihood of a repeat event.

In the language of risk developed in Chapter 3, then, the safety case regime successfully reduced the actuarial risk of a repeat event. This was facilitated by a political risk reduction strategy by the government that allowed the regulator significant latitude, whilst also reassuring the population that the problems revealed by Longford were being addressed. Further, government was able to convince industry of the need for a significantly enhanced focus on major hazard risk and repel industry advances for a weakening of the regime. Actuarial, socio-cultural and political risks were effectively managed.

An effective regime, however, is only as good as long as it can be sustained. The safety case regime was particularly onerous, one that required significant resources of both time and money by both the regulator and the sites concerned. The obvious danger, then, was that industry would eventually be successful in pushing back against government and weakening the regime. This was particularly the case for Victoria with its ageing chemical industry. The MHF regulator commented, 'The chemical industry in Australia is, you know, decreasing and depleting and decamping to other countries and they run on the smell of an oily rag. They're always under threat and they're always looking for cheaper ways to do things ...' (4, p.10)

Nonetheless, five years after the safety case regime had been put in place the regulator remained confident that they had government support to enforce compliance with the new regime and that the government would not undermine regulatory authority. In response to questions about whether complaints from industry directly to government would be heard the (then) senior MHU senior manager argued:

> Well in the end if they [industry] are not going to listen, they don't believe [in] the legislation that's sitting there, their only alternative is to make a commercial decision to be out of the market. ... [I have told the MHFs] 'go for your life!' Everybody's tried [to talk to government] but in the end if you want to operate in the state of Victoria under an MHF regime you need to have a license. To get a license you have to satisfy the guy in there[2] and the panel[3]. To demonstrate adequacy you have to go through the whole process. And there's no exception. (4, pp.12–13)

But there were challenges. Pressures were mounting on the MHU both internally, from within Worksafe as a whole, as well as from industry. Other divisions within Worksafe complained of the unequal division of resources given to the MHU when compared with other areas:

> We were seen, and probably still are, as over resourced you know. There's only 50 sites, 'how come you've got 50 people?' [other divisions say] ... So my opposite

numbers across the organization, there are five other fellows that I get along very well with but always are gagging about, you know (that) I've got too many bods and not enough work. (4, p.4)

Further, the unit was seen as somewhat elitist, which created internal jealousies:

The fact of the matter is that the whole of the branch virtually was recruited from outside the organization. There was this specific target in terms of the qualifications and the experience of the staff. As a consequence there were targets on our backs everywhere we went ... (4, p.4)

Demands from industry for changes to the regime also increased through the first licensing round in 2000–01. Complaints were made about the lack of guidance given to sites about what was required. Some of these complaints were valid, if not entirely unexpected, given the innovative nature of the safety case regime implemented in the state in 2000. To begin with both regulator and industry were learning about how the new regime would work in practice. Certainly, more effective guidance could well be expected to reduce the pressure on industry, whilst also retaining the necessary rigour of the regime. However, the demands of producing more and more guidance material could drain a regulator's resources and take away from the emphasis on the sites taking responsibility for reducing their own MH risks.

The mounting pressures on the MHU resulted in an internal restructuring of the unit. Two years after the implementation of the safety case regime the unit lost its special independent status and was made a division of the regulator and, as such, was given no priority for funding over other areas of health and safety. Senior personnel, both management and technical advisors, also left. The *Safety Science Monitor*, an Occupational Health and Safety journal, ran an editorial in 2002 with the headline 'Has Victoria's Major Hazard Watchdog Been Muzzled?' which stated:

On the afternoon of September 17, 2001, the leadership of the Major Hazard Division within the Victorian Workcover Authority was ambushed and removed from office. The Director was told that she was no longer the Director and the Chief Technical Adviser was told that his contract would be paid out and that he was not to return to the office.

Does this mean that the Major Hazard Division has changed direction and will now go easier on the companies it regulates? VWA[4] spokesmen repudiate any such interpretation and say simply that the Division needed more project management skills. It is hard to see how this justifies ambushing the incumbents in this way. (Hopkins and Larsson 2002)

These changes to the MHU suggest that WorkSafe felt it had to respond to criticisms, both from its other divisions as well as complaints from industry. Their capacity to maintain the rigour of the regime was under threat and was exacerbated by the difficulty in retaining good people at the top of the organ-isation. Partly, however, the regulator was a victim of its own success. Victoria's high profile MHF regime was imitated by other jurisdictions around Australia, most notably the National Offshore Petroleum Safety Authority (NOPSA). Some valuable members of staff were lost to this new agency. However, it was also apparent that the intense pressure on the Victorian MHU increased the attractiveness of positions outside of the Victorian regulator. A senior regulator argued:

> It's a very political appointment, [the] director of the division that runs major hazards. Because it's a tripartite position: unions, government and operators [all have influence]. So you've got three bosses and it's very difficult to keep all three of them away from your door. Admittedly a couple of the fellers who came in here were caretakers and just threw their hands up in the air and ran away. ... I think the WorkSafe culture is extremely demanding of that particular position. (4, p.10)

The difficulty of the position was illustrated by the fact that the unit had expe-rienced five directors in the previous five years. Clearly, regulation is about politics and the support of the regulator depends in large part on how the government of the day decides to deal with the political risk it faces. The expe-rience above suggests that government had shifted away from unequivocal support of the MHU to demanding the regulator negotiate effectively with the political demands from three exacting masters. Being an effective regulator, then, needed considerable (perhaps even unrealistic levels of) political skills. Certainly, in the case of the MHU this was a position that few could stomach for an extended period.

Despite this pressure, at the time of the research the MHU had managed to retain significant authority. It was still able to withhold licences from those it considered not able to manage their major hazard risk and had developed a monitoring regime which focussed on sites it considered the most at risk. It had responded to the demands of sites for greater guidance and had worked hard to provide adequate documentation. Further, it had extracted a price for this guidance material – namely, that there would be no extensions given on licence renewals during the 2008–09 round as there had been in the initial licensing round. Sites no longer would be able to extract extra time to demon-strate their capacity to reduce risk. They needed to manage risk and their regu-latory responsibilities in a timely manner. The regime had been in place for sufficient time, the regulator reasoned, to allow sites to adjust and ensure at all times that they had in place an adequate 'case for safety.'

Sustainability of the Victorian regime post-Longford needs to be under-stood in a broader context. Whilst the MHU was at the forefront of control of major hazards another regulator controlled risk management of the extensive gas pipelines that run across the state. Clearly, major disruptions in supply could occur not only because of a catastrophic breakdown of production, but also a significant disruption in supply. This regulator, the gas division within Energy Safe Victoria, also had implemented a safety case regime that covered the integrity of the gas pipeline system from the MHF gate to the consumers' doors. This regulatory framework had similarities to the MHF regime but had an emphasis on security of supply as well as safety and had to deal with the dispersed nature of the gas network.

Post Longford, the security of gas supply had been considerably enhanced through ensuring a greater diversity of that supply. No longer would Victoria be held to ransom by failure at a single source. Supply hubs had been installed that allowed gas flow normally destined for other states to be redirected to Victoria when necessary. However, the gas pipeline regime demonstrated additional threats to the sustainability of a safety case approach. Gas supply in Victoria had been privatised and a market structure comprised of competing gas retailers set up. Such a regime placed a priority on economic modelling that dictated what resources could go into maintenance and repair of the gas network. An engineering ethos of the need for a system to have sufficient redundancy could be undermined by an economic ethos that emphasised efficiency and cost of the network. Economic regulation was primarily controlled by the Essential Services Commission (ESC) and to an extent their concerns were separate from the gas safety division of Energy Safe Victoria (ESV). At times, however, economic regulation could impinge upon safety. The gas safety regulator explained:

> There are some things that are purely safety, some things that are purely service, but some of them, and supply is the classic in gas, overlap, it's both. The Essential Services Commission's driver is ODRC – Optimised Depreciated Replacement Cost. All you're allowed to earn money on for your regulated asset base is the minimum number of assets that you need prudently to manage the next few years. So you're not allowed to build something for the next generation and charge this generation for the privilege. (10, pp.10–11)

Money that was used to create redundancy in a system, a benefit from an engineering perspective, was seen as 'gold-plating' when viewed from an economic paradigm. In short, this generation should not pay for the next generation's problems. Nonetheless, the response to Longford in Victoria, then, demonstrated the best that was possible in reform. The expertise and acumen of the regulator was critical to this end, as was the existence of a suitable model (safety case) that understood both the technical and human demands that needed to be met to reduce risk. But selection of this regime was not under the total control of the regulator. A particular method the government chose to reduce its political risk (when a denunciatory approach failed) provided the regulator with both discretion and resources.

Even in this 'best case' scenario sustaining the regime was difficult. Over time, the government acceded to industry pressure. Some of this could be seen as helpful in fine-tuning the regime. But sustaining the regime came at a considerable cost to the leadership of the regulator and changes at the helm were common. Finally, the experience of the gas safety regulator highlights the multiple intersecting elements of any hazard reduction regime. Here again political risk reduction remained a key priority. Diversification of supply ensured lower political risk. Economic models based on minimal redundancy also ensured lower political risk for incumbent governments (by virtue of being able to control cost and price) but arguably left a more ambivalent legacy for their successors.

Northern Territory

The response to Longford in the Northern Territory (NT) provides a useful contrast to Victoria. In this jurisdiction resources were scarce (the population of the NT being around 200,000 compared with around 5 million in Victoria). The number of staff in the whole NT occupational health and safety regulator, NT Worksafe, was around the same as numbers of staff exclusively dedicated to the Victorian MHU. From these scarce resources the NT regulator had to deal with the full breadth of OHS issues 'from major hazard facilities to workplace bullying' (3, p.1). The resources dedicated to each of the problems and to MH risk was then significantly lower, '1/20th of a person' (3, p.7).

Nonetheless, following Longford the NT had implemented a safety case regime. The regime, however, was quite different in character from the Victorian model. Safety case was enshrined in a code of practice for major hazard facilities that was called up under existing legislation *Work Health Act 2005* (NT).[5] This code of practice had been developed by a national body, the National Occupational Health and Safety Commission (NOHSC).[6] It was implemented without modification. The NOHSC code was developed prior to Longford in 1996 in response to the Piper Alpha disaster. Until Longford, however, no state or territory in Australia had either implemented the code or drawn from it to regulate major hazards in their jurisdiction.

The NOHSC code was recognised as a less onerous safety case model with a less prescriptive mandate around the process of generating a site specific risk management regime. It set out general principles rather than developing the comprehensive structure Victoria had implemented in the wake of Longford. Implementing the NOHSC code at NT MH worksites also was not mandatory. MHFs could choose either to use the code on site, or utilise an alternative route to ensure the safety of their facility, as long as the necessary level of risk reduction was achieved. Following the code could be used in court to demonstrate risk reduction and so provided some assurance to sites in terms of fulfilling their legal responsibilities. Overall, however, the regime was a much weaker version of the Victorian model.

Yet, the MH risk itself was much lower. The NT had only two major hazard sites one of which, a storage facility, was considered by MH standards to be relatively safe. The two sites were also new and argued to be 'state of the art' (3, p.5) in terms of technological control of risk. Arguably, then, the NT safety case approach was appropriate for the much lower risk posed by MHFs in the NT. Further, it was commensurate with the resources of NT Worksafe. The regulator argued that they simply did not have the resources to implement a Victorian approach to safety case. Indeed, it was struggling to find the necessary engineering skills in the whole OHS arena. A review of NT Worksafe had recommended that another engineer be employed but the position remained vacant due to lack of applicants.

A generalist engineer also would not necessarily be able to understand the risk control features necessary for a major hazard site. The regulator recognised that the kind of engineers required for MH work were in short supply. The likelihood of finding someone with the requisite skills who was willing to work for the NT regulator was low.

Nonetheless, the regulator was confident that the two sites were safe. This assessment was based, as mentioned above, on the age of the MHFs in the NT. Plant design was also required by law to have been verified by a qualified designer who had to be independent from the designer of the plant. This verification process was paid for by the company concerned. The company that controlled the MHF site was also considered important. Both MH sites were owned and operated by major multinational companies who were considered to have the necessary expertise to control their MH risk. Further, it was argued that the sites had too much to lose if a major incident occurred:

> I'll put my neck on the line and say that I don't believe our major hazard facilities will be any less safe[7] than the ones that are being put through the million dollar rigour of our southern counterparts ... there's too much money being spent. No industry spends a million dollars on something just to be able to say they've got the files on the desk. (3, p.22)

This did not mean the regulator had no involvement with these two facilities. The approach taken was to build relationships with both sites and to use these relationships to leverage high standards. The regulator had also decided to focus on the implementation of proper procedure and argued 'I'm very much focussed on going right down to the shop floor ... to make sure that the people on the ground actually implement all the systems that they'll put in place'[8] (p.9). This was a sensible strategy, one that used the skills the regulator actually had. Many disasters occur because proper procedure has not been followed; Piper Alpha exploded in part because of a faulty permit to work system, for example (Miller 1991).

Enforcement was also considered important. However, the regulator had found that prosecutions and fines were of little use. Penalties were too low and the process too slow. Halting production was a much more powerful tool:

> [If it is unsafe] we just shut them down, make sure that they don't work in that area. And that costs them a lot more in productivity than it does by trying to fine them or trying to even [take] them to court because [it costs] tens of thousands of dollars to take them to court and they get fined a thousand dollars. (3, p.14)

The political environment of the NT took a distinct form. The regulator had a close relationship with politicians but also was cognizant of what was happening on sites. This, the regulator argued was an advantage of a small jurisdiction:

> I can be dealing with the Deputy Chief Minister one minute and the labourer on the construction site the next in my role as the Manager of Prevention at WorkSafe. I see what's really happening at the coalface as well as what's happening at the higher level. (3, p.16)

It was not clear, however, how much political support NT Worksafe would have if faced with strong lobbying from MNCs who threatened to withdraw their investment from the territory. It was clear that this regulator could, and did, take action against recalcitrant contractors or 'cowboys' attracted to the rugged nature of the NT lifestyle. Retaining political support for action against a major MNC, however, is quite another proposition.

Nonetheless, it is possible to argue that NT Worksafe was addressing the actuarial risk of disaster in an appropriate fashion. To date, it also appeared that there was political support for the approach taken. Political risk management did not negatively impinge on the control of actuarial risk, partly because the safety of these plants was not of current political concern. The level of political risk associated with the possibility of disaster was low.

Again, however, it is important to consider the sustainability of this method of MH control over time. Here the picture suggests potential threats. These in part arose from the demands of other states under a process of harmonisation. Other states could be dismissive of the NT approach and push for a more rigorous safety case model to be implemented. This may be positive, but had the potential to detract from a focus on the hazard, 'I don't care what anyone says. I won't be convinced otherwise and yes I do have arguments with my peers, because a lot of them are just focused on paperwork and I'm saying 'what's the outcome here?' (3, p.3). Further, the resources were simply not there, 'For me to put in place what Victoria has I would need to invest a million dollars a year, half a million dollars a year. That's almost our total budget. It's not going to happen' (3, p.21). This regulator was critical of what he saw as 'empire building'. He was particularly dismissive of the dangerous goods area in general, which he saw as an area more of political advancement rather than actually focussed on risk reduction, 'It's a dog's breakfast ... individual regulators protecting their little bailiwick' (3, p.18).

The strategy NT Worksafe employed to counter the demands from other states for a more rigorous approach in their jurisdiction was to employ consultants with the necessary MH expertise to monitor site activities. Again, this appeared to be a useful approach. Nonetheless, the quality of the consultancy and the degree to which their recommendations are implemented also needs to be considered.

But there were legitimate concerns about the capacity of the NT regulator to manage MH risk in the long term. Over time, the territory would face several threats including ageing plant, revisions to the MH sites as well as possible changes in site ownership, all of which can heighten actuarial risk. Further, faith placed in a high-profile MNC to keep a site safe may be misplaced. Evidence for this was demonstrated by the Longford incident which, as it will be remembered, was run by Esso Australia, considered at the time to be a paragon of MH risk control. Important, too, was the generally high turnover of employees in the NT with subsequent losses of corporate knowledge, lapses in training and communication also potentially posing considerable risk.

The NT approach, then, arguably was appropriate for the level of risk the MHFs posed. The confluence of actuarial, socio-cultural and political risk dedicated to the reduction of MH risk was to an extent at least evident in the NT. Nonetheless, there was a considerable imbalance of power and knowledge between the MNCs who owned the MHFs and the regulator. The regulator conserved his resources to try to use them to best effect, but ultimately was dependent on the good faith efforts of the MHFs themselves.

New South Wales

At the time of the research New South Wales (NSW) was an outlier in terms of the control of MH risk. As late as 2006 it had not implemented any form of safety case legislation in the eight years following the Longford disaster. Reform to its major hazards regime was occurring, but was painfully slow. Finally in 2008, ten years after the Longford disaster, it brought in a regulation entitled the Occupational Health and Safety Amendment (Major Hazard Facilities) Regulation 2008 (NSW). The level of control in the decade preceding the new regulation could not be considered commensurate with the level of risk. NSW had a similar industry profile to Victoria, with a number of ageing plants within the boundaries of major population centres.

The reasons for the slow response given the risks it faced required careful analysis. As with all the jurisdictions, the lack of a dedicated MH regime should not imply there was no regulation covering these industries at all. There was a plethora of regulations dealing with general occupational health and safety, dangerous goods, environment and emergency management under the control of NSW WorkCover. Secondly, there existed a related regime under the control of another government department, the Department of Infrastructure, Planning and Natural Resources (DIPNR) responsible for planning issues associated with hazardous industry. This planning process comprised several features that are part of a safety case type regime. Nonetheless, NSW itself had identified that it had some limitations in terms of risk control and MHF, particularly in the area of low probability but high consequence events. These limits were those that were revealed by the Longford incident: the need for a tightly focussed regime that could target high-hazard industries and to engender a regime that satisfied both regulator and site that risks were being adequately controlled. A collaborative, but accountable regime was still needed in that state.

Politically, however, reform of the MHF regulation was not a high priority. Quite simply Longford happened in Victoria (a neighbouring state) not New South Wales. The disaster did not feature prominently in parliamentary debates. Indeed, the only two references to Longford were from within the incumbent government during question time; 'Dorothy Dix' questions (one in 2001 and again in 2004) that allowed the government to demonstrate that it was doing something about major hazard regulations in the state. Further, in the wake of September 11 the 2004 question emphasised as much the possibility of a terrorist attack on such facilities as an internally generated breakdown of risk controls. Finally, the response of the parliamentary opposition was to question the need for more regulations, not to identify whether there was an unacceptable risk to NSW citizens from its major hazard facilities.

Political priorities on both sides of the NSW Parliament, then, lay elsewhere. The long and tortuous passage of relevant legislative and regulatory reform can in large part be explained by this low level of political risk. Reform to major hazard regulation was pushed off the parliamentary agenda by other 'more important' issues, including a bill to control dangerous dogs in the aftermath of the mauling of a child by a pit bull terrier.[9] The sheer weight of 'more pressing' legislation and regulation to go through parliamentary council meant that items considered a low priority (as this one was) just got pushed to the bottom of the pile:

> ... Parliamentary council don't always have the same timetable as you so if they are busy with other bills that they're doing, your legislation might go on the backburner until they've got time to draft it so it['s] just finding, loading everything up and trying to get all of those things done seems to take some time. (7, p.3)

There was also some concern expressed by MHFs with the possibility of more regulation. The picture here, however, was mixed. Some sites in NSW saw the new regime as inevitable and necessary. Some had experienced benefits in Victoria from sister sites located there and were keen to have similar legislative and regulatory certainty. Some had even begun to move towards a safety case approach and were frustrated by the length of time the reforms were taking. From their perspective such tardiness was a waste of their time and money. Other sites, however, were clearly less keen to have the regulations in place and pressured the NSW Government to minimise the impact of the change. Clearly, the NSW Opposition saw little gain in pushing for change.

The low political risk was met by a problematic bureaucratic structure and ethos around the regulation of major hazard risk in NSW. There were two potential sites for the new major hazard regulatory regime: DIPNR[10] and NSW WorkCover. The split nature of responsibility was the source of political tension. A NSW regulator commented:

> ... there's been quite a lot of work done in trying to work out how it will set up, it had to get a cabinet approval, there was a whole lot of disputes about where it should sit. For a long time it was with the planning authority [DIPNR] so they were responsible for it and then at the very last minute when they swapped funding again to finalise the process and cabinet decided that they didn't think it was appropriate for them, it should be WorkCover, so then we took over the process and so now we're the lead agency. (7, p.3)

The problem in moving the responsibility to NSW WorkCover, however, was that much of the expertise around controlling major hazard risk was found within DIPNR, whose existing regulations were closest to a safety case type of approach. DIPNR expertise existed both in the technical detail and the relationship necessary for a successful co-regulatory regime.

In contrast, there was also a level of discomfort within NSW WorkCover over the ethos of a co-regulatory safety case approach. The OHS regulator had considerable experience with a prescriptive dangerous goods regime and felt comfortable with it. However 13,000 sites were licensed under this regime and the regulator admitted to being rather 'overwhelmed with information' from the inspection and audit regime they had undertaken. The move to a different regulatory philosophy was challenging for some within this organisation, particularly those working in the dangerous goods area. The NSW regulator commented:

> ... we've got a first draft of the reg[11] and people internally weren't happy with that ... I think it's the dangerous goods people there I think that get very up tight about it so there's also a bit of arguing going on at the moment about what's in the reg ... (7, p.13)

The lack of political will underpinning the lack of progress in NSW, then, was exacerbated by competing philosophies and jurisdictional tension between relevant bureaucracies.

Extensive consultation did, eventually, result in a comprehensive regime. Indeed, in some respects it learnt from Victoria in its design and was able to incorporate emerging security risks into the regime. But, there were some key differences that could threaten its integrity. In particular, the resources put into the implementation and monitoring were much lower. This was argued to be because the number of MHFs was lower in NSW. However, until the notification process was completed the actual number of sites remained unclear. It was anticipated that there would be only nine staff from NSW WorkCover dedicated to the MHF area, with another three from the Department of Planning and one each from the NSW Police and Fire brigade. This spread of personnel raised the possibility of an inspection and registration process combining quite distinct regulatory styles and, critically, whose members would report to different political masters. Further, in 2008 there were allegations of bullying and harassment by one member associated with the MH process that did not bode well for a smooth collaborative relationship between agencies dedicated to the reduction of MH risk (Lynn 2008).

In addition, the regime in NSW was designed to be cost neutral to the regulator consistent with the prevailing competition framework that stipulated that industry should pay for the cost of its own regulation (for a succinct description see Government of Victoria 2007 section 3.2.13). Victoria had a capped regime and in the NT costs were divided between regulator and MH site. Cost neutral funding can work well (indeed as we will see below, APRA also was a cost neutral regime and used this relationship with industry effectively) but it does require a strong and united commitment to risk reduction and the political will to ensure that fees payable by industry are sufficient to cover the necessary regulatory resources. Whether this would eventuate in NSW was not clear at the time of the research.

The reform experience in NSW, then, was quite distinct from both Victoria and the Northern Territory. Despite a commensurable risk of a MHF disaster, when compared with Victoria reform was painfully slow. The reasons for this were multilayered: there was some industry resistance to enhanced controls as well as bureaucratic complexities and tensions between regulators that exacerbated a timely passage of reform. Cultural change also needed to develop as the necessary co-regulatory regime was, for NSW WorkCover at least, challenging. Yet these hurdles stemmed in large part from a lack of political will. Longford happened in Victoria; it was not a concern for NSW. The current regime was 'good enough' and anyway there were more pressing concerns to deal with.

THE REGULATORY RESPONSE TO SEPTEMBER 11

The regulatory response to September 11 was decisive and dramatic. The political emphasis was for visible changes that could ensure that airlines would keep flying and trade flowing. To achieve this, both trading partners (in particular the United States) and the public needed assurance that they were safe from attack. The overriding purpose of regulatory reform was the reduction of political risk. That is, the success of reform would be measured by its capacity to maintain economic activity at the same time as reassuring the public that the government would keep them secure. Indeed, the aim was for regulatory reform to enhance political fortunes, as the Howard government's response to the *Tampa* crisis had managed to do in the months preceding the September 11 attacks. The Labor opposition also saw security as an avenue for political advancement and systematically set about trying to find weaknesses in the government's security net and so further its own political interests. They were assisted in this by the particular nature of the threat since the potential for terrorist attack was – in the public imagination at least – limitless. Yet, for a government such tactics from an opposition needed to be muted, particularly where they threatened core economic interests. The actuarial risk assessment made by government bureaucracies, then, was shaped by economic concerns so that a narrative was built up around what made a site 'vulnerable'. Here, the co-regulatory regime could be used to good effect and sites encouraged to 'dig their own regulatory grave' (Haines and Sutton 2003 p.17) to satisfy the demands of the regulators.

Sustaining a regulatory regime associated with counterterrorism had a particular character in contrast to the regimes discussed above. Two elements were particularly noteworthy. Firstly, there was the massive influx in resources in the aftermath of September 11 that led to the creation of a 'new empire', one with which successive governments would have to deal. Secondly, government was increasingly concerned to move the costs from their own agencies and on to business. A reduction in security control was not tenable politically, but the costs were considerable. Here, the elastic nature of the terrorist risk was stretched to create economic models where business, not the public at large, was argued to be the principal beneficiary of regulatory control and hence should be asked to pay for the costs involved.

The regulatory framework that governed counter-terrorism at air and seaports was, at first blush, quite similar in philosophy to the co-regulatory structure of the MHF regime. The regulatory framework put in place in the aftermath of September 11 required active, ongoing and demonstrated commitment to risk reduction by regulated sites, the air and seaports. The principal regulator, Office of Transport Security (OTS) required sites to develop site-specific security plans that were both approved and audited by the OTS.

Ports and airports needed to submit to the OTS a detailed security plan based on an assessment and management plan for security risks within the particular port or airport. Designated secure areas had to be created (so called 'sterile' areas) where only those adequately screened and accompanied or with the proper security identification card (ASIC or MSIC) could enter. As with the safety case regime, the security plans also needed to contain emergency procedures in the event of an attack. Finally, strict reporting requirements of suspicious occurrences to the OTS were required.[12] Plans were subject to audit and review by the OTS that could result in additional measures being required of sites.

There was legislative and regulatory coverage to enable the new regimes in both the aviation and maritime arena. In the aviation area, there were two acts: *Aviation Transport Security Act 2004* as well as the *Aviation Transport Security (Consequential Amendments and Transitional Provisions) Act 2004,* underpinned by Aviation Transport Security Regulations 2005. In the Maritime area there was the *Maritime Transport and Offshore Facilities Security Act 2003* also underpinned by regulations. These acts enshrined the transport security plan requirements. In addition, there were enhanced international security regulatory obligations to be met. For example, Australia needed to comply with reforms to the International Maritime Organization regulatory regime, in particular amendments to the Safety of Life at Sea Convention, 1974 (SOLAS Convention) in particular the introduction of the International Ship and Port Facility Security Code (ISPS Code).

Counter-terrorist regulatory reforms at airports were those most visible in the immediate aftermath of the terrorist attacks in the United States. There was an immediate impact on the airline industry, namely the bankruptcy of US airlines. Australia, too, had experienced the collapse of Ansett Airlines and the aviation industry was under considerable stress. The pressure on government, then, was to keep the airlines flying. A senior regulator commented:

> ... ten airlines went bankrupt in the United States and had to be bailed out by the United States Government. ... The US government is providing billions of dollars of assistance to those airports. ... The impact for Australia was significant also there was a drop in transport and the use of aviation. ... So there was no question they [airports and airlines] needed to demonstrate that they were secure; they needed public confidence back. (5, p.5)

In order to keep the industry afloat the travelling public needed to feel adequately protected. This was an overriding concern of the government that brought together the two aspects of political risk management together in one set of policies around security at airports. A security regulator commented, 'The driving force was public perception because that influences political perception. It influences political will and it influences the regulatory model that's applied' (5, p.5).

What was considered adequate protection of the travelling public, however, was constantly changing. There were always 'new risks and vulnerabilities' (5, p.5). These then had a direct impact on the security plans prepared at airports. What was adequate at one moment might change at the next. Changed perceptions of risk had a direct impact on regulations, '(new threats) changed the whole threat picture, which then changed the risks, the risk mitigation strategies, and therefore the security plans' (5, p.5).

Legislation and supporting regulations were in a state of constant flux. In the aviation area, the *Aviation Transport Security Act* was amended four times between 2004 and 2008. *The Aviation Transport Security (Consequential Amendments and Transitional Provisions) Act 2004* was also amended once. Changes to regulations were even more frequent. The Aviation Transport Security Regulations were amended six times since coming into force in October 2005. The marine area was not immune, as political attention broadened to include maritime security. Again, the regulations were amended most frequently. In the Marine area, the *Maritime Transport and Offshore Facilities Security Act 2003* was amended once from 2003–08, and the regulations six times to 2008 since their promulgation in 2004.

The pressure on regulators to generate regulations and to comment on reform proposals, then, was considerable. There was a steady stream of high-profile media stories around drug offences, the actions of baggage handlers (particularly at Sydney airport) that led to successive demands for change. Further, security became a focal point for political point scoring between the opposition and the government. Kim Beazley, the (then) leader of the opposition ALP in an address entitled 'A Nation Unprepared: Australia in the Fourth Year of a Long War' argued, 'Target hardening of our mass transit systems and iconic building and other sites must of course also be relentlessly pursued. We must ensure these important services and locations are simply unattractive, too difficult, for would-be terrorists' (Beazley 2005 p.1).

Recent media stories were used by the opposition to push for more reform, particularly around tighter security at regional airports. The government would then respond with an inquiry or review, the most important of which was the Wheeler Inquiry (Wheeler 2005) into security of airports, that would then feed into more reform, 'We have a Council of Australian Government Ministers on the 27th of September [2005], there are 17 recommendations out of Wheeler, there are 11 recommendations coming out of CoAG. Those will result in new systems being developed and legislation, regulation, education and training and so on' (5, p.7).

The political dynamic generated more and more reform. A security regulator argued, '[There is] the constant need to amend the legislation and regulations. I mean, if industry thinks it's bad, try writing the damn stuff' (5, p.7). The chance to consider review proposals carefully was a luxury and the turnaround on policy documentation swift. Twenty-four hours was a luxury, with often only a few hours available for senior regulators to comment on complex and lengthy documents, 'I get them at two o'clock in the afternoon and they [the relevant Minister's office] want comments by four o'clock' (16, p.6) commented one.

Further, the security regime necessarily required various government departments (such as Customs and the OTS) enforcement and intelligence agencies (State and Federal Police, ASIO and the Office of National Assessments (ONA) for example) to work together and much time and effort was spent on creating a collaborative approach to solving the complex security problems at sea ports and airports. There were successes and the experience of the Sydney Olympics in 2000 created some good working relationships. But, 'whole of government' was not always easy. Different cultural expectations between departments and jealousies between enforcement agencies meant that collaboration could be challenging. Some regulators saw culture as determining legislation and outcome, 'Culture is the way we do things around here, and that impacts the way they draft their legislation, which they then say 'I come to that because my legislation says that.' But you can actually trace it back to culture and the way they work' (5, p.17). Distrust between police forces, a finding of the Wheeler Inquiry, also made 'whole of government' type approaches difficult as one commented, 'It's been a difficult and hard lesson for me to learn about the sort of culture, various cultures and the distrust between police forces' (5, p.17).

However, the structure of the relationship between a minister and the regulator was also critical to understand here, as was the competitive nature of the political environment. Within government, ministers were vying for prominence and their capacity to have engendered prominent reforms a key indicator of their effectiveness as ministers. Regulators were clear who their political masters were (that is, their respective ministers) and this critically affected their policy proposals and their relationships with other bureaucracies:

> ... at the end of the day we certainly make sure that we've designed or built something that is going to work and that my Minister can look the Prime Minister in the eye and say 'you've told me to do this, I've done it.' And even though our colleagues in the department across the road are doing something, [and] we're not, I'm not that interested in how they're going to do it. Because it's hard enough for me to get it right for this organization and my Minister and that's at the end of the day the public servant's aim: what's the Minister's reaction going to be to this? And I guess I don't really care if my friends in tax [or] if the treasurer said this is a crummy proposal or this is a ridiculous method of regulating this ... (16, p.17)

Success or failure, then, was assessed by the 'government displeasure index' (5, p.8). Public perception of security fuelled by the media and urged on by the opposition underpinned government, which then sought both to reassure and demonstrate political authority. To the extent policy achieved this security regulators could, at least for a brief moment, enjoy 'government pleasure'.

Public and opposition pressure, though, was not the only hurdle to be overcome. Privatised airports guarded their revenue and pushed back against what they saw and 'over the top' costly security requirements. Enhanced security, for example Customs requiring more space to process passengers, could immediately affect an airport's revenue. A regulator explained the nature of the discussion:

> When we [the regulator] want more space he [the airport manager] says 'it's x dollars a square metre' and we say 'you've got to be kidding!' He said, 'Well if you're not here and RM Williams[13] is going to be here and that's on the spot [you want], that's where I'm going to get my money.' (16, p.5)

Certainly, the Office of Transport Security (OTS), one of the main regulators here was keen to try to accommodate business as far as possible. They recognised that a good relationship was important. The aim was to convince air and seaports that good security would be in their own interests. The security plans were underpinned by a comprehensive penalty regime with penalties ranging from infringement notices to criminal fines. However, active enforcement through the relevant penalty regime under either the *Aviation Transport Security Act 2004* or *Marine Transport and Offshore Facilities Act 2003* was not a high priority at the time of the research and feedback from industry was carefully listened to, 'we're trying to set the regulatory framework, but what we're trying to do is help the industry,' the Office of Transport Security argued (5, p.12).

A key question at this point is whether the new regulations actually made the air and seaports safer from a terrorist attack; that is, whether actuarial risk had been reduced. This was a difficult if not impossible question to answer. Each regulator could point to indications of success, where particular sites were working well and collaboration between agencies effective. Yet, there was a hesitation to identify whether the regime had reduced the risk of a terrorist attack. Rather, regulators would point to 'government displeasure' or media attention (or preferably its lack) to gauge their success. This should not be taken as a criticism; indeed it is not hard to understand why a regulator would not want to claim their success based on the fact that no terrorist attack had occurred, since tomorrow's news might prove otherwise.

Yet, at the same time the OTS claimed they were an 'outcome focussed' regulator. But it was not clear how the outcomes they nominated (relationship with business, public concern, government displeasure) related to the actuarial risk of attack. The OTS recognised this disjunction, and attempted to modify their risk reduction strategy to one they argued was 'intelligence led, risk-based security, outcome focussed' (5, p.4). Reducing the risk of attack was important, but the challenge of identifying who the likely attacker was, or what the avenue for attack would be was considerable. Transport security plans required a constant stream of reporting back to the OTS about suspicious occurrences to feed into other sources of intelligence, but obtaining accurate information was difficult. Intelligence and threat assessments were done but it was still difficult to analyse and gauge accurately whether an attack was being planned, '[they] will never be of the level of granularity that some people in the industry would like, which is "Can you tell me what time and what day and where this thing's going to occur?" It's rare that you'll every get to that level of granularity' (5, p.6).

Profiling for terrorists also was problematic. Regulators were conscious that 'our profiles are only as good as the information that's fed into us from security agencies' (16, p.17). Broad categories were also no help in trying to identify which cargo might be suspect or where explosives might enter Australia undetected. The response from Customs illustrated this point:

> With narcotics we can get it these days just about right to the source country where we are going to hit. We are going to hit everything coming out of country x if it's shipped directly to Australia. Don't even think about it, because it's going to be full of coke.[14] But [identifying] a source country for terrorists is very, very difficult. What do you do there? I mean if you plug every country in the world there, what are you going to do, close the airport? (16, p.17)

Such challenges then had a direct impact on the monitoring of trade through ports and airports and, to a lesser extent, the flow of passengers through (mainly) airports. Customs routinely scanned about 7 per cent of all cargo. Advance reporting of goods bound for Australia from the point of departure meant that considerable profiling of cargo could occur before a ship entered an Australian port.

Yet, regulators acknowledged that some contraband, such as drugs, made its way through their scrutiny, '... On the public record, the Customs Service says that we think we'd get about 10 per cent of all narcotics that are imported into Australia and we've been saying that for about 15 years' (16, p.15). Full screening of all cargo was not considered a sensible use of resources and was considered to slow trade to a level that was unacceptable to business. Cargo companies pushed back against regulations arguing that 'People pay us good money for speed and these measures are going to slow the whole thing down' (16, p.6). The political influence that business had using arguments about slowing business was considerable. So, regulators were not only pressured by business to keep trade flowing but also by politicians. Measures that had an appreciable drag on business would not occur, 'over my dead body, or rather the Prime Minister's dead body' commented one. The opposition ALP demand that 90 per cent of all cargo should be screened (Beazley 2005) was ignored.

So, the actuarial risk remained unmeasured and unmeasurable beyond perception and what might be termed informed common sense. But, vulnerability remained since, as one security analyst during a security conference put it, 'terrorists are smarter than your average bolt' (Windeyer 2006).

The shaping of where the next attack might come from was based on analysing past attacks. These assessments could be extended to include possible future threats, or vulnerabilities, but only when business would not be too severely affected. Airport freight was perhaps the clearest example of this narrative construction of risk at work. There was, as many would have experienced, mass screening of passengers at airports, 'we then take off your shoe buckle and all your shoes and all the other bits of metal. At the same time there's a guy here having a look at your carry on baggage, through his x-ray machine. And before this your checked-in luggage is x-rayed for explosives. ...' (16, p.16). But, for cargo the rules were different, 'And when you are sitting up there in the plane having your own orange juice, there is 50 tonne of cargo going into the belly of that plane underneath the seat you're on, that's not screened for explosives' (16, p.16).

The reason for such disparity was not hard to find. People were reassured by the screening process; indeed, many would complain if they felt screening was too lax. Informal disapproval of fellow passengers who challenged security measures also was at work. These measures were important in reassuring the public it was safe to travel, and helped to keep the airlines flying. Freight, however, was another matter. Airline profits were tight and profit on passenger tickets slim or non-existent. Freight was more profitable:

> I think the general public, (a) they don't see it [the lack of freight screening], they don't realise it. By the time they're getting on its already being loaded. And (b) there's no money in airline tickets. Where they [the airlines] get their money is in cargo. And you don't ship air, you jam a package that size into a plane if you can. Shipping empty space is not good. (16, p.17)

The security regime across various regulators, then, had generated considerable changes. These changes, though, were strongly influenced by the needs of industry that in turn affected the economic fortunes of government. Financial concerns and public reassurance shaped the security response. Clearly, the risk that terrorists might use some avenues of attack had been reduced. But, measures of success were difficult and certain areas remained vulnerable.

The sustainability of this regime also had particular characteristics. Technological innovation to allow swifter screening from a greater distance remained an important source of future security. Security regulators knew where there were vulnerabilities and sought technological solutions: radio frequency identification, mobile x-ray technology, ion mobility spectrometry to test for explosives as well as more dog teams trained in explosives. Technological solutions, however, could also be quite problematic as regulators dealt with an ever-expanding number of companies purveying their technology and hoping for a regulatory seal of approval. Technology also could create problems with some electronic entry systems requiring identical key strokes to be entered. Simple typographical errors in cargo manifests could be responsible for costly freight delays. Technological advancements, then, could promise much but also could create additional difficulties.

Equally as important was the human and logistical impact within the public service of such a massive injection of resources into the security area. Personnel in the OTS had increased over 800 per cent (from 30 to 250) in the four years following the September 11 attacks. These numbers were expected to grow as greater demands were made on cargo screening. As one regulator stated, 'We started a new empire' (16, p.18). Such an empire, however, had some difficulty in retaining staff. Staff turnover was felt at all levels and included the director of security, with successive directors moving on to other positions within the public service. To an extent, the OTS could be viewed as a place for rapid advancement and, when opportunity arose, the possibility for public servants to move to more rewarding positions in the public service commensurate with their new found status.

Yet, empires cost money. Who was to pay for security was a constant source of tension between the government and business. In the immediate aftermath of September 11 the Federal government could fund their security initiatives safe in the knowledge of public support. Certainly, the opposition did not seem to raise the issue of funding, or whether public resources were being used effectively.[15] Regulators would try to convince ports, airports, airlines and shipping companies that the cost of security should be seen as a cost of doing business and so that there should be full cost recovery. Not surprisingly, business did not see it this way. A security regulator explained:

> [Industry says] 'Ok, now you're expecting me to outlay 93 million dollars in the maritime industry to implement this regime, what effect is it having on my bottom line?' Hardened cockpit doors on some aircraft, too, the aircraft owners are saying that takes out one seat the impact of that one seat is 17 thousand dollars a year. So, that's the sort of issue you have, but I suppose I often ask the question, 'What would happen to your business if there was actually a security incident, if … one of your aircrafts is hijacked … you'd be out of business.' (5, p.9)

Here, the capacity to model costs became critical. Some costs were easier to measure than others. Estimating the loss to business income due to a terrorist attack could be undertaken, albeit with some assumptions being made. Yet, coming up with any figures that estimated with any degree of accuracy what specific reduction in threat could be attributed to what particular security measure was impossible. The costs, then, tended to fall on those with least political leverage, which also meant that significant outlays by government itself continued. Cost neutrality remained a hope more than a reality.

The security reforms in the aftermath of September 11 then bore some resemblance to the co-regulatory approach evident in the MH regime. But, co-regulation was starkly contoured by the demands for political risk reduction: of reassuring the public whilst keeping industry on side. Such a risk reduction strategy had a complicated relationship to the reduction of actuarial risk, since measurement of whether and by how much terrorist risk had been reduced was difficult to gauge. Success remained measured by criteria based on government satisfaction and measures of public reassurance. Such measures meant that reducing security coverage was not possible, yet pressure from business meant that extending coverage was restricted to weaknesses revealed by past attacks. Even this partial coverage created 'new bureaucratic empires' that over time generated their own internal dynamic.

REFORMS IN THE WAKE OF THE HIH COLLAPSE

There were two main regulatory regimes that were affected by the collapse of HIH: prudential regulation, the responsibility of the Australian Prudential Regulation Authority (APRA) and securities and investments regulation, under the control of the Australian Securities and Investments Commission (ASIC). Both regulators were the result of an overhaul of financial regulation in Australia that resulted from the Inquiry into the Financial System in 1997, chaired by Stan Wallis (hereafter the Wallis Report) (1997) that resulted in a major consolidation of 11 financial regulatory agencies across Australia bringing together state and federal regulators into a streamlined system of regulation (Black 2006; Palmer 2002). It is worth considering regulatory reforms in each of these two areas separately not only because of their technical differences in terms of the specific actuarial risk each was charged with managing, but also because the political pressures on each of the regulators differed quite markedly. So, whilst there were similarities, for example both were affected by political demands that they cut 'red tape' by virtue of the upswing in the economic cycle and growing business confidence, there were key differences. Firstly, APRA came in for much harsher criticism in the aftermath of the HIH collapse. Paradoxically, this gave it greater momentum in implementing reforms than its sister agency ASIC. Secondly, APRA was able, in the area of insurance, to define narrowly its areas of responsibility to protecting existing policyholders of Australian insurers, so that it could more easily control its supervision activities. In contrast ASIC's mandate included, at least implicitly, potential as well as existing securities investors entailing responsibility for a much larger number of regulatees, which meant that the level of control it exerted was much less. Its position as a regulator charged with reducing risk, in order to facilitate the normal risk taking inherent in investment, also meant that it sat at the centre of powerful contradictory imperatives.

APRA

The success of the reforms that were made to the regulation of Australian insurance companies in the wake of the HIH collapse resulted from a concerted effort by APRA that was facilitated by government support and from the tight definition of their regulatory responsibilities. Criticism of the APRA by the HIH Royal Commission kept the regulator in the public spotlight which, together with a sweeping review that aimed to reverse what was seen as a 'compensation culture' within Australia, provided the parameters of significant political support of the prudential regulator. The management of political risk by the Howard government shaped the prudential regulatory reforms in the wake of the HIH collapse. The collapse of HIH Insurance posed significant risks to the incumbent government in terms of perceptions of both its economic management and of its concern about the welfare of the popula-tion. As will be remembered from Chapter 4, HIH was renowned as an aggres-sive insurer which pursued market share with low premiums. Their demise had two immediate effects: on existing policyholders of HIH and more broadly on the insurance market. Both these posed significant political risk in terms of high public anxiety around insurance and threats to the economy and in partic-ular key insurance industry sectors such as health, with a threatened collapse of medical indemnity insurance. The strategies government employed to quell public anxiety and to counter economic threats to the insurance industry that resulted from the collapse differed quite markedly from each other. Both, however, make sense when considered in light of the twin demands of politi-cal risk: public reassurance aimed at restoring political legitimacy and main-taining key markets in order to facilitate revenue flow to government.

The response to the stranded HIH policyholders was one of providing immediate financial assistance. For eligible policyholders, government became the 'reinsurer of last resort' (Spigelman 2006 p.7) by establishing the HIH Claims Support Scheme together with the insurance industry and the Insurance Council of Australia. The scheme was announced on May 14, 2001 only two months after the collapse and began operations on July 7, 2001. Eligibility was restricted to individuals, small businesses and not-for-profit organisations (Auditor General 2004). The scheme was funded to a maximum of $640 million (Auditor General 2004) and had paid $245 million by June 2003 having processed 12,000 claims (Coonan 2003). This swift action by the government stemmed considerable public anxiety about insurance policies with HIH. Government could present itself as supporting 'the battlers': individuals, small business and not-for-profit organisations.

Yet, the public and in particular industry concern remained centred on the price and availability of insurance. After the collapse of HIH there was a sharp increase in premiums across many insurance lines (Spigelman 2006). Further, many community activities were unable to be run because of an inability, in the absence of HIH, to obtain public liability insurance or because of prohibitive cost. There was frequent media coverage about the cancellation of community events including town fetes, surfing carnivals, adventure activities as well as growing anxiety around medical indemnity insurance with a potentially catastrophic impact on the health sector. The critical role access to affordable insurance played in everyday Australian life was evident in the front pages of daily newspapers (Spigelman 2006).

The response of the government to the insurance crisis was instructive. It interpreted it as a liability crisis, one generated by growing litigation and a 'compensation culture'. Increased cost of insurance was due to too much money being paid out. The need was, then, to restrict public liability claims – to reform the law with regards to negligence. It commissioned a review of the Law of Negligence chaired by the Hon. David Ipp (hereafter the Ipp review (2002)), to investigate the laws of negligence with a view to drastically curtailing the right to sue and to generating national uniformity. The details of the negligence reforms need not concern us here, save for understanding that they led to reforms of the laws of tort across the states (tort being a state matter), albeit not at a level anticipated by the government. National uniformity certainly was not achieved (Ipp 2007; Spigelman 2006; Wright 2006). Nonetheless, the response pacified the concerns of the insurance industry about their long-term viability.

Whilst increased premium levels were evident, the reasons for the rise were not. Certainly, it was not clear that there had been an extraordinary growth in public liability claims (Wright 2006). Hence, this response of the Commonwealth Government to the rising cost of insurance needs careful scrutiny. It should be remembered that before its collapse HIH Insurance had an aggressive competitive presence in the market and was instrumental in keeping premium levels down. HIH collapsed at a time that the 'insurance cycle' was in a downswing and profitability low. Not surprisingly, when HIH collapsed the insurance industry took the opportunity to raise premiums and with them their profit margins. Further, concern about 'long-tailed' risks meant that insurers became particularly risk averse and eschewed writing certain classes of insurance. The collapse of HIH provided an opportunity to the insurance industry to regain profitability by raising premiums and pulling back from certain markets.

As the insurance industry regained confidence the industry cycle turned to an upswing. Not surprisingly, the Commonwealth Government could claim that its swift action on tort law reform had been a success (Ipp 2007). However, it was more likely that the removal of a major competitor, changing judicial attitudes to compensation and the promise of legal limitations to insurers' vulnerability to potential litigants together restored confidence within the industry. Increased profitability was achieved (Somogyi 2005) and over time there was a decline in premiums in some, but not all, insurance lines (Spigelman 2006).

Pressure on the government from the public and from the insurance industry had been dealt with. But, there had been significant criticism of APRA in the Palmer Report (hereafter Palmer 2002), which had been commissioned by the HIH Royal Commission, and which highlighted the regulator's lack of attention to the growing problems at HIH Insurance in the months before the collapse. This criticism needed a response.

Given the extensive reforms set in motion from the Wallis report in 1997 there was no desire for the government to initiate another restructure of prudential regulatory oversight. Neither was it necessary. The Wallis reforms were largely seen as appropriate for effective prudential regulation (Black 2006; Palmer 2002). Indeed, many of the reforms considered central to APRA's long-term success had begun before the collapse of HIH, but were provided with significant momentum after HIH's demise (Somogyi 2005). What was needed, however, was for APRA to live up to the potential of those reforms in terms of adequate regulatory oversight of the insurance industry.

APRA, then, had the political mandate for a strong regulatory response to HIH and a systematic overhaul of how it went about the task of identifying which regulated institutions were at risk. APRA transformed from a rather trusting 'hands off' approach to regulation of the insurance industry under the previous fragmented regulatory structure[16] to an intensive, comprehensive and integrated 'hands on' approach. In terms of the general insurance industry it reinvigorated efforts towards a reauthorisation process of all general insurers. This was combined with an increase in the absolute minimum capital requirement from $2 million to $5 million. As a result of this process, a number of smaller insurers either had to go into 'run off',[17] merge or be taken over by larger companies. Steve Somogyi, a member of APRA remarked in an address to the industry, 'APRA treated re-authorisation as a matter of substance rather than mere form – an additional opportunity to take stock of each company's soundness, and a useful discipline on companies to put in the work needed to meet the new requirements.' (Somogyi 2005 p.3)

The framework of regulation of insurance that became fully fledged in the aftermath of the HIH collapse comprised three layers. The first was the head of power vested in the *Insurance Act 1973* (Cth) substantially amended in the general insurance area by the *General Insurance Reform Act 2001* (Cth).

These were underpinned by comprehensive reforms to prudential standards. These standards were mandatory. Standards were further enhanced by a suite of guidance notes to assist insurers and their actuaries' compliance efforts. In addition there were reformed financial reporting standards given effect by the *Financial Sector (Collection of Data) Act 2001* (Cth) (Somogyi 2005).

There were several noteworthy components of the new prudential standards. The first round of reforms, completed in 2002, narrowed industry discretion around how policy liabilities were calculated and reported. A Liability Valuation Standard was developed that structured more tightly how these liabilities were to be calculated. Insurers also needed to accept the advice of their approved actuary – or explain to APRA why they had not done so. There were also changes to the amounts of capital for insurers to put aside to ensure that claims on their policies could be met. The calculation of the minimum capital that would be required of an insurer for a given level of risk was tightened, and the buffer of reserves they needed to hold to ensure they could meet those liabilities was increased. APRA also was given the authority to require insurers hold a higher 'buffer' of financial reserves if APRA felt they were at higher risk of failure to meet their liabilities. There were also extensive reforms to what was expected of risk management practices and, in particular, increased expectations of the board to have a risk management strategy to reduce financial and operational risks, increased expectations around independence of the board and 'fit and proper' tests for key personnel, directors, senior managers and advisers. Finally, reinsurance became more tightly controlled with an extensive approvals process put in place (Somogyi 2005).

A further round of reforms to the regulation of general insurance was also instigated, known as General Insurance Reforms Stage II. These further tightened and clarified the 2002 reforms in areas including risk management and reinsurance. Further, changes to audit and actuarial reporting led to the appointed actuary being required to prepare a Financial Condition Report (FCR), which as the name suggests reported on the financial condition of the insurer and in particular their calculation of liabilities and how accurate these proved to be in the light of their experience of claims. The FCR then needed to be considered by the CEO and Chair of the Audit Committee of the board (as set out in the Prudential Standard GPS 310 Audit and Actuarial Reporting and Valuation 2006). Claims of sufficient reserves could then be assessed in the light of history and problems with these calculations identified.

Clearly, there were multiple reforms in the area of prudential regulation as there were in counter-terrorism security regulation. The difference, though, was the level of direct political control of those reforms. As discussed above, often security reforms were politically driven in response to media stories and criticism from the opposition. Political control was direct and intrusive. In the case of the APRA reforms, they emanated from a review that predated the HIH collapse (the Wallis Inquiry) and were heavily shaped by what the regulator itself considered necessary. APRA had discretion and control in a similar manner to the MHU in Victoria.

A critical part of APRAs overall approach was its risk-based approach to identifying which of its regulated organisations needed greater oversight. The approach was comprised of two separate elements. The first, PAIRS (probability and impact rating system), was designed to assess the level of risk a particular institution posed in terms of APRA's objectives. For example, insurers specialising in long-tailed risks that are inherently more difficult to calculate would incur a higher PAIRS rating. PAIRS was based on a series of scores across a range of risk and risk management assessments undertaken on each individual regulated institution (APRA 2008a; Black 2006; Somogyi 2005). The second component SOARS (supervisory oversight and response system) was designed to define what level of oversight the regulator needed to undertake of each individual regulated institution. SOARS was structured in a traditional risk management fashion according to an estimation of the impact in the occasion of company failure combined with an estimation of the probability of such an occurrence (APRA 2008c; Black 2006; Somogyi 2005).

The combined effect of these reforms can be understood as a systematic attempt by APRA to achieve real reductions in actuarial risk of failure of a prudential institution. The political setting described above created the space necessary for APRA to undertake a series of reforms that it felt best able to reduce the risk of another HIH.

It was clear from the data that although APRA was aware that in the event of another collapse they would be held up to scrutiny, yet they were somewhat detached in a manner quite distinct from the security regulators described above. APRA put its faith in the rigour of its processes and its capacity to communicate with industry and government. As Julia Black described it, PAIRS and SOARS were used to 'define the parameters of blame' (Black 2006). Whilst APRA was aware of the possibility of being placed again in an uncomfortable political spotlight, five years after the collapse of HIH there was a quiet confidence that their improved practice would, to an extent at least, shield them from blame:

> ... when push comes to shove if there's a disaster, the fingers will be pointed straight at us again, that's a risk we can't remove. We can try and mitigate it again, which is our own risk management. We can try and mitigate that by explaining and reinforcing what we can and cannot do ... (8,[18] p.19)

Clearly, the development of PAIRS and SOARS was open to criticism should another insurance company go into liquidation. However, there were some interesting elements of APRAs approach. APRA had developed ways to test, and retest, their judgements around the prudential risk an institution posed.

PAIRS and SOARS were used to reduce the inevitable subjectivity in evaluations by increasing their technical expertise and levels of peer review. Firstly, they had employed people with particular technical skills from industry. One particularly innovative method was called 'the grey path.' Here APRA directly targeted individuals in the prudential sector who were coming to the end of their career. APRA could not compete on salary with private industry, but could compete in providing diverse and interesting challenges to those whom they employed. Secondly, they employed young graduates with key technical skills and gave them diverse experience of prudential regulation. They recognised that after a few years these graduates would leave for greener pastures in industry and so tailored their roles to suit the period they were expected to stay with the regulator. It was acknowledged that technical experts at the beginning of their career would come and go. Methods of building up technical expertise were combined with longstanding regulatory experience of a number within APRA who had been involved in prudential regulation for a considerable period. Diverse technical expertise, long-term industry and regulatory experience were used to develop a comprehensive peer review approach to PAIRS and SOARS.

APRA prized reflexivity. Those with deep knowledge needed to broaden their horizons, and those with a broad view needed to deepen their knowledge:

> ... people in the life insurance technical team, who are actually those people with the deep technical skills, and we see [their] capacity over time [improve] in broadening them, and we also run out people who've got broader skill sets through the technical teams to deepen their knowledge. (8, p.3)

The aim of the regulator was to combine technical expertise with effective communication. This was accomplished within APRA itself by 'getting the mix right' (8, p.6) of expertise, regulatory and industry experience. This had the potential to breakdown 'groupthink' around risk (Sunstein 2005). It was also seen as critical for prudential institutions to become reflexive around risk, an aim that was given effect through the requirement for boards to develop appropriate risk-management protocols. For these to be effective, boards needed to understand prudential risk, and in particular reinsurance strategies. A senior prudential regulator commented on one particular case:

> We did have at least one company, when we bought that reinsurance management strategy requirement in at 2002, where the management put the strategy together and gave it to the board. The board looked at it and said 'We don't understand this make it simpler'. ... We want something that's understandable to everybody rather than the way you would run this business ... (8, p.5)

Clearly, then, part of the success of APRA had been in developing a rigorous framework for increasing the resilience of Australian prudential institutions.

But, in the insurance sector this needs to be put into a particular perspective. APRA saw itself as protecting current policyholders of Australian based insurers. This mandate was deliberately narrow. Their principal concern was whether Australian insurers had properly assessed the risk they were underwriting and insuring, 'our role as a regulator is to ensure they can actually pay their claims for the liabilities they take on' (8, p.12). APRA's remit in insurance regulation began at the point of the insurance contract, 'We have a relatively narrow regulatory remit in this in that if you write a contract in Australia then you are an Australian insurer and you have to have a licence here ... these are the rules that you have to abide by' (8, p.17).

This narrow remit was important and allowed APRA to conserve its resources and maintain adequate oversight and knowledge of a tightly defined area. It allowed the regulator to distinguish what was, and what was not, its concern. Further, the number of general insurance companies within Australia was declining as mergers were taking place, with around 130 insurers in 2005 (Somogyi 2005). Regulating these insurers was no small task and technically complex requiring an understanding of brokerage, underwriting, reinsurance and retrocession (the insurance of reinsurance) and strong communication skills. But again in a manner similar to MHU, there was some commensuration between the size of the regulated industry and the resources of the regulator (including their technical expertise) needed to provide adequate oversight.

But, the narrow remit also meant that risk reduction was concentrated in a particular regulatory space. Problematic practices that fell outside APRA's remit were not of concern. Hence, the growing practice of self-insurance was not regulated by APRA. Whilst in some areas, such as workers compensation, self-insurance was subject to oversight by other regulators this was not as clear in other areas with potentially significant risks left with no oversight. Individuals and companies signing international contracts with international insurers based offshore also were subject to little or no prudential regulatory oversight. Further, practices such as increasing excess payments to decrease liabilities were not a concern to APRA. For them, the decrease in liabilities was where their focus lay. This narrow remit provided the means by which some could escape regulatory control.

Finally, then, what were the prospects for sustaining the rigour of the enhanced APRA regulatory regime around insurance? Here there were similarities with the other two risk areas. In particular, there was a marked increase in emphasis on providing guidance and explanation to industry of what APRA required. The insurance industry had pushed back at APRA in light of the reforms and had been critical of their lack of concern about the health of the insurance industry. In particular, there had been greater resistance by industry to the Mark II reforms. APRA responded through a series of presentations, discussion and response papers on these reforms (see for example APRA 2005; 2006; 2008b). APRA wanted to remain true to the lessons of HIH through the Mark II reforms but was finding it more difficult:

> ... HIH happened some years ago now. The appetite for change was very high then (government says) 'you do whatever you have to do to APRA to fix this'. Three years have passed and now we're still implementing or trying to implement change in relation to that, but the climate's changed ... (8, p.20)

The way APRA worked through this was to provide more assistance in helping insurers comply with mandatory requirements and introducing some flexibility through providing prudential practice guides. Also, APRA stepped up its peer review process to ensure greater consistency in how it assessed risk across companies and to create documentation to assist new recruits in their assessment of risk. A regulatory style was developing of reaching out to industry and improving consistency in risk assessments, whilst also retaining regulatory autonomy through requiring increased buffering against risk or stepping-up oversight of a particular institution. Maintaining flexibility, autonomy and consistency may well prove challenging into the future.

APRA was also fully funded by industry. The Wallis report had recommended that the prudential regulator be cost neutral to government and this had been achieved. Yet, the combination of being funded by industry, being a 'hands on' regulator and developing increasing amounts of guidance material had the possibility to lead to some role confusion. One senior regulator reflected that 'we look awfully like consultants sometimes' (8, p.17). The lurking danger for APRA was of being held responsible for an insurer's failure thus increasing pressure on government to rescue a failing institution.

The reforms to prudential regulation in the wake of the HIH collapse can be understood as effectively targeting actuarial risk. The ripples from the collapse led to heightened political pressures around the cost of premiums and the affordability of insurance. The government responded swiftly to this pressure by providing assurance to stranded HIH policyholders that might draw on public sympathy, should their plight remain unattended. Yet, in responding to the insurance crisis the government chose to emphasise the need for greater individual responsibility for poor decisions to wind back the 'compensation culture' as they saw it. This response gave a clear signal to the insurance companies that they had government support. This systematic approach to reassuring the population and supporting industry enabled political threats to government legitimacy stemming from the HIH collapse to be reduced. The government, then, had little interest in constraining the discretion of the regulator in order to bolster their political fortunes. APRA, however, was under considerable pressure to respond to the failures highlighted by the Royal Commission and the Palmer report. Interestingly, it had the structure to be able to do so with the Wallis reforms already in place. Their task was to make this new structure work.

Enhancing actuarial risk management was central to their approach. PAIRS and SOARS provided the mechanisms for defensible and responsive risk management. Innovative strategies were developed to enhance technical skills, increase peer review and improve communication both within the regulator and within regulated firms. What is intriguing here is that broadly speaking financial regulation was shifting from self-regulation to co-regulation as health and safety shifted from command and control to co-regulation.

The instrumental focus of reform also was important. APRA had a tightly defined mandate which it pursued with a dogged determination and to good effect. Yet, this also provided a means of escape for the regulatory regime as a whole for companies that decided to self-insure or use internationally-based insurance cover.

Long term threats to these improvements, then, could come from exploitation of this narrow remit. Yet, APRA also experienced some industry resistance as conditions for the insurance industry improved. As one regulator put it 'the climate had changed' and so even though the reforms were in line with recommendations flowing from the HIH Royal Commission, industry was more forceful in their criticism of Mark II reforms. APRA worked to allay concerns. They increased the flexibility of what was asked for but demanded much more diligent oversight by boards of the prudential institution. Further, they retained their discretion in terms of judging a company's level of risk of defaulting on their obligations to policyholders.

ASIC

The Australian Securities and Investments Commission (ASIC) sits at the centre of Australia's financial regulatory framework and, as such, felt the full impact of the contradictory pressures that impinged on the investment market. The reforms that followed the collapse of HIH provided a fascinating insight into the Australian government's attempt to regulate in an area where maintaining investment to enable sufficient financial skim-off to the government treasury is in chronic tension with public reassurance about their financial wellbeing.

To an extent, this awkward position was equally as relevant to APRA as well as ASIC. But ASIC faced a different set of circumstances that meant regulatory options open to APRA were not available to the securities and investments regulator. In particular, ASIC was not relieved of industry pressure by virtue of independent government initiatives; in the same way pressure on APRA emanating from the insurance industry was lessened by the Ipp review. ASIC's mandate was to provide a robust investment climate by protecting the interests of both investors and potential investors. The breadth of this mandate left little opportunity for government to appease the business community as a whole through measures outside of ASIC's mandate. In contrast to APRA, then, the single site of contest between business, government and the public were the regulations themselves.

This fraught political context meant that ASIC was a regulator that needed to act in the face of considerable constraints. Constraints shaped by government need to reassure the public on one hand and to respond to business demands for deregulating and 'removing red tape' on the other. This regulator was constantly pushed in conflicting directions.

The immediate aftermath of HIH provided a window of opportunity for ASIC to strengthen its controls over business practice. But, by 2006 this had changed with government more responsive to business demands to deregulate. Malcolm Rogers,[19] Executive Director of Policy and Markets Regulations at ASIC commented that:

> Regulation is effected by its political environment. I mean the speech that I've been making internally is that the period between about 2000 and 2003 was the sort of high water mark in Australia in the present little bit of the cycle [that is] that regulation was the answer to things. There's now a very active debate which is being charged up by changing political circumstances. The Business Council of Australia is running out that there's far too much regulation in the country it's an overreaction, its strangling business and burying our global aspirations under an unmanageable burden. And that does mean that we are at a different part of the regulatory cycle (6, p.9).

This regulatory cycle, propelled by the varying level of political appetite for regulation, determined the legislative tools and enforcement discretion that ASIC was afforded. Major reforms, culminating in the *Corporate Law Economic Reform Program (Audit Reform and Corporate Disclosure) Act 2004* (Cth) (also known as CLERP 9) or the ninth set of reforms under the government's Corporate Law Economic Reform Program, had come into force progressively from 2004 in the aftermath of the HIH collapse. Yet, even as these reforms were being implemented industry pressured government to instigate a major program of reducing 'red tape,' arguing that such intrusion threatened investment and with it economic growth. The government responded, creating a 'Deregulation Taskforce' (Regulation Taskforce 2006) under the chairmanship of Gary Banks chairman of the Productivity Commission tasked with reducing the regulatory burden on business.

The impact of industry pressure was to push government to curtail the discretion of the regulator. One clear example here was the shift away from principle to prescription in the CLERP 9 reforms. The reforms following HIH were ostensibly underpinned by a principle-based approach to regulation, where the substantive concern (of what constituted a 'true and fair' view of accounts, or of an 'independent' relationship) would remain paramount and where the regulator could retain discretion in terms of how they judged adherence to these principles. However, during implementation industry pushed for greater and greater certainty. This meant a greater level of prescription which, in turn, curtailed the discretion for the regulator. Malcolm Rogers explained:

> Financial services reform is overwhelmed by a need for commercial certainty and has become in my view far more complicated than it ever should be because everybody [in industry] wanted their questions answered [by ASIC]. And both the government and ourselves thought we were being helpful by answering them but it's turned it into far more complicated and difficult piece of legislation than it really ought to be. (6, p.12)

The responsiveness of government to demands for tougher regulation or to demands for deregulation (or greater 'certainty' and 'clarity' in regulation) depended on a risk assessment of its own liability in both economic and in political terms. Within the financial sphere this regulatory cycle could be understood as a multi-layered drama aimed at reducing political risk. Reducing political risk entailed protecting the investment climate (by responding to demands to reduce the regulatory burden and to clarify principles through prescriptive rules) and reassurance of the population (by responding to demands to reform and enhance regulation). This latter component of reassurance contained a potential threat that in the event of future financial collapse demands would be made of government to step in and fund the financial disasters created by the market. Regulation needed to be carefully crafted to prevent a situation where government would be seen as morally (not just legally) obliged to step in and ameliorate financial hardship. The impetus to regulate, then, was fuelled by the hope that regulation could reassure the public (that is, reduce socio-cultural risk) and appease industry without government being seen to stifle investment, or being pushed into a position where it bore financial responsibility for financial collapse and mismanagement. Malcolm Rogers explained:

> In the case of politically catastrophic failures they create such political pressure on governments to intervene … with HIH where there was a lot of consumer damage being done and it's simply not politically acceptable [for government not to act]. … if that were to occur in superannuation at some stage in this country in the next five years, remembering that we've effectively privatised the superannuation industry now, the great risk for government, and the pressure on government, will be to underwrite superannuation losses in the same way that they physically underwrite bank deposits. And if they are forced into that position, as they were in HIH, where there was at one stage 700 million dollars of commonwealth tax payers' money in the HIH bucket, then they are quite likely to introduce regulation that they think minimises the chances of that occurring again. … (6, p.9)

To achieve adequate reduction in political risk, government needed regulatory reform that reduced both actuarial and socio-cultural risk. Reforms needed to both reduce the risk of another catastrophic collapse whilst also reassuring the public, should another catastrophe occur, that their best chance of financial security remained with the capitalist market place. Reducing socio-cultural risk involved convincing a sceptical public that the market could work to further the public interest. Reducing socio-cultural risk required reforms to target greed and profligacy (particularly when associated with failed companies) which could be seen as high profile examples of exploitation of the public good. Reducing socio-cultural risk for a capitalist democracy, however, needed to be accomplished without resorting to the wholesale guarantees made by the welfare state.

The complexity of this political risk landscape meant that reform could sometimes appear illogical from an actuarial point of view. Malcolm Rogers commented, 'Legislators never get it absolutely right and they always put stupid bits in. Well there are bits of CLERP 9 that just don't make any sense at all, there's no possible public policy reason for them to be the way they are.' (6, p.11)

The CLERP 9 reforms, then, can be understood as an amalgam of attempts at reducing both actuarial and socio-cultural risk in a context of fluctuating political risk. However, the various sections of CLERP 9 cannot neatly be divided into those aimed at reducing one or other of these risks. Each of these risks exerted pressures across and within reform attempts. Nonetheless, it is possible to understand how attempts to reduce actuarial risk were made by increasing transparency of accounts and the independence of both the board and auditors. The actuarial logic here was that good information underpinned sound investment decisions. In doing so, good companies would thrive and risky investments with a higher probability of failure would be seen as just that. Ideally for the government, high risk ventures that failed exposing investors to loss of their money would then be understood as a private rather than a government problem.

Specifically, CLERP 9 sought to strengthen the transparency of accounts and the independence of both the board and the auditors. It was hoped that it could retain a principle-based approach to accounts with a priority on a 'true and fair' view and where CEOs and CFOs signed off on accounts as an accurate representation of a company's financial health.

Transparency also was to be enhanced by strengthening the obligations for continuous disclosure, by standardising accounting and auditing rules, giving auditing standards the force of law and bringing accounting standards in line with international accounting standards. In this way, investors were argued to have greater confidence in what accounts actually showed. Greater independence was to be achieved again through a range of measures including the need for an independent chairman (that is, not the CEO of the company), by increasing the number of non-executive directors, mandating convening an audit committee of the board and finally increasing the independence of the auditors (ASIC 2009; Brown and Tarca 2005; Clarke and Dean 2005). Auditors were also to be made more independent by mandating rotation of audit partners every five years (with some capacity for a seven-year rotation) and by limiting the number of retired auditors who could join the board. There was also the need for auditing firms to demonstrate that there was no conflict of interest in the provision of audit and non-audit services with an expectation that non-audit services would not be provided by the company auditor (Brown and Tarca 2005; Clarke and Dean 2005). Government oversight committees were also restructured with the strengthening of the Financial Reporting Council to include oversight of the Australian Accounting Standard Board (AASB), the board responsible for the generation of accounting standards as well as the Australian Auditing Standards Board (AUASB) responsible for setting auditing standards. Disputes about compliance with financial reporting standards were to be heard by the Financial Reporting Panel (FRP) (Brown and Tarca 2005).

Part of the CLERP 9 package of reforms was that financial reporting was also to be harmonised with international standards. Australian financial standards were to be brought into line with international financial reporting standards, standards developed through the International Accounting Standards Board (IASB). These standards were considered to be a more progressive principle-based approach to accounting when contrasted with the more prescriptive approach of the United States. Harmonised reporting, too, was considered to enhance Australia's global competitiveness, to reduce the costs of access to capital and to provide accessibility and transparency of cross-border financial reports (Financial Reporting Council 2002; cf. Jones and Higgins 2006). By 2005 Australia was to be fully compliant with international financial reporting requirements as stipulated through the Australian version of international standards (labelled AIFRS).

The contours of socio-cultural risk management were most easily recognised in sections aimed at constraining the self-interest of directors and executives. These included strengthening shareholder access to remuneration packages, requiring shareholder approval for certain termination payments and through mechanisms such as expensing executive stock options in executive remuneration packages (Clarke and Dean 2005; Blake Dawson Waldron 2004). Self-interest was further to be constrained through enhanced financial reporting obligations on CEOs and CFOs, which had criminal penalties attached for false or misleading statements (ASIC 2009; Blake Dawson Waldron 2004).

The nature of these reforms aimed at curbing self-interest is intriguing.

Since Adam Smith it has long been argued that the strength of the market arises precisely because it is driven by self-interest. Actuarial risk assessments that follow Smith, then, might be expected to take a different approach. From a neo-classical economic perspective there is at least some strength to the argument that a promotion of dependence of boards on a company's financial health, for example, might better serve the interests of the shareholders than independence, particularly if self-interest indeed is the primary motivation at play here. This could arguably be more effective in aligning self-interest and dependence with the public interest (Clarke and Dean 2005).

Yet, the reforms were premised on the notion that greed and self-interest were at the root of the problem (Clarke and Dean 2005). What CLERP 9 promoted was the need for greater independence and disinterestedness in financial reporting. The shaping of reforms in this manner is open to various risk interpretations. The first is that neo-classical economics framing of the actuarial risk paradigm was not entirely convincing to either government or regulator. Rather, neo-classical assessments were embraced in good economic times and eschewed in the bad. Financial crises generate risk-assessments based on the need to curtail and control self-interest. The market simply does not work in the way predicted by standard neo-classical economic models. The second possibility is that independence and objectivity are key elements of socio-cultural not just actuarial risk. This makes some sense as socio-cultural risk involves an assessment that individuals make about their place in society. A society premised on the benefits of the uncontrolled pursuit of self-interest would leave many uneasy both about the nature of the society they live in and anxious about where they may fit within such a society.

Whatever the motivation for reforms promoting independence, however, the challenges of *ensuring* such independence were considerable. The particular method CLERP 9 enshrined to ensure such independence was subject to some criticism. Independence was to be achieved through prescribing and proscribing certain relationships between auditors, boards and executives (ASIC 2009). CLERP 9 increased the level of prescriptive rules around what independence meant in practice. The rise of prescription brought with it the danger that compliance with the rules would substitute for the capacity of an individual to provide a robust critique of company practice (Clarke and Dean 2005; Holloway and van Rhyn 2005). Indeed, as the HIH case showed, proving a substantive lack of independence is very difficult (Allan 2006; Owen 2003).

The accounting profession not surprisingly also raised concerns that the CLERP 9 reforms curtailed their independence and professional discretion (Allan 2006). Yet, it was understandable given the aggressive accounting practices that were revealed by the collapse of HIH that further controls of the audit process were deemed necessary. Malcolm Rogers pointed out that the auditing was dominated by the industry (essentially four global accounting firms) rather than the local professional bodies. The influence of professional bodies, then, was weaker than the four big accounting firms, '… the Institute of Chartered Accountants and the CPA Australia are not themselves as influential bodies as their key members, so a traditional approach to professional self-regulation doesn't work in that environment.' (6, p.6) Professional ethics were under constant threat of being subsumed under commercial concerns, as auditors served the interests of their (paying) clients.

What was not considered in the CLERP 9 reforms, however, was that the institutional relationship between auditor and company, namely that the company pays the auditor to audit the accounts, might itself be a source of ethical and actuarial compromise. With financial self-interest of both auditor and company remaining focussed on the need for a 'clean' audit a very real possibility remained that processes and relationships would substitute for independence. Rules would be met but independence sacrificed (Clarke and Dean 2005; Holloway and van Rhyn 2005). Alternative reforms, aimed at creating a different institutional relationship such as socialising the audit by pooling company resources and hence funding audits effectively independent of a financial conflict of interest were not considered.

Clearly, socialising the audit would mean greater involvement of government. But such a model was not unprecedented in the research. Arguably APRA's licensing regime and targeting of regulatory controls provided some model from which to develop such an auditing regime free of commercial conflicts of interest. Malcolm Rogers, however, was not convinced that the government would be a better commander of audit services. He suggested that perhaps getting rid of a government-mandated audit and letting the market price risk might be a better approach. But, an assumption that government can absent itself from the market, in the light of reality of political and socio-cultural risk (if not actuarial risk), suggests that this approach also was unlikely to be embraced.

The CLERP 9 reforms, then, need to be viewed in light of complex and competing dynamics. Firstly, the reforms were shaped by the regulatory cycle and the level of government appetite for intrusion in the market. The CLERP 9 reforms were quickly followed by the business sector keen to curtail the discretion of the regulator and pressured government to 'reduce red tape.' It is not clear that they were successful, only that this spurred greater prescription. Nonetheless, the regulatory cycle was propelled by political risk and the response to both public concern and industry pressure to create a climate conducive to business investment. Secondly, reforms needed a narrative of how actuarial risk was to be reduced. Actuarial risk was shaped in a manner somewhat at odds with a neo-classical assumption of the primacy of self-interest working in the public interest. Efforts at creating transparency can be understood as commensurate with neo-classical perspectives, but the reform emphasis on independence requires a more complex appreciation of risk. It suggests a wavering political adherence to the neo-classical world view and also a stronger role for socio-cultural risk in shaping reform. Self-interest does not convince a sceptical public in the manner that independence and criminal penalties aimed at curbing the aggressive pursuit of self-interest can. Finally, reforms in this area need to be understood in light of a government warding off public demands for security that might heighten the chance of fiscal crisis, whilst also shaping reforms based on 'independence', 'accountability' and 'transparency' that do their best to reassure.

CONCLUSION

The breadth of the reforms described in this chapter in response to the three disasters reconfirms the importance of disaster as a generator of regulatory reform (Hancher and Moran 1998). Yet, these three areas: safety, security and finance point to a more complex understanding of the reform impetus. Regulatory reform can be fuelled by political battles for legitimacy exemplified in this research by the ratcheting up of security reforms under critical scrutiny from government, opposition and media. Ancillary reforms could also be fuelled in the wake of initial reform attempts by industry pushing back and demanding that government respond to their needs for greater certainty (as in the case of the CLERP 9 reforms). As Hancher and Moran (1998) point out a regulatory crisis is broader than a particular disaster event.

The effectiveness of regulatory reform able to reduce the risk of a repeat disaster (that is, actuarial risk management) rested in large part on political support for the actions of the regulator and an adequate technical expertise of that body. Both the Victorian MH regulator and APRA were provided with such support (at least initially) and were able to employ people with sufficient levels of expertise to understand what was needed to control the particular form of actuarial risk at the heart of their respective regimes.

Yet political enthusiasm for a regime for reducing a particular risk did not ensure effective reform. The security regime illustrates the fate of a regime where political support was high, but also was accompanied by high levels of political intrusion. Here the regime was designed not to reduce actuarial risk so much as to counter the criticisms of the media and the political opposition. In national security the result was a new bureaucratic empire, one which could craft with industry a regulatory regime that was compatible with the needs of a mass transit and trade regime, whilst providing grist for political contests and leadership opportunities for public servants to use elsewhere in the bureaucracy.

Political enthusiasm for reform was also tempered by the needs of the economy. National security reforms were designed to ensure public confidence whilst ensuring trade was left relatively unhindered and airline profitability relatively secure. In the regulation of financial securities and investments political enthusiasm waxed and waned with the economic cycle. The securities and investments regulator could never be confident of political support. The degree to which a particular industry was seen as central to securing economic growth and fiscal skim-off (elements of political risk assessment) determined the level of discretion a regulator could retain in intervening in the everyday activities of that particular sector of industry in order to reduce actuarial risk.

Political support also could be tempered by broader policies aimed at responding to the particular disaster. So, reforms after Longford in Victoria included increasing the diversity of gas supply. In doing so, the government no longer had to rely on MH regulation as the sole protection against future loss of supply. With less at stake from the regulations in terms of actuarial risk of a loss of supply, government support for the regulator also appeared to decline.

Government required the regulator to respond to the demands of industry for greater clarity in the safety case regime and resulted in considerable compliance documentation being developed by that regulator. Whilst such clarity could assist industry in reducing actuarial risk, it also curtailed the discretion of the regulator over their enforcement activity. Enforcement discretion was an important component of the sustainability of an effective actuarial risk reduction regime. APRA retained such discretion. Arguably, for APRA the Ipp review provided the backdrop for it to retain enforcement discretion by appeasing industry concerns about their profitability. The Victorian MHU also retained at least some enforcement discretion, but appeared increasingly constrained. Other regulators were not in such a strong position. ASIC, for example, experienced considerable pressure from industry to clarify regulatory expectations and in the process of doing so constrained their own enforcement capacity. What is intriguing in the case of ASIC was that it was industry that pushed for greater and greater levels of rule-based prescriptive controls rather than principle-based regulation as a way to ensure 'market certainty' and to constrain regulatory discretion.

Where political attention was not focussed on the particular actuarial risk the reform trajectory was quite distinct. NSW WorkCover was provided with little political support for reform, despite considerable actuarial risk being present. Low levels of political risk resulted in a slow pace of reform. Further, the opposition was concerned more with promoting the need to reduce 'red tape,' rather than pointing to the possibility of a disaster at a local MHF. These low levels of political risk translated into low levels of support for the regulator, to regulator inertia and, in the case of NSW, allowing conflict between regulators for resources and control to fester. Intriguingly here it was the regulator, in particular NSW WorkCover that promoted the benefits of prescription in terms of ensuring certainty of compliance. Prescription, then, could be fuelled by industry, by government (as in the case of security controls on small airports) and by regulators. Prescription promises a certain environment for a wide range of regulatory actors.

In sum, reforms were shaped predominantly by political risk management. Arguably political risk management through regulatory reform appeared to be targeted in the first instance at reducing socio-cultural risk, whilst protecting investment and fiscal skim-off. It was only when socio-cultural risk management failed, for example with the failure of the industrial manslaughter legislation, that the Victorian government moved in a comprehensive manner to control actuarial risk. Further, when security of gas supply was achieved by the diversification of supply, control of actuarial risk of an industrial disaster appeared again to be slipping from the political agenda.

The particular nature of actuarial risk does appear to influence the nature of reform. Again, however, the position of actuarial risk with respect to political risk is important to understand. In particular where the actuarial risk is tightly embedded in the market, efforts at actuarial risk management were dampened while socio-cultural risk management efforts predominated. So, counter-terrorism security regulation was designed to reassure the travelling public whilst protecting airline viability and protecting trade. Financial regulation was designed to 'stop greed' (a socio-cultural concern) but not at the expense of fully dismantling the ideology of the pursuit of self-interest as the engine of productive risk taking.

Yet, there was a loosening of political adherence to the importance of market self-regulation. This was because self-regulation could not protect the government against political risk. Both prudential and securities regulation shifted from a prioritising of self-regulation towards, for APRA, co-regulation and arguably for ASIC even further in the direction of prescriptive command and control approaches. At the same time MHF regulation was shifting (albeit hesitatingly in the case of NSW) away from prescription towards co-regulation. It was the NT where self-regulation had reappeared, justified in this case by the superior resources and technical expertise of industry when compared with the resources and technical expertise of a regulator in a small jurisdiction.

Finally, it is worth emphasising the conditions under which the more effective regulatory regimes appeared. In the case of both the Victorian MHF and APRA, political support allowed the regulator to narrow the goal of its activity. In both cases the economic health of the industry was not seen as a major concern for the regulator. The financial health of Victorian MHFs and the insurance industry were either not seen as critical (because such industry was no longer central to the economy) or in the case of APRA because this was dealt with by other reforms.

This narrowing of regulatory goals was both positive and negative in the control of actuarial risk. It allowed for development of a comprehensive regime that could be more easily monitored in terms of its effectiveness. But, at the same time it provided the means by which the regime as a whole could be sidestepped by industry. Narrowing the regulatory target also broadened the area of regulatory absence. Where reducing the regulatory target and ignoring the financial fortunes of industry was not possible (as was the case for ASIC and the OTS) regulations were framed to minimise impact on industry – even if this undermined the capacity to reduce actuarial risk.

NOTES

1. Each quotation from interviews undertaken as part of this research is referenced by a tran-script number and by the specific page of the transcript where the quotation appears. The University of Melbourne ethics clearance required the names of interviewees not to be used unless specific permission was given.
2. The particular enforcement officer who works on site to assess the site's safety case regime.
3. The review panel that assesses the safety case licence application or renewal.
4. Victorian WorkCover Authority the health and safety regulator that encompassed the MHU.
5. There is now new legislation Workplace Health and Safety Act 2007.
6. This organisation underwent a number of changes subsequent to the development of the Major Hazard Code; it was renamed the Australian Safety and Compensation Council and then, with the change of Government, Safe Work Australia.
7. At the time of interview one site was operational and the other being commissioned just prior to the commencement of operation.
8. At the time of the research, one of the sites had yet to begin production and so the operation of safety case at this site was still to be fully worked out.
9. The bill being discussed was the Companion Animals Amendment Bill (NSW) 2006.
10. Department of Infrastructure, Planning and Natural Resources.
11. Regulation.
12. This can reach down to the level of reporting doors found open into secure areas for example.
13. A clothing outlet.
14. Cocaine.
15. The exception here was the funding of Australian involvement in the Iraq war. The argument here was that money used to deploy Australian troops could be put to better effect in counter-terrorism at home, and in particular in the regulatory regimes at ports and airports.
16. Eleven regulators merged to form APRA, both at Commonwealth and state level.
17. That is they could write no new business only pay out on claims from existing policyholders.
18. This was a group interview with three senior representatives from APRA.
19. Malcolm Rogers agreed to be interviewed on condition his comments were attributed to him personally and not to ASIC.

6. The challenge of compliance – major hazard risk

Regulatory reform is argued to be principally about changing the behaviour of those targeted in the legislation. But, as the previous chapter explained, regulatory reform entailed more than a concern with actuarial risk, more than simply reducing the risk of repeat disaster. So, with reforms moulded to reduce socio-cultural and, importantly, political risk as well as actuarial risk, what was their impact on the ground? The next three chapters explore the response of those worksites, the major hazard facilities, seaports and airports that found themselves responsible for a considerable increase in their regulatory responsibilities. This chapter focuses on the Major Hazard Facilities in three jurisdictions, Victoria, NSW and the Northern Territory. Chapter 7 analyses the response of sea and airports to their increased security responsibilities and Chapter 8 considers the impact of financial reforms.

The challenges for MHFs in the three jurisdictions were diverse. For Victoria, safety case reforms had produced positive results, but maintaining standards was an ongoing challenge. In the NT compliance was primarily couched in terms of what industry demanded, rather than the regulator. For NSW frustration was expressed at the time taken for reforms to be implemented with stalled efforts at improving standards evident on the ground. In each jurisdiction, then, political risk management by state and territory governments affected whether and how actuarial risk management was achieved. Further, the experiences of the MHFs also illustrate how they, too, were concerned to reassure various audiences of their competency to operate, a process that was both socio-cultural as well as actuarial in orientation.

VICTORIA

As we saw in Chapter 5, the safety case regime in Victoria that followed the Longford Gas explosion was considered to be the most effective in terms of reducing the risk of repeat disaster. As explained in Chapter 5, the strength of this regime was its combination of the high level of political support provided by the Victorian government, the resources provided to the regulator and the particular design of the regime. Political, socio-cultural and actuarial risk concerns all were met through the reforms, the Victorian Occupational Health and Safety (Major Hazard) Regulations of 2000. This scheme was co-regulatory, or perhaps more accurately meta-regulatory, where sites needed to develop a comprehensive regulatory regime through which they were held accountable by the regulator, the Victorian Major Hazards Unit (Vic MHU). To be licensed as a major hazard facility in Victoria all sites meeting certain criteria (such as holding above a certain quantity of a given list of chemicals) had to first register with the regulator, then to develop a safety case document and apply for a licence to continue to operate in the state. This document was rigorously assessed by the regulator and, if approved, a licence issued. In order to develop such a 'safety case' document, sites needed to undergo an intense period of self-assessment by way of hazard identification, followed by design and implementation of measures able to control such hazards and a demonstration that such controls would reduce the risk to an acceptable level. The control of major hazards was then supplemented by an internally developed and integrated safety management system designed to deal with the everyday occupational health and safety hazards, as well as an emergency management plan. This portfolio of risk management protocols, the 'safety case' document, was then required to go through a stringent approval process undertaken by the regulator.

The reform process that emerged post-Longford was a combination of regulatory design and political support that generated a metaphorical 'jolt' to the MHFs to improve their practices, and to demonstrate that improvement to the regulator, in order to be licensed. The message received by the case study sites[1] was that substandard safety levels would not be tolerated by either the regulator or the political elite. One site chemical engineering expert commented, 'The regulators had done their homework and had the minister onside. He had a breakfast for the CEOs to make sure the CEOs got the message that this was important' (20 p.7).[2]

The safety case regime was understood by MHFs as a non-negotiable demand for a significant improvement in their control over major hazard risk. This demand was described by one as 'very aggressive' (19, p.4). MHFs understood that if they were found wanting no licence would be forthcoming. One said 'WorkSafe was really going to demonstrate to Victoria that, "unless you meet a standard we're closing you down"' (21, p.5). This propelled the MHFs studied to take stock of what they really understood about their sites and what they did not. One shop floor operator who had worked extensively on the licensing process argued:

> Safety case hit us over the head really, really hard saying, 'You need to know more about your industry.' And we had to show that we knew it. That's probably the big thing. A lot of us did know a lot of things about the place ... But how do we know that that knowledge had transferred from their minds across to others? I think

Longford has really dragged us to realise you have to know things. Safety case was a real interesting way of doing it. (21, p.4)

At its best this impetus, together with the legislative and regulatory framework, generated a 'case for safety' that bridged the gap between regulation and everyday practice. Responsibility for risk reduction was passed from the regulator to the MHFs. Meta-regulation with its initial emphasis on self-regulation came to the fore. The case study plants understood and accepted that the responsibility for creating a safe site was theirs alone. One manager commented:

... At the end if the day I feel that the pressure is on the right side of the equation. It's not the matter of the authorities saying, 'I gave you the OK, so therefore if anything happens I [the regulator] am responsible ...'. It doesn't work like that. (22, p.5)

Each MHF needed to interrogate their production processes, operating procedures and everyday practices to identify what hazards there were, whether they were covered by existing controls and if not, how they could control them. This effort was extensive and intensive. For example, meetings and workshops with machine and process operators alone took, at one case study site, a year of daily meetings of between 3–4 hours each time. The overall process was seen as effective by all the MHF sites in improving safety. A typical comment was as follows:

I would say that the major hazard facility licensing process has clearly improved the level of safety on the site. It's forced us to look at things at a depth that we hadn't previously and otherwise wouldn't have. It forced us to justify a lot of things that we were happy with but, you know, had never been forced to justify in the past and therefore forced us to revisit them and forced us to make some physical changes on the ground too. (19, p.4)

But, there was also intense frustration centred on the lack of guidance MHFs were given in terms of what the regulator wanted. One commented that 'Quite frankly it (the safety case regime) is the most challenging project I've ever worked on in my career simply because we weren't sure that we knew whether we were going to the point that we would be able to satisfy the regulator' (20, p.2). Another commented that they were not sure that the regulator even knew what it was they required, 'I don't think they really knew what they wanted, it was make it up as we go on. 'You give something to us (and) we'll tell you if it's good enough after we've read it' (they told us). They couldn't tell us what was expected beforehand' (15, p.9).

A crisis was generated at each of the MHFs, then, in terms of how to respond to this significant new demand. Critical decisions needed to be made around whether or not to engage with this new regulatory regime and whether they could do this and remain profitable. Most of the plants in the study faced serious competition from interstate and overseas suppliers. Further, the chemical industry in Victoria has ageing infrastructure (around 30–40 years old in many cases) and costs needed to be watched carefully. Change in business strategy by MNCs had seen most of the sites change owners in the previous ten years, with a regular change in who held ultimate control at each site. It is not surprising, then, that some potential MHFs chose not to engage with the regime. Plants that could initially have been caught by the regulations decided to reduce their inventory of hazardous materials and so avoided the safety case regime altogether.[3] They were then no longer considered of sufficient risk to warrant either the effort required to produce a safety case, or the rigorous level of scrutiny undertaken to ensure compliance with that regime by the regulator.

Others, including one of the MHFs in this study, decided as a result of the first round of licensing to close their operations in Victoria. After obtaining their first licence, senior management at this MHF made the decision that the regime was too costly and too onerous and decided to move to China. The safety case manager argued, 'It was a huge drain on our resources. … the safety case originally was estimated by the regulator to cost $350,000 and it cost us 1.2 million' (20, p.12). A particular concern for this site was the amount of effort they felt had been put into working with regulators to develop a common understanding of the new regime. As we have seen above, a number of sites were critical of the lack of knowledge of some inspectors. An inspector was dedicated to each site and an intense education process took place between MHF and regulator. Regulators would then develop the requisite expertise on a particular site. However, turnover of staff at the regulator, the Victorian MHU, meant that some MHFs faced the prospect of a new inspector at the next licensing round. For this site, the time needed to educate another inspector was stated as a further reason for their move offshore.

The other case study sites decided to remain in Victoria and continue their operations as an MHF for the foreseeable future. The reasons for their decision to stay grouped around two separate but interdependent factors. The first was the expertise in controlling major hazard risk that could be gained by remaining in Victoria and subjecting themselves to the safety case regime, expertise that could then be passed on to sister sites in other locations. The second was the business gains some argued would flow through increased production opportunities brought about by more effective risk management, or lower ongoing costs that could be achieved by complying with the regime.

The value of expertise generated by MHFs that became licensed was multi-faceted. At one level, the expertise was purely of a technical and organisational nature, namely how to reduce risk and ensure a sustainable level of safety that could be disseminated throughout a given major hazard site. This was clearly important. But, the expertise gained also encompassed knowledge about how a MHF can thrive in the midst of a residential community. A number of MHFs were located within major cities and hence surrounded by residential suburbs. This was the case with most of the MHFs in this study. As such, they faced pressure from nearby residents who believed that they were inappropriate in the neighbourhood and should be told to move. A key form of expertise for owners of one MHF, a major Asian consortium, was gaining an understanding of how a hazardous facility could be seen as a legitimate 'citizen' of a suburban community despite the risks involved. The safety case process with its attention to the reduction of actuarial risk and its focus on the communication of risk and emergency management to the local community was seen by this site as a means to prevent local protest against MHF operations. This particular case study site was acutely concerned with risks to its legitimacy, that is the political risk faced by MHFs in urban settings (Haines 2009b). The lesson the owners wanted to learn from their facility in Victoria was how to undertake a profit-making and hazardous enterprise whilst also being able to reassure the local community that they were safe. It was this lesson that was critical to them in their other locations throughout Asia.

A robust business case in terms of increased long-term profitability was the other reason that sites decided to remain in Victoria. Again, this variable was multidimensional. It could include a calculation of the critical mass of a certain kind of industrial process that a particular MNC needed to retain in order to remain viable in that industry. Closing down a site in Victoria might mean that the MNCs international viability in a particular processing industry would be undermined. This was the reasoning that changed the decision of one case study site on the eve of a decision to close:

> We were told the plant would close and then at the eleventh hour our CEO, who happens to be an Australian, put the stops on that and said, 'Well hang on a minute, I don't think (this is right).' ... At the time it was a business decision. He said, '... You're not really looking at the bigger picture.' And they did that. They revisited it and decided yes, we'll continue to [produce] because Australia needs to have a critical mass ... if we close that plant down it would have affected that critical mass. This site has always been a very important resource for expertise for other Pacific countries. (19, p.13)

Clearly, the concern with critical mass only affected those owners with plants in multiple locations. Owners and managers with only one plant in their total operations, that is, the one site in Victoria, needed a different rationale to stay. Their business case had to be constructed differently. In this research, the rationale was that improved safety could allow greater cost savings (for example, reducing the number of workers on a site) or by increasing production. Improved risk management, reducing the probability of an adverse event meant that it was considered safe to increase the amount of a particular hazardous chemical on site and so to increase production. The manager of one such site argued:

> ... Since we've gone through the safety case regime we've gone from 110,000 tonnes a year to 140 plus if we could get hold of the [chemical] to run the plant. Now that hasn't happened by accident that's happened because actually a lot of the work that we did in the safety case identifying what was really critical and important ... (15, p.21)

This improved level of safety arose out of successful resolution of a persistent hazard that dogged this particular site. The problem involved a combination of elements: a poor design of liquid monitoring equipment in a process line, contamination of liquid chemicals in pipelines designed to carry gas and the challenge on cold nights of preventing condensate entering compressors. Liquid in compressors that have been designed for gas can lead to catastrophic failure of the compressor. This complex problem came to a head when the combination of these three factors resulted in a toxic liquid release that overcame all the engineering defences of the site, except the last physical constraint against the flammable liquid contaminating the local area and creating the fuel for a potential explosion and fire. The engineering solution to this problem, which took three years to implement fully, then allowed the company to argue that its safety was now such that a greater amount of hazardous materials on site posed an acceptable risk given the enhanced controls it had in place.

A decision to remain subject to the Victorian MHF regime required sites to implement a safety case that would meet the approval of the regulator, allow them to reach their long-term business goals and ensure a sustained reduction of risk. This was difficult. As described above, meeting the expectation of the regulator was complicated by the fact that sites were unsure about what those expectations were. Indeed, one site had misread the regulator's expectations and appeared in danger of being refused a licence. Here, the site had procured the services of a consultant used to working with safety case regimes in the offshore oil area and was confident initially of their application for an MHF licence. However, the regime in Victoria was significantly different with a much greater emphasis on ownership of the regime by the particular MHF concerned. The regulator was particularly keen to avoid an 'off the shelf' solution to a new regulatory problem. It was also concerned that the site had not taken full responsibility for control of their hazards. The use of the consultant in the regulator's view was compounded by the fact that the site had recently undergone a significant restructure as a result of a change of ownership, a change which was not reflected in all their documentation. The regulator, the Victorian MHU, rejected the initial application and gave this site a very short time window (six months) to revise their application. When the application was finally accepted it was for three rather than five years and came with certain conditions attached.[4]

The task MHFs faced in convincing the regulator that they were safe led some to overstate what risks needed to be, and would be, attended to. Some realised in the aftermath of the first licensing round[5] that they had generated too many indicators of risk that would require too many controls without a sufficient prioritising of what was, and what was not, critical in terms of control. One safety case manager explained:

> We had too many action items and too many KPIs [Key Performance Indicators] for the small company that we are. We ended up with a system that we couldn't manage. … We didn't have the time to go through and sort it out … to do a reality check. Do we have the resources? Is this the right fit for our business? (23, p.19)

However, reducing the risks identified and the number of controls put forward to the regulator in the second licensing round was a difficult proposition. Sites wanting to scale back their list of potential hazards realised that they were vulnerable to a perception of them 'watering down' their controls, an impression they wanted to avoid. This led to ambiguous outcomes, where one manager suggested in the same interview that the MHF would reduce the standard of control of risk, 'We probably went too far (in identifying hazards) and we weren't getting value for it. So we're going to drop that a bit …' and later in the same interview that they wouldn't reduce the number of controls presented to the regulator, 'we have said consciously no we won't, we'll maintain the same standard that we did then.' (19, p.12)

At this point it is worth remembering that one component that led to the Longford explosion was the provision of too many alarms, and a lack of priority placed on which alarms required immediate attention. A similar dynamic is at play here. Recognition of multiple risks and a presentation of both the risks and the controls might reassure a regulator that a complex risk assessment had been done, but poor prioritisation might also undermine the capacity of an MHF to maintain a clear focus on critical issues, those that could most easily lead to a catastrophic failure. A successful safety case regime required controls to be prioritised with critical controls, those that would result in a significant increase in risk if they were disabled, given priority over less significant risk, 'you need to concentrate on those big issues, OK, that underpin the others … like if there is no system of managing contractors, or work that is taking place by fitters with no permit to work' (22, p.15). This prioritising was complex and the task of capturing actuarial risk extremely challenging. One site manager explained that through their hazard analysis on site they found, 'two and a half thousand different scenarios of getting killed on site and ten and a half thousand control measures that prevents a major hazard incident happening' (22, p.6).

A complicating feature here was ambiguity around terms such as 'critical control', or 'critical event'. There could be different views expressed about what constituted a critical control, for example. Further, the understanding of the importance of a particular critical control or whether a certain event should be considered 'critical' could be uneven throughout a particular site. So, whilst a manager or a shop floor supervisor might understand the critical nature of a particular monitor, or a particular emergency management process, this knowledge might not be shared more broadly. As a result, procedures could be ignored if they were considered too onerous or serving no purpose, or if the pressure of production overwhelmed an appreciation of the risks being taken. These problems were certainly anticipated by the regulatory regime, yet continued to trouble the MHFs in this study.

The regulatory regime was designed to generate a shared understanding of what was, and was not, critical to the safe operation of a site. To this end, the regulations required safety case documentation to be drawn up on the basis of extensive workshopping with shop floor supervisors in each of the areas of the plant. The extent of the resources devoted to the workshopping process has been commented on above. Most managers and shop floor employees interviewed for the study considered deploying resources in this manner essential to the success of the overall safety case process. Procedures needed to be developed by both managers and those shop floor operators actually working with the equipment. For managers it might be important, for example, that procedures require recording an exact reading of particular gauges, not just a 'tick' placed in the box contained in the relevant documentation. Their task often involved building a comprehensive picture of the safety levels across the site, so a particular measure that did not appear to mean much to a process worker or machine operator in a particular location may have significant meaning for those monitoring records across the site as a whole. There were also dangers in developing procedures without shop floor input since procedures that could not be practically implemented on a day-to-day basis were destined not to be implemented at all.

Hence, the workshop could be illuminating for both managers and shop floor employees. Managers could learn how equipment was actually used by operators, rather than what they thought was occurring. Shop floor operators could get a sense of the systemic nature of risk and risk management across the site as a whole. One such operator commented:

> I was quite surprised about how well thought out the place was. I hadn't really given it that much thought up until I got involved with it and the amount of engineering thinking that went into the place initially. I've got a respect for that as a result of doing the safety case. I learnt what the place was about why we do certain things the way we do. Why it's situated where it was. Why it was laid out how it was. All those things that I'd never really thought of I just accepted it. ... It gave me a fantastic insight into what we're about. (24, p.6)

These shop floor participants were key individuals in the safety case development and implementation process. Their role was one of translating this complexity back to their work units as a whole, a role that required both skill and diplomacy. One logistics technician involved in the workshops explained:

> I can understand a little bit more because of being involved [in the process], like acronyms and things like that. … But just feeding it back into the blokes without the acronyms was the hard bit. Just trying to de-layer all the influx, because there was a hell of a lot of information that was passed to us … (21, p.7)

At times assessing what each individual present at a workshop needed to know, though, required considerable judgement and a level of obstinacy. Workshopping was a human process, one where issues of saving face come into play. This employee was aware of issues that he did not understand:

> I'll sit in the meeting and the site manager would just go bang, bang, bang! But being part of the process and knowing some (of the acronyms) you could actually get a gist of where they're going. But sometimes you sit back and go, 'I didn't understand a word you said' and just bide your time and it's obviously above what we need to know. (21, p.7)

There were complex decisions being made by the shop floor representative. There may well be aspects of the plant that he did not need to know. Indeed, it would be surprising if there were not. Yet at another site, workshopping was in danger of glossing over critical issues – such as a person responsible for fighting a fire on a production line not understanding exactly how to operate fire monitors[6] and hence control the amount of suppressant available. Yet, pointing out this misunderstanding could be seen as unhelpful by those present in a workshop, even disloyal. This shop floor operator explained this lack of knowledge and the dangers of exposing ignorance:

> Then it came down to workforce knowledge … [now] fire monitors were a control method and a critical control method. So they wanted to know what the workforce knowledge was of fire monitors. Everyone around said 'oh yeah, great, great, great.' Then the consultant who was taking us through [said to me] 'OK what do you think?' And I said, 'It's poor. My colleagues don't understand about fire monitors.' And that got a real retaliation from middle management, towards me. … [they] really attacked and said, 'How can you say that? How easy is it to operate a fire monitor? You go over and turn a valve and you've got water coming out of it.' … It developed into an argument and the consultant said could I demonstrate it? And I said, 'Yeah I can.' So I grab two STLs, Shift Team Leaders, and I said, 'OK my role now, I will be the fire chief of this fire.' So we've got a fire burning over here and I said to them, 'Put that fire monitor on.' And they did it. They did exactly what management said they'd do. They turned a valve, they pulled a valve and the water came out. Beautiful. Just prior to them putting it on I did check to see what the flow rate was on and it was on its lowest flow. So I went to the two guys operating the

monitor and I said, 'I need maximum water flow out of that monitor.' So they mucked around with the defuser and they changed the defuser which takes it from a straight jet to full or something in between. So they were playing around with the defuser on the fire monitor and I walked back up to them again and I said, 'I want maximum water flow.' 'Yeah, we're giving you maximum water flow.' 'No you haven't. I want maximum water flow.' And I put the pressure on because we've got a fire here, we're playing fire brigade now type stuff. So I put the pressure on like we're in a fire situation. They had no idea what I was talking about and I went back to them and I said, 'Guys I need maximum water flow.' And then they said, 'We don't know what you mean.' And so then I got the dial and turned the dial and everyone just stood there and said, 'Wow look at the difference that the monitor made! Water flowed out of it.' And I turned to the consultant and I said, 'That's what I'm saying. They don't know this and the reason they don't know it, no fault of theirs, no one's ever taken the time to show them.' (32, p.7–8)

This graphic illustration of what was assumed, but what was actually misunderstood, provides a useful illustration of the relational aspect of the safety case approach. A workshop can be a place of learning, or a place of (misplaced) assurance. There will be those who do not understand what is going on all the time and this may well not be a problem. Constant (and perhaps unnecessary) interruptions create tension, disruption and fatigue yet ensuring that essential knowledge is transferred and understood is critical to an effective risk management.

This relational dimension of regulation and compliance brings to the fore the importance of socio-cultural dimensions to risk and risk management once again. Workshopping can be likened to a drama and, as such, contains a ritualistic element. The skill in generating an effective workshop was the capacity to comprehend the need for assurance whilst also ensuring the necessary actuarial risk was being addressed. Safety case workshops could break the normal routine at a worksite and expose the inconsistencies between procedure and practice and the assumptions made by managers of shop floor staff and by shop floor staff of managers. They could educate, illuminate and prompt a more effective means to reduce the risk of a repeat disaster. But they also could perpetuate inconsistencies in the process of reassuring participants and the regulator that all is well.

Combined with this was the challenge of ensuring not only that written procedures were well drafted but that they were followed. Most (but not all) acknowledged this as an ongoing challenge[7] and, as a result, revisions to written procedures to ensure their ongoing relevance to shop floor operators and middle management was commonplace. Revisions to written procedures could not, however, prevent wilful circumvention or disregard of those procedures. The same shop floor operator involved in the fire monitor incident above provided the clearest illustration of this problem. He had been the direct victim of an attempt to circumvent commissioning and training protocols, a decision that had nearly resulted in a serious incident, if not his own demise. The problem revolved around a demand for him to work a new piece of equipment, one on which he had no training and that had not been commissioned for use on the site. The production manager, together with the shift team leader, decided that this operator needed to work this piece of plant to meet production targets for the day:

And I said, 'Look, I had no training in this system. I don't know the system's ready. I don't think we should be touching it because we haven't got the training.' And of course the production manager he said, 'No don't worry, it's like for like [similar to the old machine]. It's OK to operate. ... I went and had a look at it and I thought no, it's not like for like, its not you know. I could nut it out, but I was not feeling comfortable. So I spoke to my STL, my shift team leader, and said, 'Look I'm not really comfortable in that system.' Production manager was called up. Production manager was getting quite cranky with me, Just do it [he said]. We've got this production to make.' ... I said, 'Look, can you just humour me. Show me all the paperwork to say that it was commissioned.' So he brought up a whole, as thick as this, document (demonstrates), fairly thick document ... and put it in front of me and it was like a salesman, a car salesman you know. ... I said 'Look, just leave it with me and let me have a bit of a read before I say yes to it ... just let me have a bit of a read.' [He said] 'We haven't got time for you to read it!' At which my answer was well I'm going to read it. I'll read it and I called him back and I said, 'These things haven't been signed off. This is not signed off yet.' (32, p.22)

At this point the production manager called the relevant sections and managers (maintenance and instrumentation managers) and got them to agree to approve the use of the machine, sight unseen, without proper commissioning. The production manager signed the documentation on their behalf. The machine operator was then told to start the machine up, triggering additional problems:

I still felt uncomfortable. OK boss, yep. Alright, under protest I'm going out and we'll do this. So we went out to the system and we found spades, blanks [metal plates] in the [pipe] line [that] were not supposed to be there because it was said those blanks were taken out. So I called my STL and said, 'Hey look, we've got a blank in the line.' 'Oh just one, OK' [he said]. So we took that one out. OK now we'll do it. So I'm starting to line it up. [I find] there's another blank in the line. 'Oh, look there's another blank in the line' [I said]. So with that the production manager was calling and saying, 'Oh, we'll just take them out.' I said, 'No, no. ... This is not right. ... Before I go any further I'm writing an email and I want to send this email off to managers saying I'm going out under absolute pressure here.' ... So I did, I typed that email up. I must admit they were extremely unhappy with me. (32, p.22)

The end of this debacle was when the machine operator found water in the equipment in a place where it had the potential to cause an explosion. Indeed the presence of water in a similar machine had been the cause of a previous explosion on site that had resulted in the death of the operator two years earlier. With the revelation that water was in the system the machine operator finally refused to start the equipment. Three critical problems stood out in this scenario where production pressure overruled genuine safety concerns: a lack of training, a circumvention of commissioning procedures and the presence of water in the system. Any one of these presented a high risk, but the presence of all three was potentially catastrophic.

This scenario does not invalidate a safety case regulatory approach. But it does point to the inevitable limitations to any regulatory framework. Even the best regime requires the commitment to the aims of the regime by all those involved. Good outcomes rely on good people as well as good processes. One redeeming feature of the above narrative is the response of senior management to the above incident. They were appalled at the event and made sure that those responsible were reprimanded. As is well known, the commitment of senior management to a particular safety regime is important (Hopkins 2001; Reason 1997). But such commitment is not sufficient to ensure good outcomes.

The capacity of good people to work with the safety case regime effectively required layers of accountability where their actions to pursue and promote both compliance and safety were rewarded. Successful implementation of the safety case regime depended on the measures in place to prompt compliance and to pick up problems before disaster occurred.

There were such layers of accountability. The regulator was an important player here, and the presence of the regulator was common especially during the licensing process. But, some sites had seen less of the regulator as they were considered more competent in maintaining the requisite levels of safety. No regime, even one resourced in the manner here, is going to be able to have enough inspectors to monitor all MHFs to pick up every sign of a potential disaster in the future. Here sites had to rely on other means to ensure ongoing and sustained commitment. This could take the form of adherence to internal procedures, not only those generated on their particular site but procedures generated by corporate headquarters either in Australia or overseas. Those MHFs that were part of a larger group of sites, often owned by a multi-national corporation (MNC) benefitted from the additional support provided. This could be significant with visits and in some cases structured safety audits from head office that could point to problems on their site. Others benefitted from the audits by insurance companies although the positive influence of insurers was small. Indeed in the case of MNCs insurance could be purchased centrally and could bear little relation to the risk management practices of the MHF in Victoria (Haines 2009a). Within the site itself, the prompting of local safety committees or safety representatives could be important. But here the committees and representatives needed to be concerned with major hazard risk, not just the more mundane (yet no less important) safety concerns. But, such individuals had to be listened to and interviews with these representatives indicated that although their experience was generally positive, this was not a universal experience.

One final element was the perceived need for increased security at MHFs. The MHFs in the study were aware of the need for some security before the September 11 terrorist attacks, but security was primarily concerned with ensuring that people were safe and did not end up in any danger. Substantial perimeter fences, for example, were not necessarily a high priority since plants could be located in the middle of scrubland with little visibility from nearby roads. Certainly, there were processes for being allowed on site with sign-in and supervision procedures and, at some sites, the request to leave all electronic devices at the front office. Again, however, the primary concern was to know who was on site so that in the case of emergency all could be accounted for. Preventing a deliberate act of sabotage was not uppermost in mind. Some felt more vulnerable to protest action by environmental and human rights groups by virtue of their profile in the media over some event in the past, but again their concern fell short of feeling threatened by acts of sabotage. The need to prevent a terrorist attack was seen as a somewhat incongruous concern by interviewees. Engineers, for example, were puzzled at the government focus on counter-terrorism security at MHFs and felt the motive behind the demand that they reduce this risk was a combination of misunderstanding and politics. Those interviewed considered other targets far more accessible and had the potential for a considerably greater political impact:

> Now I understand that some chemicals can go bang, but I also know if you get a chlorine tanker that goes and unloads chlorine at the local swimming pool, [and] you put it in the middle of Bourke Street[8] and open the tap, you're going to kill more people than any explosion down here. Can you see what I'm saying? ... And what we're saying is 'why us again'? (20, p.20)

Terrorists also did not fit the normal risk profile. Risk management principles did not include terrorism in a standard equivalent to an engineering standard for safety, one defining an acceptable outcome involving terrorism, did not exist. Probability and outcome were not quantifiable:

> ... If the definition of the safety case is that I have to prove to you that [we are safe], I need a standard of a security standard then I would say, 'Well we have a standard, let's discuss the standard, not the process'. I mean I have already a plan, a security plan for the site. Is it good enough or not? Unlike MHF where the issue of the inherent hazard is quantifiable, terrorism is not. (20, p.21)

Terrorism and counter-terrorism security, then, were not seen as needing the same priority as safety. The need for security was more removed, less pressing and more open to political manipulation of what was and was not required.

The experience of the MHFs in Victoria reflected the success of the reform process. There was a significant increase in safety. The regulatory regime had anticipated many of the common failings that generate ongoing and chronic problems in compliance, ill-thought through procedures creating unrealistic expectations and complex elements coming together in an unanticipated way to create a catastrophic outcome (Reason 1997). The regulations created the potential for an environment to be created where hazards were controlled effectively. But, the challenge of controlling such hazards was never-ending. The examples of failure above were anticipated by the regulatory regime, but the regime alone could not prevent such a situation eventuating. Distractions were a constant, not the least being the need to keep producing in an industry where competition was intense. For some, this meant avoiding the regime. For those who made the decision to engage with the safety case requirements, creative leadership was required to develop a business case that could engage fully with the safety case regime whilst also maintaining a vision for long-term profitability. Effective compliance also required considerable skill at all levels of the organisation in the dissemination of necessary information about hazards and supporting those routines that enshrined a mindfulness of the potential for an incident, whilst challenging those routines that glossed over looming problems. Effective risk management at these sites, then, was a technical and interpersonal challenge. How to prevent a terrorist attack, though, was a challenge of an altogether different order, one that was seen as more difficult and one that should be given a much lower priority.

MAJOR HAZARDS: NORTHERN TERRITORY

Research into the reception of the safety case regime in the Northern Territory by MHFs was more limited than in the other two states. This was for several reasons. Firstly, there were only two MHFs in the jurisdiction. Both were owned by MNCs and were very new with commissioning taking place in late 2005–06. Confidentiality requirements of the ethics approval process also mean that a detailed case study of one of these plants, or both, is impossible without identification of the plant. Nonetheless meetings and interviews did take place with the two MHFs and some general conclusions can be drawn.

Firstly, it is clear that the principle driver for MH safety was the MNC internal standards, not the external constraints by the regulator. Both were owned by prominent global corporations, and both were specialists in their particular field of processing and storage of hazardous materials. At one MHF, monitoring of safety levels also was undertaken in one case by more than one MNC, as a number of MNCs saw they had a joint interest in maintaining the safety of the plant. There was, in Rees's (1994) terms a community of fate here with the joint interest of companies lying in the safety of this one particular MNC.

The newness of the technology at this particular MHF meant that there were considerable levels of safety built into their infrastructure and equipment. Hence, issues of ageing and maintenance leading to heightened risk were not of serious concern. Face-to-face meetings were held so that the regulator understood what technology existed at the plants to reduce risk. At one plant, the paperwork required by the regulator did not really fit the nature of the technology of the plant. Insurance audits were also cited as a positive influence on safety levels, but one that took place in the context of considerable scrutiny by MNC headquarters.

The importance of having 'good people' as well as good processes was also emphasised. The transient nature of the workforce in the Northern Territory was discussed and the need to identify potential employees that were sufficiently careful and cautious was noted. Careful recruitment strategies were supported by what was termed a 'no blame' culture (Reason 1997), one that encouraged reporting of near misses so that learning about how to improve safety could take place. When asked for an example of what constituted a reporting culture, a manager gave an example of a spillage where blame could be laid at the feet of the operator but where an alternative approach focussing on corrective action would be taken:

> Occasionally an operator will have an incident in the gantry where they'll spill a little bit of product onto the ground. Now, I mean, I could quite easily get very angry with that and start yelling and screaming and, you know, 'get out of the yard,' type approach, or say, 'well, okay, explain to me what happened ... how do you think we can fix it to stop it from happening again?' ... There['s] two approaches, you can get cross or you can try and fix it so it doesn't happen again. (54, p.8)

Finally, mention was made of security with the heightened level of security demanded when chemicals were transported to the local port being noted. However, the need for security on sites meant that counter-terrorism security was seen as just another layer, albeit one that emphasised the port environs rather than the MHF facility itself.

Overall, the material from the NT MHFs mirrored the understanding of the regulator, NT Worksafe. The facilities were new and the dominant catalyst for high safety levels was the MNC's internal procedures and engineering controls rather than regulatory oversight. At the time of this research such a situation appeared to be working, although the paucity of data on these sites means that there needs to be caution in drawing strong conclusions here. The long-term safety challenge these sites pose, however, may well prove to be significant. In one case where there was multiple MNC oversight, perhaps a greater level of confidence might be warranted as long as there remains a confluence of self-interest in maintaining the safety levels of the site. The conclusion here is stark for those with concerns about self-regulation. The example of MHFs in the NT was one of a vast inequality of resources and expertise between the plant and the regulator, a situation that is unlikely to change. The safety of both employees and local communities relies on these MNCs remaining committed to safety in the long term.

NEW SOUTH WALES

The MHF regime in New South Wales was finalised in 2008, with regulations set to commence on 14 July of that year. The process of notification and registration means that it was unlikely that all relevant sites would be registered until 2010 at the earliest. The two case studies analysed in NSW were undertaken in late 2006, so provide an insight into the activities made by sites in preparation for the new regime and their experiences with a scheme with a decade-long gestation. Both MHFs also had sister plants in Victoria, so were able to learn from their Victorian colleagues about the experience of preparing for a safety case registration.

As described in Chapter 5 political risk framed the government response to Longford in NSW. The disaster had not occurred in that state and more pressing concerns from a political risk perspective had taken precedence. Reassurance by the NSW State Government about the safety of NSW citizens had not included tighter control of that state's MHFs. Financial concerns of the state also appeared to shape the government response, leading to a distant relationship between regulator and site as well as a high cost charged to sites in gaining safety case registration.

In contrast to Victoria, the safety case regime in NSW was termed a registration rather than a licensing regime. The focus of the NSW scheme aimed to ensure that sites understood that managing major hazard risk was their responsibility not that of the regulator. Some at the NSW sites agreed with this interpretation of the difference between the two. However, as noted above, the Victorian MHFs were clear that they held the responsibility and that gaining a licence in Victoria was a privilege not a right and one which the regulator was willing and able to revoke. Those that had experience working with the Victorian regime and the potential framework of the NSW regime felt that the difference was purely semantic. Both states were emphasising site responsibility.

The emphasis of site responsibility also needs to be understood in light of the experience of being regulated in NSW. This experience was one of a distant and punitive regulator. The director of safety and environment on one site stated that, '… if its really that bad and you haven't done the right [thing] you'll go to jail. That's fine. But they [the regulator] don't want to know anything in between. … I don't think they've got the structure to be involved.' (43, p.15)

The cost of gaining a licence versus registration in NSW is also important. Purely from the differences in terminology, one might expect that if licensing did mean greater regulator responsibility then the cost in Victoria would be greater. Licensing suggests a higher level of oversight and hence greater cost. In fact, the opposite was the case with the cost to a site for registration in NSW anticipated to be considerably higher than the cost of the Victorian licence. This difference arguably could be understood as a signal that NSW was making a greater investment in MHF regulation than Victoria, and hence might be expected to take more of the burden of responsibility for the outcome.

This understanding of greater responsibility for the NSW regulator by virtue of the cost charged to sites would be a misreading. The reason for the higher cost expected in NSW related to the underlying budgeting logic of what fees would be charged in each state and had nothing to do with the allocation of responsibility between site and regulator under each regime. NSW was expecting MHFs to bear the total cost of their own regulation, a principle known as cost neutrality. Victoria subsidised the cost of licensing in that state. The different costs related to different budgeting and held no insight into the rigour of either regime.

The cost to be charged to the MHF in NSW also did not equate to resources put into the regime. At the time of interview, the major hazards division of WorkCover NSW only had two inspectors and one administrative support officer. The regime was expected to have 12 staff when fully implemented. But this was still less than Victoria. There was speculation at the sites about the reason for the difference in cost and approach. The parlous state of NSW finances was cited as one reason why NSW was pushing for full cost neutrality and the reason behind having a more distant and punitive approach.

The cost of the regime did affect how sites interacted with the regulator. A concern was with how a MHF was to be defined for the purposes of the registration fee, namely whether it was to be defined by ownership or by process. At one site, for example, there were four separate production processes taking place. It made a considerable difference whether a single registration fee would cover all four or whether four separate fees would be required, as one major hazards engineer explained '… I certainly don't want to say I've got four major hazard facilities because at 55 grand a pop [\$55,000AUD] there's some economics involved. So what's a facility? Is it defined by geographical boundaries?' (37, p.15)

The major question, though, is whether the NSW sites felt that the new regime when it eventuated would improve safety and, if so, what preparation they were undertaking to get ready for the change. In terms of an improvement in safety both sites felt that safety levels would improve. One described the safety case as 'a breath of fresh air' (37, p.10) one that would bring all those on site to a common understanding and appreciation of the hazards and risk controls on the site.[9] The improvements in the safety case regime revolved around its capacity to disseminate information on major hazard controls throughout the site and in the demand for a demonstration to the regulator of how the risks on site were reduced to an acceptable level. This demonstration of risk reduction was an intriguing element where expert knowledge needed to be broken down into its constituent elements and communicated to the regulator. One engineering expert explained:

> You need to unpack the intellectual property that is being built into those engineering standards which is an amalgam of operating experience, environmental requirements, personal safety issues and process safety issues, right? Unpack it into a safety report [to the regulator] which shows the discrete layers of protection and also does a quantification of their performance. (37, p.11)

This process allows expert knowledge to be contestable. But this contestability depends upon a regulator contesting the knowledge and keeping the MHF accountable, which was at the time of the case studies under considerable doubt. As explained in Chapter 5, there was one NSW regulator, the planning bureaucracy, which had at the time an engaged relationship with major hazard sites. Yet, this regulator was not to be involved with the new regime. The site manager commented, 'It sort of does leave DIPNR (the planning regulator) sitting out there a little bit which worries me a bit because they're quite a, you know, good bunch of people.' (38, p.14)

The potential for a greater level of engagement by NSW regulators was welcomed by some, but not all, on the two case study sites. Those with little experience of Victoria viewed the high level of regulator engagement in that state with some suspicion, feeling that 'IR (industrial relations) is intermingled too much with safety in Victoria' (38, p.3).

The uncertainty around the reform process also had led to significant costs expended by these sites in preparation for the anticipated new regime, costs that could, but did not always improve safety levels on site. Personnel changes on one site reached $250,000 per annum in order to prepare and then institutionalise the new regime. This money had largely been expended by bringing an engineering expert from Victoria to NSW to assist them in preparation of their safety case. This engineer had led the preparation process and worked hard to bring improvements in process safety across the various production processes on site. He had been assisted in this by considerable groundwork laid by virtue of this MHF's previous ownership, a US MNC that was very involved in monitoring their constituent sites across the globe, described by one engineer as 'overpowering. It was very invasive and overwhelming' (39 p.7). By virtue of this increased expertise and experience with MNC oversight this MHF considered they had a good grasp of what would be required by the new regime and had most, if not all, elements in place. They argued that the new NSW regime would simply make an internal, self-regulatory regime mandatory and, as such, would make it easier to maintain the necessary standards.

Nonetheless, the delay in legislation did create problems. Both the case study sites had anticipated a much quicker response in NSW than actually occurred. The MHFs had undergone internal hazard identification processes in preparation for the impending regime. But, the motivation for change was in danger of being dissipated, 'it's not creating the drive, the incentive to see it all the way through' (37, p.16) one safety case expert commented. At the other site the delay meant that one review had been largely wasted and the MHF was looking at a whole new review process:

> We galloped off from the start and then we sort of lost our incentive to keep going because it was just like it wasn't going to happen, and then by the time we got to this stage where it looks like, yes, its almost about to happen with the legislation [stalled] we have to go back to the beginning and start reviewing [again] ... we started 18 months ago and 18 months have passed and if we submit something now or in 6 months or 8 months time or something, they are going to say, 'well hold on, this is two years old. Go away and do it and start again.' (36, p.18)

This particular site had undertaken extensive preparations, over and above their normal regime. As part of their hazard identification process, they had undertaken extensive consultation with their shop floor operators, 88 half-day workshops that represented a considerable investment in time and effort. Together with the engineering-led hazard identification process the workshops had identified hundreds of potential risks. But little had happened. The items had not been systematically prioritised (an essential step in a safety case process) and feedback on action to the shop floor operators had not taken place, 'a lot of the actions, proposed actions that have come out of the work-shopping sessions, they haven't been, there's been no (systematic) attempt to put them into place as yet' (36, p.20). A recognised danger in this scenario is the lack of trust by shop floor operators in site management that is generated by a lack of follow up (Reason 1997). The issues raised by shop floor operators had either not been addressed, or, if they had the results had not been fed back to those with the concerns.

The regime slowly developing in NSW as experienced by the sites was rather haphazard with bursts of effort followed by periods of stagnation. Without involvement from the safety regulator, sites fell back on their internal processes to ensure they controlled MH risk. One of the NSW sites was interesting in that it was one of the few where an insurance company was playing a significant role in maintaining risk reduction on the site. The MHFs systematic approach to the reduction of risk had been helpful in securing lower cost insurance, in this case business interruption insurance. The site had undertaken an extensive search for an insurer that best suited their needs. This included presentations of their risk management strategy to a number of potential insurers internationally. Most insurers were not interested in the measures this site had undertaken to reduce risk.[10] One, however, was vitally interested and offered a 25 per cent discount on its premium to the site by virtue of the MH risk-reduction regime implemented on this site. Further, the insurer had its own testing laboratory and lists of standards and test results that insured firms could use. As such, they were an ideal example of 'secondary regulators' (Grabosky 1997), regulators in the private sector. This firm was selective in who they would, and would not insure; they required attention to risk before they would offer an insurance contract to a potential client. Clearly, this level of oversight would not be available to all MHFs in NSW. Ultimately, an active regulator was still essential for the success of the control of MH risk in NSW.

Political risk was also obvious in shaping the security focus of the NSW safety case regime. Chapter 5 noted that the security emphasis of the safety case regime in NSW could be seen as an improvement on Victoria. The case study material, however, sheds some doubt on a prominent security focus being an improvement to a safety case regime. Both the case study sites in NSW noted the emphasis on counter-terrorism security as a prominent aspect of the intended regulatory regime. Indeed, much of their dealing with the regulator revolved around the security dimension of the impending safety case requirements. Yet, the detail of the level of security requirement was unavailable. There was concern expressed that the detail about how security was to be managed on site was only to be drafted after the main regulation, Occupational Health and Safety Amendment (Major Hazard Facilities) Regulation (2008) came into force. This was seen as problematic; one commented, 'I don't know how that would work or how long it would take but I've got fairly severe concerns about how the whole thing's going to happen with no guidelines from WorkCover, two people in the unit at the moment' (36, p.12). This lack of detail concerning security was consistent with an analysis that looks to the primary role played by political risk management here. That is the emphasis on security was not intended to capture the attention of the NSW MHFs but rather to signal to the broader public that the NSW government was taking the threat of terrorism seriously.

The case study sites in NSW shared the concerns of their Victorian counterparts in what heightened security at the sites could actually achieve. The aim of the sites was to achieve a level of security, 'trying to stop people coming in through a gate, not a terrorist barging through with a tank' (38, p.24). Wilfulness required a completely different risk paradigm:

> ... all my mathematics and calculations don't apply. I mean I've got fancy human error rate tables and all of that but a human error rate table means nothing to someone

with a certain bent and orientation and wilfulness. Just all that, you can't do risk assessment on that sort of stuff. (37, p.23)

Despite these views about reducing the risk of a terrorist attack, heightened security was seen to be a good idea. There were security issues at the two sites, namely a problem with trespass (people using the MHF land as a shortcut to shops), occasional vandalism and a greater problem with theft. A perimeter fence, even a substantial one, was seen as a limited deterrent against a terrorist, as more effective in reducing the incident of trespass and theft.

Even in terms of reducing theft and vandalism, however, there were significant costs involved. One of the sites shared property with adjoining MHFs, so the issue of cost loomed large as they had a joint pool of money for security. The compromise position was to invest money in security cameras rather than in upgrading perimeter fencing, the latter seen as too expensive.

Heightened security, though, could create frustration and occasionally create considerable tension. In one case there had been an altercation between an employee and a security guard who had asked to do a bag check on an employee. The security emphasis rankled this engineer on this particular day:

I mean the guy had a very long day, he was an engineer here. He just had enough and the guy [security guard] said, 'Give me your bag'. He said, 'Come on mate, you see me walk out of there everyday. You know, you know me. What are you doing this for?' The engineer says, 'No [I won't do it], I just need to go home.' ... And he walked on and the guy literally tackled him to the ground. And, then another one [security guard] came along and sat on him. So it certainly made for an interesting [time]. We didn't change the policy [of searching bags] but we sort of made people aware that it's better to let someone look in your bag than going through all of this. (40, p.14)

Heightened security could also reassure employees about their own safety. But calming their anxieties around security created a conflict with the overall reduction of major hazard risk on the site. At one MHF, the night shift operators had requested that their building be locked at night to prevent intruders coming in. Discussion about this was taking place with the site manager who was sympathetic to their concerns and willing to entertain locking the building. The approval to lock the buildings by the site manager would signal to operators that their concerns for security had been heard and they were valued. This was, in part at least, reassurance and as such a socio-cultural orientation by the site manager to show that operators were valued. But, in light of the actuarial risk of explosion such reassurance was problematic. This control building was a designated safe place on the site in the event of a catastrophic release or fire. A rule of MH safety is the need for safe places. The locking of this building became a major concern for other engineers on site, 'For safety reasons they haven't put locks on them because you need to be able to get into the blast proof building [quickly]. ... You don't need card readers and locks on doors and things like that because it may inhibit getting in.' (40, p.8) Heightened security with swipe cards and tighter control over exit and entry had the real potential to conflict with the need to act quickly in the case of disaster. These discussions were ongoing.

Overall, the experience of NSW MHFs complements that of the NSW safety regulators, Workcover. Political risk was seen as the main driver for change, and since political risk was low around major hazard risk, progress was slow. The safety case regime was experienced by the sites as costly, in terms of registration fees, with doubts expressed about whether the regulator had the expertise necessary to oversee it. Regulators were seen as distant yet punitive. Preparations made by sites for the new regime could be wasted and valuable motivation to improve safety lost. Sites needed to draw on their own resources, both for those with experience of rigorous company procedures and those without. Here, there was an indication that insurers could play a prominent role in reducing MH risk, but that most chose a more limited role. Finally, the one area in the safety case that was emphasised, counter-terrorism security, was creating problems of its own. It was seen as useful, but only in terms of preventing theft, trespass and vandalism rather than in dealing with the risk of a terrorist attack. But the control of security could create very real challenges for a site whose primary duty was to control the safety of employees in the case of catastrophic failure.

CONCLUSION

The reduction of actuarial risk, such as in the prevention of a catastrophic explosion or fire, was in evidence across the MHFs studied across all three jurisdictions. To a significant extent behaviour that led to the reduction of actuarial risk went on outside of the gaze or influence of the safety regulator. Control and oversight beyond that provided by the regulator was important in all three jurisdictions. Even in Victoria, where regulatory oversight was the most comprehensive, MHFs needed to develop other sources for oversight and accountability to ensure adequate actuarial risk reduction. Accountability in terms of the reduction of actuarial risk derived from various sources both within and outside of the MHF in question. Internal processes and procedures were critical in all case study sites, procedures that could be enhanced through the oversight of MNC headquarters. Further, in a minority of cases the activities of insurance companies could play an important role in reducing risk. In two jurisdictions, NSW and the NT, these alternative sources were the primary means of accountability in terms of actuarial risk reduction and hence for the levels of safety at MHFs.

The regulatory regime MHFs laboured under, however, was important. Significant reforms in Victoria had led to particular improvements in MHFs in that state, with a regime that had the potential for ongoing and sustained improvements in MHF risk. Part of the reason for this was that the Victorian regime required engineers on site to deconstruct their knowledge and question their understanding of the level of risk their site posed and the adequacy of their risk controls. They needed to be able to explain their reasoning to each other and to the regulator. This made them accountable in a manner not evident in the NT or NSW. Even so, conceptualising what was required and developing adequate language to communicate actuarial risk in a robust fashion was challenging both for the Victorian MHFs and for the MHU. Both had developed hard-won expertise that was essential to sustaining this level of risk reduction and, at the time of this research, unique to Victoria.

A particular strength of the safety case regime was in the dissemination of information on the MHF site. There was a human and communicative dimension to this regulatory framework. This was a potentially powerful tool. But, the communication and dissemination of knowledge was a very human process. Technical expertise was important, but this was embedded within human interaction that could either work for or against knowledge around actuarial risk being shared. Employee concerns about security (in NSW) and the need to retain credibility (in Victoria), classic socio-cultural concerns, had a complex relationship to actuarial risk reduction. Whilst there could be a complementary relationship between socio-cultural and actuarial risk concerns, there could also be tension. Workshopping at one site in Victoria provided an example of how assumptions of technical competency, assumptions that maintained smooth relationships, could undermine the dissemination of critical knowledge. In NSW, too, reassurance around counter-terrorism security conflicted with actuarial risk reduction in the case of explosion and fire.

Finally, the analysis of the MHFs here suggests that the control of political risk is not the preserve of governments alone. The two dimensions to political risk, economic viability and legitimacy, also were important to the MHFs in this study. They needed to reconcile themselves to the increased costs that were associated with the safety case regime or avoid the need to comply. They would challenge their respective state governments where costs imposed were seen as excessive. But this did not mean that they were not preparing for an impending regime. The lobbying of business for reduced regulatory costs should not be conflated with a perception that business was not in active preparation for a new regulatory regime, as the research in NSW showed. Further, delays in implementation of an expected regime were costly. Ultimately, business cases developed by each MHF in each location needed to reconcile the costs of the regime with ongoing profitability. In the case of MHFs owned by

MNCs this task could be undertaken in light of the company's operations as a whole. Success was framed within business models in various ways yet, as Victoria showed, when compatibility between success and compliance could not be achieved the result was either relocation or changes introduced to operations, so the safety case regime was avoided altogether.

MHFs also recognised the need for a 'social licence' (Kagan, et al. 2003), a legitimacy afforded to them by their own workforce and, for some at least, by the local residential community. This concern was greatest in Victoria, arguably as a result of the Longford explosion itself. At its best, legitimacy was established through reduction in both actuarial and socio-cultural risks. Maintaining the necessary attention to both these risks was challenging.

The political risk management strategies of state governments had an effect on the level of compliance by the case study sites. In Victoria, the public and compelling demands for a safety case regime were not seen to be consistent with the actual level of knowledge held by the regulator. This caused uncertainty at the MHF sites around the actual substance of compliance and generated a certain amount of resentment that the MHFs were educating the regulator about MHF risk. The waning of support for the MHF regime in that state over time as the memories of Longford faded and as staff came and left the regulatory agency meant that this education process would need to be repeated, a task some did not relish. In NSW the emphasis on counter-terrorism within the safety case regime was seen as somewhat incongruous and politically motivated. Only in the NT did the political risk management of government not seem to affect the MHF sites in that territory. This could be attributed to the significant imbalance of resources with the MNCs having both financial and human resources far in excess of the territory regulator.

NOTES

1. There were six case studies undertaken in Victoria. One of these primarily involved research on community consultation (see appendix for research methods). Five were involved in the chemical industry, whilst the sixth was an oil refinery.
2. Each quotation from interviews undertaken as part of this research is referenced by a transcript number and by the specific page of the transcript where the quotation appears.
3. Although they remained subject to a range of other regulations covering dangerous goods, hazardous substances and occupational health and safety more generally.
4. The second time around, the site received a full five-year licence without any conditions attached.
5. The first round of licensing took place in 2001–02, the second mainly 2006–07. Of course, those licensed for three not five years needed to apply for relicensing before 2006.
6. A fire monitor is a form of pump that enables water or some other fire suppressant to be directed onto a fire at high pressure.
7. The one site manager who denied this was a problem was directly contradicted in an interview with a shop floor operator from the same site, even though the manager was also present at the interview. This was the only interview with shop floor employees where a

manager elected to stay for the interview. It was also an interview where the shop floor employee was particularly critical of some of the procedures in place at the plant.

8. A main street in the centre of Melbourne.

9. It should be remembered that the new regulations were not covering an area untouched by legislative mandate. Indeed, the (then) current regime had a three-year third-party major-hazard risk audit requirement that would be removed under the new regime.

10. A frontrunner in the final negotiations was the Insurer AIG, but this firm had no interest in risk reduction strategies on site. Presumably it felt that money was made through reinsurance and other financial instruments used to spread risk. As we have seen, AIG suffered significant, almost catastrophic, losses during the financial crisis. The successful insurer in contrast had avoided high-risk financial instruments and had successfully traded through the crisis with little ill effect.

7. The challenge of security at air and seaports

The obligations on airports and seaports to the counter-terrorism security regime in Australia that followed the 11 September 2001 attacks in the United States were considerable. The impact of these new responsibilities was, for airports in particular, a re-orientation of their fundamental purpose away from service and business to a policing role. Ports of both kinds are transport service centres with multiple relationships with other facilities in close proximity (often on the same site) such as cargo agents, flying clubs or pilot schools aimed at moving people and freight to their destination, or training the generations of the future to do so. Each port was a vital hub, some essential to Australia's interconnectedness internationally, others to a region and yet others to a remote locale such as an indigenous community, an offshore island settlement, or a mine.

The character and identity of both sea and airports over the past two decades had already changed significantly. Seaports were corporatised and airports had been privatised during the 1990s and early 2000s, transforming many airports from government-owned infrastructure to businesses, profit-making and profit-seeking entities in intense competition with one another. Yet, in the wake of the counter-terrorism reforms both sea and airports were re-identified as a possible location for a terrorist attack or the entry point of a terrorist into the country. For some, such as major airports, this reorientation began suddenly as the attacks unfolded in the United States. For others, the smaller airports and seaports, it was slower but nonetheless could still engender radical change. Initial security measures at airports, such as revamped screening of on-board luggage was supplemented by wave upon wave of new measures spurred by an incident overseas, a media exposé or an attack by the parliamentary opposition.

The response by the air and seaports to these mounting responsibilities was vigorous, with their respective industry associations playing a leading role in communicating the concerns of their industry to government. Each new counter-terrorism initiative proudly announced by the incumbent government needed to be shaped through industry lobbying and negotiation to protect existing assets and future business in danger of being threatened by the costs of compliance with security measures. These costs were considerable and continual calls were made for government funding for investment in required security technology. The Federal government responded favourably, increasing the budget for counter-terrorism that covered much, but not all, of the costs involved and only at airports, not seaports. Ultimately, costs were shared by tax payers, the users of sea and airports and the facilities themselves. Not surprisingly the regulator, the Office of Transport Security (OTS),[1] was a central player in negotiations and in developing the regime. Initially, in the aftermath of the September 11 attacks, the OTS was seen as both powerful and ill-informed. Over time, though, this view softened and they were considered more responsive and receptive to the concerns of both air and seaports.

This negotiation between regulator and ports shaped a narrative of how the threat of terrorism could be mitigated. Such a narrative needed to reassure the travelling public and key trading partners (in particular the US) of their security. But, to many on the ground the regime remained somewhat illogical, an overreaction with weaknesses still able to be exploited by those with sufficient knowledge of how an air or seaport functioned. The difficulties associated with a calculation of an actuarial risk of attack meant socio-cultural and political risk concerns as well as preserving trade relationships with the United States were the driving force behind reforms. Nonetheless, seaports in particular began to see advantages of the new regime, aided by the reality that it was supported by a well-resourced and high-profile regulator. Strict access control, as required by the regime, could be an effective tool in controlling and organising work and keeping 'nuisance' requests for access at bay.

AIRPORTS

Airports in Australia are incredibly diverse. High-profile international airports, those most often brought to mind as the target for a terrorist attack, are only a small minority of over 150 airports in Australia that receive regular scheduled flights. A secondary tier of airports grow and decline, based on the fortunes of particular budget airlines and business strategies. There are regional airports designed to service local needs and tourism as well as remote airstrips with perhaps a tin shed designed to meet the needs of outback communities. Finally, there are the multiple flying clubs with their requisite airstrips scattered around the country where individuals can learn to fly and pursue a dream. This diversity was matched by the range of individuals that took part in this research who found themselves faced with onerous responsibilities under the new security regime: businesspeople with a broad international experience; aviation and other engineers with a variety of technical expertise to council workers with backgrounds ranging from tradespeople to postmen.

The terrorist attacks in the US had a widespread and immediate impact on aviation in general and airports in particular. One regional airport manager commented that Al-Qaida '... found the ideal medium to generate world wide panic' (45, p.7).[2] As Chapter 5 outlined, there was a cascade of counter-terrorism security regulatory reforms that resulted from this seminal event. At one level the regulatory framework was co-regulatory, similar to the safety case reforms. Airports with regular scheduled flights, known as RPT airports, had to develop a Transport Security Plan (TSP), identifying their exposure to a risk of terrorism and putting in place risk management strategies to reduce that exposure. Yet, most evident were specific measures promoted by media debate or the most recent attack aimed at the United States. The scrutiny of airports within Australia by the media and the government opposition was intense, even or arguably especially of smaller airports. The manager of one such small airport described the levels of anxiety around the airport, 'Now at that stage (just after the attacks) we were in the media, they were saying, "why don't you have armed guards? Why don't you close down?"' (45, p.7).

September 2001 was not a good time for airports or the airline industry in general. In addition to the terrorist attacks was the collapse of Australia's second largest airline, Ansett, which was grounded on 14 September leaving thousands of passengers stranded across Australia. As a result of both events airports reported steep declines in traffic that was their lifeblood. One manager of a regional airport stated, 'It was a huge loss of income for us that year. I mean the passengers went from the year before in a corresponding month (it was) nearly 8,000 passengers, to September 2001 (when) it went down to 5,000' (51, p.10).

A manager at a major airport agreed but argued that it was the loss of Ansett, not the terrorist attacks that posed the greatest threat to Australia:

> So what was the biggest shock? The 9/11, which happened overseas – it didn't happen in Australia – or Ansett falling over? ... [There was] a huge amount of job losses ... I remember seeing a figure that was between 50,000 and 60,000 jobs that were either with Ansett or in industries that supplied it. ... (With September 11th) it was going to have an effect on the international traffic going through and, okay, we had to beef up the security measures. But there were still aeroplanes flying etcetera. But when Ansett fell over, it was just boom! (55, p.7)

Others saw security and airline viability linked. Vulnerable airlines could be bought to their knees by the attacks as Ansett had been by the reaction to September 11, 'And of course the biggest thing that September 11th did was kill Ansett. ...' (11, p.10) one manager commented.

The government regulatory response, as argued in Chapter 5, was focussed on political risk with its twin foci of keeping the economy moving whilst reassuring the broader population that their security was uppermost in the government's mind. Airports understood the drive for security, 'I can understand it because the PM[3] is the head of the country and he wants the country to be safe and secure. ... he would see his greatest challenge, is to ensure no terrorist attacks on Australian soil. Which is all very admirable' (12, p.20). But, from their vantage point the regulatory strategies employed by government to reduce that risk were problematic. The airport manager cited above continued '... it's how you achieve that (security) that he (the Prime Minister) has not been admirable on' (12, p.20). Both the regulatory tools used and implementation process that unfolded were seen by airports as designed as much to appease the public and enhance the reputation of the government as to reduce the risk of attack. Indeed, combating media headlines and the attacks of the opposition were, in the view of a number of interviewees, a principal concern, 'their (the government's) sole purpose is to ensure they do not get criticised publicly about airport security' (49, p.18) commented one.

For the incumbent government to reduce their political risk the counter-terrorism measures employed needed to be visible and plausible. In academic jargon, they required 'face validity' and to grab attention in media and political debate. So, the major focus was on tangible symbols of security: fences, cameras, signs, screening points, identification and policing. Each of these has legitimacy as a means to counter the threat of terrorism, particularly to a casual observer. Fences keep people out, cameras identify undesirables, identity cards determine who is legitimate and who is not, screening points identify explosives and police catch terrorists.

These very visible measures cascaded onto the diverse airport settings described above. In interviews managers, maintenance workers and business engineers would protest exclaiming 'one size doesn't fit all!' (55, p.10). Fences came in for particular criticism. Clearly, in a city setting a substantial fence has a security function and the city airports saw some value in upgrading their fencing. But, fences would be only a minor irritant to a determined terrorist, 'that fence wouldn't stop anyone, it wouldn't stop a 12-year-old if he wanted to get through it, all he needs is a pair of pliers,' (14, p.37) one quipped about their brand new fence. No fence, however strong, would be sufficient. One airport manager commented on a post-implementation audit of his security plan, 'He [the security auditor] said even the palisade [high security] fencing will only stop people for about ten minutes' (45, p.28).

Further, fences were expensive and, in many locations, restricted in their reach, 'they have a terminal building here and the fence starts 100 metres this side of the building and finishes 100 metres that side of the building. And all you've got to do is walk 100 metres and go around it' (49, p.9). Breaches of fences were also commented on, 'if some kid jumps the fence to get his football over the other side of the airport, I just, I don't care, you know. He gets it, but to them [the government] it's make sure no one gets into the fence. And there's this great drama' (49, p.22). Another recounted, 'the only breach we've had is a buffalo through the security fence. The fences only keep out honest people' (p.12, 18). Indeed, on occasion fences kept passengers and pilots in when they wanted to get out causing some consternation. For instance one respondent commented that, '[small airport] has got a security system and they've actually left a spot where you can climb up onto a step and skirt around a piece of steel to get in, because otherwise you can't get off the airport' (47, p.9).

CCTV cameras were also seen as a good visible measure of security. They were considered particularly valuable by the Australian government in the wake of the 2005 attacks in London where CCTV helped in identifying the culprits. Airports, too, particularly the larger airports saw some benefit to these cameras. But the capacity of the CCTV technology and its widespread use suggested more of a political than and actuarial motivation behind their implementation. Some airports were disappointed in the quality of the output, 'the cameras that we got were not high quality cameras and we are not getting the imagery that we expect to get' (45, p.17) said one manager. Visual monitoring, a considerable cost, could be undertaken elsewhere provided the infrastructure was in place. Other locations with dubious benefits from CCTV still received public funding under a government initiative entitled 'Security in our regional skies'. One manager recounted the fate of funds released under this scheme for a security upgrade at a remote and very small airport, one that had no regular passenger air services:

> Last year they come out with this you beaut strategy to make our smaller airports safe. ... Now there was $500,000 [given] for this particular airport. A security fence was built for about 20% of the boundary and then a CCTV camera was installed which then went back to Canberra. ... (But) there's nobody there! It's not only worse than nobody there, there aren't any passenger RPT[4] aircraft that land there. (55, pp.19–20)

It was pointed out to the relevant official that perhaps this was a waste of money. However, the response was that it was too late to give the money back, 'well that's on the budget [they said], we can't go back and say it's not needed' (55, p.20).

Fencing and cameras did have some value, however. They were effective in reducing vandalism and theft. Aircraft fuel, Avgas, at small airports was a popular target for theft, 'Because avgas is high-octane fuel, people want to put high-octane fuel in their jet ski boat they go to the airport and they go and siphon out fuel and go off and do their water skiing ... that's all stopped now' (45, p.17). This benefit to these airports was also one the government was paying for, 'from my point of view it's fantastic because these planes, they used to sit here 24 hours a day, seven days a week, totally unsecured. (Interviewer: You don't pay for the security?) No. ... I wouldn't want to either, it wouldn't be viable!' (46, p.23).

A major initiative had been the introduction of the Aviation Security Identification Cards or ASICs for short at all airports with regular public air transport (RPT). These cards were intended to prevent someone with dubious intent from gaining access to a security sensitive part of the airport. There were multiple challenges to overcome in their introduction and implementation. A definition of 'dubious intent' needed to be translated into concrete form through a criminal record check by the Federal Police, a security check by ASIO (The Australian Security Intelligence Organisation) and a check of immigration status. The second challenge was to determine what constituted a security sensitive part of the airport. For large airports this presented little problem as 'airside' was a clearly distinct location. But at smaller airports, one where regular public transport (RPT) mixed with general aviation,[5] 'airside' could simply mean a blue square on the tarmac, 'The RPT area is two blue boxes, where RPT aircraft go. If you go inside of that block you must have an ASIC' (45, p.9). Another gave a vivid illustration of stepping in and out of the square and thus needing and then not needing an ASIC. Under the new regime, an ASIC provided assurance around security rather than the fact that this employee was well known around the airport.

The third task was determining how many people needed an ASIC. For a security card to be effective the ideal scenario would be for as few people as possible to have a card, hence making it easier to monitor who was and was not legitimately in a sensitive area. But here the security rationale met the reality of airports where contracting and subcontracting of maintenance and building works at airports, together with delivery services, cleaning and catering to aircraft meant that the number of ASICs that needed to be issued quickly rose. In the case of the larger airports this escalated into the thousands. There was sound business logic at play here. A contractor without an ASIC needed to be supervised at all times whilst airside, a situation not only costly but often impractical, and so spurred the demand for ASICs. Not surprisingly, the Federal Government not wishing to be burdened with this task delegated this to 'issuing authorities,' amongst which were the airports themselves.

Finally, there was the problem of trainee and general aviation pilots, (that is, pilots of smaller private planes). Technically, at the time of this research, they did not need an ASIC unless they were airside in an ASIC controlled zone. However, for some an ASIC was a badge of pride and of status, more so than the AVID, an alternative form of identification available at the time with less onerous clearance requirements suitable for general aviation pilots. An ASIC became the identification to have.

Greater requirements around identification brought with them concerns about getting the necessary access airside at airports. Amongst the smaller airports and general aviation pilots, in particular, there was a fear of being denied immediate access to airside locations in emergency situations:

> ... you get the air ambulance rolling in, you get an ambulance officer who might be
> one day from Moree, the next day he might be from Wee Waa, the next day he might
> be from Narrabri and you don't know who that is. Does he have an ASIC – no. Well
> then he can't come on the airport – what do I do, let that person bleed? You know,
> how do we get them from the fence to the aircraft? How do we get that last 80
> metres sorted out? (58, p.13)

There were limits to the strict regulation of the ASIC and access regime.
Airport managers needed to make complex decisions about who should and
should not be trusted. In regional and remote airports airport staff were clearly
part of their local community and managers had responsibility for maintaining
ongoing harmonious relationships. Denying access could sour relationships. In
one case, denying a businessman access to a security sensitive airport led to the
lobbying of a politician and a change in the rules to allow this individual access
to his personal jet. In other cases, where those concerned had less political
access, those on the ground had to find ways to accommodate both the regulations and the needs of the local community. Local demands did not necessarily fit with the ideals of a remote government and a bureaucracy in Canberra:

> Let me give you an example, funerals. When we have a charter aircraft coming in
> with a body, an Indigenous body, that's going to be buried in the community. ...
> there would be a group of probably 50, 60 or 100 Aboriginals, all traditionally
> dressed because we are in traditional Aboriginal land. They would go to the plane
> and knock on the door with the spears and frighten the spirits away ... and take the
> body out. It's all done as ceremony. ... Theoretically under the new Act they should
> have VICs [Visitor Identification Cards] ... to be able to go out to the airport. Well
> what a nonsense! They have 200 blokes. There is a clause that says if you are a
> freight or passenger facilitator under the constant vision of an ASIC card holder you
> don't need to have an ASIC. So I ran the body as cargo and all these 200 as cargo
> facilitators. If they catch me and they don't like it what are they going to say? Fine,
> next time they will be passenger facilitators, yeah, seriously. But it affects our rela-
> tionship to our traditional community ... they would be pretty upset [if they didn't
> have access] and I wouldn't risk my guys at the gates saying to 200 Aboriginals, 40
> or 50 of them carrying spears, 'no sorry, you can't go to that aircraft. We'll bring
> the body out' I wouldn't risk my two guys out there. ... It (this airport) is in such a
> remote locality, where is the risk? (12, p.23)

Some relationships suffered. School visits to one airport were halted due to an
inability to process all the access cards necessary. The loss of these visits
disappointed the airport manager, a former schoolteacher, but he could not
now justify the time spent. This airport was a private profit-making enterprise
and the paperwork involved could not be justified. Another airport, owned and
operated by a local council, continued school visits albeit with the airport
manager conceding he was probably acting in a grey area of legality in terms
of the access regime, reflecting: 'We're probably on the border of regulatory
compliance with that ...' (50, p.26).

Details of the ASIC regime were an ongoing sore during the implementation phase. Who was to issue an ASIC and at whose cost needed to be determined, as did an understanding of what an ASIC actually meant to the wearer
and the airport. The meaning and purpose attached to the ASIC was initially in
a state of flux around security and access. Originally, there were to be several
levels of ASIC, signalling different levels of access and clearance. Ultimately,
the levels were streamlined to two, a red and a grey ASIC that covered all
airside workers, with the grey ASIC allowing access to secure areas and the
red ASIC allowing access to restricted areas. Finally, the meaning of an ASIC
was restricted to background checks with no assumption made concerning
access to a particular airport or location within an airport. One airport manager
gave a detailed description of all the changes and ended stating that, 'Now,
they are saying ASIC cards have nothing whatsoever to do with having access.
They are purely and simply a card to show that all the background checks have
been done' (12, p.15).

Once an ASIC had been issued problems surfaced with the need to have an
ASIC visible at all times, above waist height and at the front or side of the
body according to the required standards. This either meant using a lanyard, a
strap around the neck, which could be a nuisance for those undertaking
baggage handling or maintenance, or placed in a see-through pocket that might
get covered by warm clothing when cold. But the OTS were adamant, ASICs
must be visible at all times. One airport manager recounted:

> We got into trouble three months ago in the middle of winter we had a blizzard here
> and I had a female inspector … she looked and there were guys clearly unloading
> baggage off the plane in Qantas attire or Rex uniforms and she couldn't see all their
> ASICs because the guys had pulled their raincoats on and gone out. So I got a phone
> call saying she was going to fine me and do all sorts of things I said, 'Listen, let's
> be realistic.' … She said to me, 'It's your airport, you're the one that is supposed to
> be policing it.' And I said, 'That's fine, but how do I fine them because our security
> guards don't have any powers of arrest or detainment or the fines for these things.
> They haven't issued an infringement book yet' … so anyway I sorted her out but it's
> just she was having a bad hair day or something. I mean, honestly, and it was about
> minus four and these guys are getting rained on, they're clearly the baggage
> handlers. (51, p.25)

The ASIC regime grated against other regulatory aims. Lanyards, for example,
were frowned upon as a safety or choking hazard. Then, there were privacy
concerns with combining background checks with airport access. An ongoing
tension was the difference between a security check and authorising access to
sensitive or secure areas of the airport. This suited airport managers who
viewed an ASIC as simply a background check. It did not and should not
provide access which was, for them, an entirely separate question. For pilots
it seemed irrational that the ASIC regime could not be combined with access,

particularly when they were at their home airport. The reason given to them why this was not possible was that it breached privacy regulations.

For most members of the public passing through an airport the most visible aspects of security were not fences and access cards for airport staff, but screening points and police presence. Both these aspects of security were emphasised in the response to September 11. Each fell onto airport responsibilities akin to a stone in a pond with an ever-extending reach as events and anxieties increased. In terms of screening, the first step was enhanced screening of on-board luggage and tighter restrictions around sharp objects that could no longer be carried on to a plane by a passenger. This was followed by checked bag screening, first at major airports then at all RPT airports.[6]

At the time of data collection for this research in 2006–07 the topic consuming most of the regional and small airports was the move to explosive trace detection (ETD) and checked bag screening across all airports. The cost involved in implementation was considerable, and comprised more than just the equipment, the cost of which was often, but not always, covered by a Federal Government grant. Most airport managers found that government funds covered only a third of initial costs and contributed nothing to necessary restructuring of terminals to accommodate tighter security or the costs of employing those responsible for screening passengers and luggage. One explained:

> The government funded 100% of the purchase of the ETD machine. The second phase is December 2008 and we have to implement full x-ray inline checked-bag screening and, once again, the government are going to fund 50% of the purchase of the x-ray machine only. But there's a lot more expenditure than just the machine that we have to [meet]. (59, p.6)

These costs had to be borne by someone. Clearly, government grants were supported by taxes and general government revenue. When at all possible the additional cost was added to the charges for using the airport, onto the airlines (who could have their own responsibilities for screening) and finally onto the passengers. The impact of the cost of screening and additional security depended on the size of the airport and the numbers of passengers. At the larger airports it amounted to around 10 cents per passenger. For smaller airports the cost could be considerable, up to $27 per passenger in one case. Hence, regional airports and rural passengers were affected most by the increased cost of security. The irony was that part of the motivation behind widespread implementation of checked bag screening was to signal to the regional electorate that they were of equal value to their city counterparts and that they too would be safe from a terrorist attack. Rural and regional Australians travelling by air paid a significant premium for this assurance.

As with the ASIC identity card, the everyday practice of screening brought challenges. At screening locations, difficulties in assessing an object and the level of threat it posed would surface. What constituted a sharp object? Forks, for example, came in for intense discussion:

> The regulations say that a fork with squared off tines is okay, but one with sharp or rounded tines is not okay. So how do you tell that a tine on a fork is square or rounded? ... And if it was square, but it's gone sort of soft on the edges because of the wear is that acceptable or not acceptable? So some people will take that fork off them and other people won't. (50, p.28)

Knitting needles also created problems, so did objects sold in airport stores airside, such as drinks in glass bottles and didgeridoos, which could be defined as weapons. Airports close to mining sites had additional dilemmas to face, since explosives used at mine sites could be picked up by ETD machines. Indeed, there were soils in some regions of Australia that, even when unrefined, would be enough to set off an explosion detection machine. So, determining what was, and was not a terrorist threat either needed intense discussion with the OTS and a common resolution reached to be deployed across all screening sites, or it became one of local discretion.

Even when a common procedure had been developed, implementation of that procedure was still a concern. An employee determining something as a terrorist threat or as a potential explosive brought a range of emergency services into play once a suspicious package procedure was activated. At times, such a decision proved a step too far for this airport supervisor:

> The other night there was a package left outside and, you know, we've got to then start our 'security suspicious package' procedure. [We should] go through the procedure like we have to, but we did a sort of short cut. We didn't get the bomb squad from [capital city] involved. I thought it might not be a good idea, wouldn't be good publicity for us. ... It was taped up so it looked like, you know, a little suspicious. [It didn't] have any baggage tag on it or anything.

This supervisor checked to see whose it might be, but to no avail. A decision whether to activate a suspicious package procedure or not had to be made. He continued:

> It was beside the bin right? ... Normally [the owner] may have just stuck it in the bin, but the bin was full ... and being taped up like that and not open [it wasn't clear what it was]. It is stressful when you've got to come out here and make a decision ... the plane was late. So there were people sitting around with the package, right, just sitting around, standing around having a cigarette outside. And then the next plane came in so there were even more people coming in. Conveyer belts right next to the bin, like five meters away from these packages here (gestures). So the first thing I do is evacuate the area. You know. Do I then make the plane late again? The next thing I do is we call up the police. Do we call up the police and then do we

> have to wait four hours for a bomb squad to come over from [capital city]. ... I just
> picked it up shook it and ran. (14, pp.35–6)

With each terrorist incident involving the US, a new screening process would
be put in place. During the research in 2006 a plot to use liquid explosives to
blow up an airliner from the UK bound for the US and Canada was foiled.
Australia responded to this new threat by introducing a new liquids and gels
policy for carry on luggage on international flights. At the time of writing, new
body scanners were in the process of being introduced.

Police presence also was a visible sign of security. A number of the case
study airports, those considered 'counter-terrorism first response' (CTFR)
airports were subject to multiple police forces with a 24-hour presence. Private
security guards were supplemented by state police forces and finally the
Australian Federal Police (AFP). Yet, some CTFR airports were empty for
much of the day and night. For much of the time there was nothing to do and
even when there was an arrival of a plane the level of policing could be excessive. One manager responsible for three airports argued:

> ... well (at this CTFR airport) you get off the apron and then you've got about a
> 60m walk straight into the terminal. You'll have two coppers looking at you, stand-
> ing there like this looking at you as you get off the aeroplane, another one as you
> walk down the passage way, and then you'll have at least two standing around the
> baggage reclaim unit eyeing you off, and then the other three will come and join
> you. So you've got five policemen standing around watching this, probably 100
> people or less, picking their bags up. (55, p.16)

The presence of police meant that there needed to be enforcement. Without
terrorists to find, the attention of the extra police turned to enforcing other
laws, regulations or procedures at airports:

> ... well we did have problems with itinerants, drinking and carrying on and coming
> into the terminal, and in our native garden over here drinking grog all day and all
> this sort of stuff. We had to call up the police to move them on. But it was a lot
> cheaper to move them on just by calling the local police to come out and fix them
> up, or we use Chubb[7] with a bit of bluff to get them off the airport or out of the
> terminal, than having an establishment of [all these new] bloody police here 24
> hours a day. (55, p.16)

The need arose to justify such a strong police presence. They had to be seen to
be active. At times, this could undermine the capacity of those employed at the
airport to take responsibility and at other times reports of their usefulness was
exaggerated. One manager recounted an incident when:

> ... this inebriated or pissed something man, grabs hold of a jeep ... and was doing
> wheelies up and down the runway, the taxiway, and he was doing it for 20 minutes.

Now our safety or operations officer was the one that chased him, finally appre-
hended him, and he's not armed. The Federal Police came along later on a baggage
trolley tug. ... The [AFP] vehicle which was patrolling the perimeter fence wasn't
here, it was on the landside, [so] when they [the AFP] came out they didn't have a
vehicle. Now you read the headlines the next day 'Federal Police arrested this guy
blah blah blah.' The poor old Operations Officer never even got a mention, not in
the official report that went back to Canberra, not anywhere. (55, p.16)

Employees could also find themselves on the receiving end of the enhanced
police presence, with AFP officers enforcing a range of regulations, sometimes
inappropriately:

... all they're doing now is going around looking for work and encroaching on the
airport's responsibilities. ... they want to go out and book people for not wearing
seatbelts on the airside. Half the equipment out there hasn't got seatbelts because it
doesn't have to because we're not on a public road. They're looking for things to
do. Now what that has got to do with terrorism has me beat! It might have something to do with occupational health and safety, but it's not a security matter and
that's why the Federal Police were here. (55, p.22)

It is important to reflect on what was occurring during the implementation of
the counter-terrorism security regime at these airports. The majority of those
interviewed saw there was a need to respond to the terrorist attacks in the
United States. But the level and intensity of responses varied. In the face of an
unknown assailant the rationale behind counter-terrorism security was the
need to create a number of hurdles that any potential terrorist would need to
cross in order to create chaos. In the process, however, the risk of a terrorist
attack was simplified to a view that if you can see a way for a terrorist to attack
then it should be addressed and if one security strategy had identified weaknesses then another was needed to complement it. In professional jargon the
response was conceptualised as putting in place layers of security. The
strength lay in the multiple layers of security created.

The problem was that no clear boundary could be placed around what
constituted an adequate level of control, since the next terrorist might figure
out where tight controls fell away. Neither could the level of response be justified in any precise manner. As one respondent pointed out, Australian aircraft
had been subject to hijackings before 9/11, the first taking place in 1960 and
the second in 1972, and the first use of liquid explosives on an airline took
place in 1994. The response to this attack relative to those before was difficult
to explain in terms of actuarial risk. Quantification of actuarial risk, an assessment of the probability of an attack and the severity of its impact was impossible to calculate.

The lacuna created by the absence of actuarial risk assessments then was
filled by dealing with socio-cultural and political risk. Security was principally

concerned with assurance, making people feel safe, 'Well, I think it gives the community a sense of security' (58, p.15) one airport manager commented in response to what he felt were the main advantages to the regime. Thoughtfulness was well in evidence in some discussions where airport managers, engineers and maintenance workers would tease through the problem of security, trying to imagine what a terrorist could do and realising the impossibility of total control and then translating the regime into one of care and reassurance, 'People need to see something happening, whether it's just security in the uniforms. My wife's about to fly and she's doesn't enjoy flying. She sees all these things happening. A lot of people need that sort of comfort' (14, p.37).

Comfort, though, was a state of mind and an assessment of the surrounding environment either as one to be trusted or not. This socio-cultural risk assessment could be perceived of as fragile. When a new attack occurred against the US it was conceptualised as a threat against 'us' and so needed attention. Imagination and fear made the potential for additional risk control endless, '[the attacks] have ingrained in us this fear that has been a real detriment to our industry' (46, p.14), said one aero club manager. Rituals of assurance were created such as screening, surveillance, policing and identification. Despite these controls each airport manager knew of weaknesses. Some pointed to cargo that needed no screening and others commented that small aircraft could be used to devastating effect. Their concern, however, was not of a terrorist attack at their airport but that another attack using one of these methods or a media story of the potential for such an outcome would generate a wave of new requirements.

The political response was central in identifying which fears would be responded to and who would be cared for. The government could either exacerbate or calm socio-cultural anxieties. Government responses aimed to reduce political risks and were patterned by the lobbying of particular industry groups regarding the economic impact of security regulations on the one side and which gestures of concern would resonate with the broader electorate on the other.

The regulator was the mediating influence here. As we have noted above, initial experiences with the OTS were not good. Over time, however, this changed. Large, high-profile airports eventually developed a robust relationship with the regulator and became much more positive about their experience with the OTS. In particular, their experience of the introduction of the liquids and gels policy was of an ordered implementation process that had little implications for them in terms of cost and efficiency:

> That's an excellent example where they (OTS) were brave enough to say, 'We're not doing it on the 1st of March. We're putting it back to 31st of March.' [That]

allowed industry to walk through from November/December how we're going to do it, what the regulation looks like, are we going to apply it to crew or not, what do we do with baby formula? So we probably spent days and days working together around tables in Canberra to work out an agreed position ... we're all working hard to implement it, recruiting 150 extra people. So we had to recruit them, get them trained, licensed, operating. ... it all worked well, we had the right marshalling, the passenger flows worked, and people really didn't see much impact on it whatsoever. (14, p.3)

Smaller airports had less control over the political agenda but over time some of these airports, too, felt the OTS were trying to accommodate their needs. At times, though, this proved impossible and the regulator resorted to apologies to these airports to build a good relationship with them, 'They (OTS) quite honestly say "I'm sorry but we didn't write this. We were told about it and we've got to go and run it. We do know it's crazy but that isn't our choice ..."' (45, p.31).

Revenue was of concern to both government and airports. For the government, a response to the US in terms of counter-terrorism security was a prime consideration. Government needed to keep their relationships with trading partners, particularly the US, working well. This helps to understand why, at the time of writing, the liquid and gels policy remained in place only for international flights and was not extended to domestic routes. Further, every security initiative had implications for the competitiveness of each airport. Airports would fight vigorously to maintain or enhance their advantage and would lobby politicians to ensure their needs were heard. The government appeared most sensitive to anxieties expressed by threats to the larger airlines or higher profile airports about their ongoing economic viability. For example, before checked bag screening was compulsory at regional airports the large airports and airlines flying on international routes would argue it was unfair that they should bear the cost of screening passengers who had flown on regional airlines and from regional airports. This complaint dovetailed with public and media concerns evident at the time about the potential for terrorists using regional airports as a point of entry. Checked bag screening at regional airports, a significant cost burden for those facilities, was of benefit both to major centres and to government in their exhortation that 'all Australians are safe.' Hence, the government moulded a response that assuaged key industry players whilst also reassuring the broader population of their security.

Finally, all airlines and airports also were keen to keep finding additional ways to cut costs and reduce personnel. At the same time, increased security was being implemented so too was a move to self-check in where, on domestic flights at least, no visual check of identification was ever made. The security of technology replaced the security provided by people. Each of the steps made by both industry and government could be understood in terms of economic viability and, for government, the need to reduce political risk.

These economic efficiencies made by major airlines and airports fitted into the interstices of a security regime hence moulding a narrative of risk (Haines 2009a). This narrative, however, could prove vulnerable when another attack occurred or a plausible new avenue for a terrorist attack was raised.

Some affected people had neither economic nor socio-cultural capital with which they could convince government of their loss or their need for support following either the September 11 attacks or from the ensuing counter-terrorism regime. A poignant example of this was the fate of an Australian trainee pilot named Mohammed who realised there was no future for him in the airline industry in Australia. A flight school operator described the trainee pilot's experience:

> Poor guy, I mean he got run out of the place, it was very sad. I felt terribly sorry because really he was quite Australian … it was going to haunt him for years. So he went back to uni and changed courses. He was from the university too. He's Australian. (46, p.18)

Aero clubs and pilot schools that generated the technical and human expertise for the Australian industry also suffered. Their story is more complex, as it requires understanding both the impact of privatisation and increased security. Privatisation had a significant impact on airports. Each private airport as a profit centre needed, within the terms of their lease, to make money. Hence, one major airport now described themselves as a shopping centre primarily where the customers came in the form of airline passengers and their entourage of family, friends or work colleagues. Airport land, too, was viewed differently, principally as a source of revenue. Whilst larger airports built shopping centres, smaller airports leased land to factory outlets and discount shopping centres. The rent paid by clubs and pilot training schools then had to compete on commercial terms. How they were treated depended on the private owners. Some were happy with this treatment, and emphasised during interviews how well they were being treated by the new leaseholders of the land, yet even so their new dependent status meant investing in their businesses could be considered too great a risk. In short, after a substantial investment in their building they could lose their lease to another willing to pay more. Whilst shopping centres could be built anywhere, aero clubs and pilot training schools need an airport. Those affected were unsure not only of their own future, but the future of their industry. The final irony here was of a pilot training school with a number of Asian students making way for a discount shopping centre filled with Chinese and Asian goods.

The experience of airports in the wake of the September 11 attacks reinforces an understanding that counter-terrorism regulatory reforms were primarily concerned with political risk, to reassure the travelling public and key constituencies of their security whilst protecting industries and trade relationships that were seen as central to the government's fortunes. This meant that airports needed to put in place measures that were often ill-thought through, particularly in light of the diversity of airports that were charged with onerous regulatory responsibilities. An industry that when privatised was promised 'light handed' regulation found itself with intense surveillance not only by the regulator, but by the media and politicians at all levels of government. The reforms were subject to vigorous protests by the airports to the Federal government who responded by making extensive resources available to ensure implementation of new technology. The regulator, the OTS, was well resourced and empowered to ensure compliance. Over time, however, their stance shifted from authoritarian to collaborative as they experienced the deep concern that many airports had with the new regime.

The challenge of counter-terrorism regulation was significant. There was no end point in sight and no way to assess when enough security was enough. When a new terrorist attack or a media-generated anxiety arose about how a terrorist might attack, the government responded by imposing new regulatory responsibilities. Those airports with influence and resources could shape each new initiative to have the least impact on their profitability, particularly as the regulator changed its stance from intransigent to cooperative. But there were losers from the regime as airports changed in character from a service to a business and, through the security regime, towards a law enforcement and regulatory role. Amongst these were losses to the long-term sustainability of aviation industry expertise from pilot training to technical skills. But there was also the intangible loss of trust through the growth within the security regime of increased suspicion of who might or might not be a potential terrorist and where a person's name could signify a potential status as 'dangerous' and undesirable. Yet, there appeared to be no calculation by the government of these losses. Clearly, an actuarial calculation of such losses would be just as difficult as an actuarial calculation of the risk of a terrorist attack from having insufficient security controls at a regional airport. But the point here was that this calculation was not even attempted. This imbalance in what was, and was not calculated, reinforces the argument here that political risk to government was the main concern that drove not only these reforms, but also which of the concerns of airports were, and were not, listened to.

SEAPORTS

Seaports in Australia share similarities with their airport cousins but there are also some striking differences. As with airports in Australia there is considerable diversity in size and in the variety of functions they are required to undertake. In the case of the seaports studied here the number of commercial ships entering a port on an annual basis ranged from over 5,000 in the busiest port to under 50 in a quiet regional port. The major seaports that were studied were akin to small cities in size and complexity, managing road and rail operations as well as the various shipping lanes and channels and acting as landlords to stevedoring companies and bulk-user operators.

The differences in seaports when compared with airports went beyond the obvious distinction of accommodating ships rather than aeroplanes. They were distinct in their ownership and what they considered their principle function. The majority of seaports remained in (state) government hands in clear contrast to the widespread privatisation of airports. Most were state-owned corporations, a legislative structure enabled under either Commonwealth or State law (Pettit 2007). For some, this shift to corporatisation was made with privatisation seen as the ultimate goal. Corporatisation, however, rarely resulted in outright sale with South Australia the only state to have fully privatised its major port operations at the time of this research (Pettit 2007).

Finally, there was a distinct orientation of seaports towards facilitating trade. The seaports in this study saw themselves as service centres with a principal focus on enhancing trade and commerce. Ninety-nine per cent of exports and imports (by volume) to and from Australia occurred by sea (Pettit 2007). For large ports their focus was on national and international trade, with smaller ports dedicated to serve the local fishing industry, a mine or to service local islands. The ports in this study were not considered as profit centres, in marked contrast to privately-owned airports. Seaports were established to facilitate trade and this remained their primary, even sole, focus.

Nonetheless, there had been significant change in the pace and character of seaports over time. Much of this change could be understood to flow from technological modernisation and, in particular, the use of containers to move goods to and from cargo ships. The use of containers meant that ships stayed in ports for shorter periods. This in turn meant relationships between seamen and the countries they visited had changed dramatically, as one manager explained:

> I started [at seaports] in 1967 and there wasn't one single container coming through the port. In 2007, 40 years later, 2.2 million containers are coming through the port and that's 90% of the total cargo coming in through containers. In 1967, cargo was all goods and not much has changed, like 98 or so percent is still goods [as opposed to bulk produce or resources such as grain or minerals]. … A ship would come here, it would be a quarter of the size of the ships that are coming here now, manhandling every one single piece of cargo, it could be timber, it could be wool, it could be bags, it could be furniture and it was all packed in little bits and pieces all around the holds. A ship would be here for six weeks, three weeks to unload and because they always wanted to take a load back with them [three more]. People would come

here, the crew on the ship would sometimes leave the ship and hire an apartment in town and just come back to the ship during the day time, work on the ship and go and sleep ... Ship's crews made friends with people in the city and went and lived in their houses for the six weeks they were in port and come back a year later and do the same thing. Different era, different lifestyle. Nowadays a ship is here less than 24 hours and they discharge something like 4,000 containers, 10 times the amount of cargo that one of these other ships did, maybe 20 times the amount of cargo ... (42, p.21)

There is an irony here. The shift towards containerization facilitated and was accompanied by a move away from a protectionist industry policy towards lowering tariffs and increasing Australian reliance on international trade as the source for its economic security. Australia embraced international economic relationships at the same time as social relationships within the port environment shrank.

This opening up to international trade together with a change in technology led to an increased emphasis on productivity at the ports and of dockside workers in particular. With government demand for higher productivity at ports, the tension between unions and stevedoring companies rose and remained tense. Within Australia, the push for greater productivity on the waterfront came to its zenith in a long dispute in 1998 between Patrick Corporation and the Maritime Union of Australia (MUA). This was an acrimonious dispute, in which the Howard conservative coalition government was closely intertwined and where union labour was dismissed through a series of complex legal manoeuvres and non-union labour employed in much lower numbers. This dispute ended when the High Court of Australia found in favour of the MUA and required the reinstatement of the original unionised work-force (see *Patrick Stevedores v MUA* [1998] HCA 30; 195 CLR 1; 72 ALJR 873; 79 IR 339; 153 ALR 643 (4 May 1998)). Yet, the re-employment of union labour resulted in a negotiation where significantly increased productivity was achieved through a dramatic reduction in dockworkers employed. Emotions remained intense even nine years after the end of the dispute. One manager explained that there was 'hatred, voiced hatred of each other ... and a preparedness to do ill if they can. (To) cause them, not physical harm, but cause harm ... on both sides' (41, p.16). This acrimony spurred the aspirations of some stevedoring companies to achieve a zero workforce on the dockside, for containers to be loaded entirely by robots. Technology would rid the company entirely of the need for dealing with the unions.

The effect of the terrorist attacks of 11 September 2001 on the port environment was not immediate. There was no dramatic collapse of shipping companies as there had been of airlines. The impact was felt around two years later and centred on a concern to keep trade with the United States flowing. The impact when it came, however, was considerable.

Those at major ports in this study understood that the motivating force behind the security regime was to protect the United States. One manager explained that the major route for transportation of nuclear weapons was via sea, not air, and this reality shaped the US security regime at the seaports:

> If you burrow down it [the security regime] is really about America's fear of a dirty bomb coming in on a ship and being detonated in one of their major ports. ... They realised after September 11 there was no security in the ports and there wasn't. People could come and go and ships could come and go almost without notice, and they decided they [had] better start hardening up their maritime environment. (41, p.7)

The maritime security regime contained three distinct elements: the securing of ships, seaports and cargo. The first two of these were achieved through a number of amendments to the 1974 Convention of Safety of Life at Sea (SOLAS), agreed to in December 2002 and brought into force in July 2004. These amendments, known collectively as the International Ship and Port Facilities Code (ISPC), set out the broad parameters for the security of ships and the security of seaports. The security of containers entering the US was achieved through a separate mechanism, the Container Security Initiative (CSI). CSI was launched through the US bureau of Customs and Border Protection and then disseminated through the World Customs Organization.

The ISPC recognised that there were significant differences between various seaports and between ships, resulting in a regime based on tailored security plans for both ships and ports. This need for individualised security plans was given effect within Australia by the *Maritime Transport Security Act 2003* (Cth) (renamed in 2005 *Maritime Transport and Offshore Facilities Security Act 2003* (Cth)) that required both ships and seaports to develop their own individual security plans, which needed to be approved by the regulator. This legislation came into effect in July 2004 to coincide with the timeline set out in the ISPC.

The concerns of the US to protect its borders, however, were matched with the political demands of the Australian government to follow through on its reaction to the attacks of September 11. As earlier chapters have noted, this reaction was dramatic and placed Australia almost on a war footing. Some security managers at seaports well understood the extreme reaction by the government to the September 11 attacks. A former defence officer, now a port security officer, recounted his own experience of the day of the attacks when he received a top priority alert message:

> [Defence] have different ways of communicating and one of them is by signal form to our signals organization. They have an immediate message that comes out in the signal and it's called a 'flash message'. And this is a type of message when a war is declared and you're under attack. There are people that go through 30 years in the

army and never see a flash message, they're not allowed to be read out over the phone or anything. And I got a flash message ... I knew we just had 9/11 because I was just watching it on the TV ... I sat down and waited for the phone to ring and the phone [rang] and they said, 'You are the duty officer, you've got a flash message' ... It told me [we had] jumped two levels and it quite clearly said there was an imminent attack on my base. And I thought, well that was for every base in Australia! Who are we going to attack? Somebody from Mars or something attacking every base in [the country] ... the worst part about it is if you go to that type of response, you can't maintain it ... it disrupts business, it disrupts everything and nobody really said, 'Well listen, the response really isn't here. Let's go down a couple of levels.' (30, p.8)

Although delayed, when the demand for heightened security came it required a swift response by the seaports. The threat was that any country not up to standard would be denied access to the US market. One commented, 'So here's this big threat, if you don't comply and we've given you the tool to comply (with) the ISPS Code, well, we're not going to trade with you' (30, p.9).

As with the airports, the emphasis of the individualised security plans was on visible elements of security: fences, policing, background checks and access control. Despite the theory that security plans should be tailored to suit the particular circumstances of a port, it was clear that they would only be approved when particular visible elements were present. Individualised plans were given effect through generic security techniques. The pressure placed on ports to comply – with 'appropriate' security measures – was considerable, even where the usefulness of a particular measure was in doubt. Sea-borne patrols came in for particular criticism, one security officer recalled:

So what they were effectively forcing us to do was put a Chubb (security) man in a tinny[8] out on the water to protect us from a terrorist attack. I pointed out quite force-fully that the Chubb man in a tinny wasn't going to have a deterrent effect, wasn't going to have any preventative effect and was likely only to add to any body count, should such an attack [occur]. ... But the politics of it was that they wouldn't approve our plan until we did it, so we had our token man tooting out there. (41, p.2)

Fences were a dominant element in security plans. It was here that the trans-plantation of the model of airport security onto seaports created difficulties. Security managers needed to educate the OTS to understand the differences between sea and airports. Creating a sterile area in the sea around the port was almost impossible and fencing a port, both on land and at sea, clearly unviable:

They were on a steep learning curve as well because a lot of those people are ex-policemen, and from that type of background, you know. And they had no idea about ports or whatever ... the first thing they wanted to do was put a fence around our port. And we said, 'Well how are you going to do that?!' (53, p.5)

However, where fencing was impractical there was the possibility that more advanced technology might be employed instead. Security technology companies vied to secure a foothold in the security technology business of the ports, as they had attempted to do at airports. As with airports, such technology, could promise and not deliver. The idea that the seaside of a port could be secured by sonar technology was one possibility that had been tried, but had failed:

> Initially [companies] would come to us and say, 'We have perfected this,' Sonar was the perfect example. Sonar, OK, I know it works in defence organizations, but has it been commercially viable? 'Yes it is [they said] it's ready to go.' 'Where's it being tested?' [I asked]. 'Well nowhere just yet but it is available for ports.' [they said]. So we did a pilot project and they put their Sonar in. 'Which type of Sonar have you got?' [I asked] 'We've got this, we've got that, and we recommend active Sonar' [they said]. So I said, 'No we don't want active. We're not protecting war ships there. We're not protecting national assets. We only want a passive system.' My idea of a passive system is a ship to shore interface is there and you form a passive barrier … so all it was, was an intruder alarm system on the water. … Twelve months they still haven't got it up and operating … They promise everything but don't fulfil. … It just doesn't work. … It works terrific at the airport and indoors but [when it is brought] outside in a maritime environment, everything's contaminated. (30, p.21)

Other technology that controlled access could be more effective. The manager of the small port was particularly proud of his impending new 'cyber' key system that would log each person who entered the largely unmanned port. The requirement for companies and individuals to notify him each time they entered the port could now be backed up with technology. The emphasis here, though, was on compliance rather than reducing the risk of attack:

> … We've now actually got what's called a cyber key system. It's a special key that can't be picked and it logs everybody that goes in and out on which key at what time. And we can control the time that they use that key by programming the key and the lock. So we'll be telling them, 'look, if you don't comply now, we'll just put a stop on your key and you'll have to come to us every time you want to have a key to have it programmed' … (60, p.7).

Screening, too, was prominent. However, the different level of challenge for screening agencies was striking. What needed to be prevented from being taken onto passenger vessels such as cruise ships, for example, was 'a bomb, a rocket launcher, explosives, fire arms. Everything else is OK' (41, p.9). The concern then was not to find and remove nail clippers and small quantities of liquids. For this reason, screening equipment used for airline passengers at airports needed to be radically redesigned to be made useful for monitoring passengers boarding cruise ships at seaports.

In the port environment more broadly, it was an ongoing challenge to ensure all those accessing secure areas (such as the ship-to-shore interface on the dock) were screened. Many people asked for and received exemptions from screening from the regulator, the OTS. The security officer at one port considered that such widespread exclusion from screening meant the whole regime was problematic, arguing '... the list has grown because all these agencies have gone to DoTARS[9] and said, "We need to be exempt from screening for whatever reason ..."' (30, p.16).

The challenge of screening effectively for sea-borne cargo was of a different order of logistical magnitude entirely to the screening of cruise passengers. As noted in Chapter 5, the screening of cargo was undertaken according to an intelligence-led model. So, rather than checking each container (as each passenger would be screened), an impossible task, checking only took place of those containers considered to be suspect either because of the country they came from, or where there were known problems with the particular ship or freight company. Random checking of cargo was rare. This method of surveillance was considered by one port security officer to be seriously flawed:

> Well let's put it this way, how do we check containers coming into the country? Customs will tell you that they check 10 per cent a year. Look my own personal view is that they would be lucky if they checked 5 per cent. They're purely intelligence-based. I just had an interview recently with some customs surveillance. Now they're poorly funded the groups that give them this intelligence. They can't do things properly because they just haven't got the resources, the funding, the manpower ... and their skill levels are not as high as I would think to fulfil that sort of requirement. So what they do is they get their intelligence-based information, they select containers, they bring them around, they x-ray them and send them back. Now, it's not a good system. They don't choose it randomly. So if you wanted to bring some prohibited item in, you would only need to get it through a port that wasn't on the radar. If somebody says, 'there's this Indonesian ship coming in that is a bit dodgy because it stopped at this particular port,' the chances of some of the cargo being searched and x-rayed are pretty high, but if it comes via Hawaii from a reputable company well it will come (straight) through and that's exactly the same for drugs and anything else. (30, p.11)

In a similar manner to airports, there was background checking and issuing of Maritime Security Identification Cards (MSIC) to port employees and those needing to access secure areas of the port. This MSIC regime was similar to the ASIC regime awarded on the basis of a clear background check that did not also provide access to a particular port or dock. Separate permission was needed to give a person with an MSIC access to a particular port or wharf. Originally, the background checks were of a similar intensity to the ASIC regime. However, the introduction of the MSIC had created significant protests by the MUA, who were concerned at the impact on workers and had argued successfully that the level of security required was not comparable to that needed in an airport environment. A background check that was too stringent, they argued, might exclude a person from the port who had a criminal record, but had found their way back to legitimate employment. Excluding such people could be counterproductive. The weaker regime eventually implemented by government in response to union pressure was considered by some to be an appropriate one:

> ... they might have been to jail three years ago and since they've got out they've worked as a truckie and they've got, a mortgage and trying to lead a good life but because of their history they were going to have difficulties. I think that was the catalyst of tempering it down to a workable model. (30, p.14)

Others felt that the lighter regime was not effective. At the time of interview, it appeared that few applications across the country had actually been refused. One security manager recounted:

> We've done something like 65,000 checks. Ten people have been assessed as being not suitable. Two have lodged appeals to date and both have been successful. So we have in fact excluded very few people from the industry if any. Its been done on the basis of a name check only so there's always a question mark about false identification, particularly if people who have been in the industry a long time have perhaps ten years ago assumed a false identity and built up their identification. And that's not difficult to do – you can reproduce a birth certificate with false information on it very regularly. (41, p.13)

This situation was set to improve with a new background document checking system that was coordinated by the Attorney General's Department rather than by the regulator, the OTS. Nonetheless, the manager argued that what was really needed was some biometric measure:

> ... until you get fingerprints you are never going to be confident that the person that you are checking has or hasn't a record. Until you get a criteria that better reflects the sorts of people who could cause you problems, you have to be a terrorist and actually charged before you're excluded from the maritime industry. ... (41, p.14)

The introduction of biometric controls at some time in the future was seen as inevitable. What the ports wanted, however, was for the Federal government to fight unions and public resistance to bring this into effect. A security manager commented, '... we will have biometrics on the cards eventually. But it's much easier to let the federal government fight that under legislation not the port' (30, p.26).

Critically for the government, however, the security regime had been implemented swiftly enough to protect key trade relationships, despite the limited capacity of the MSIC regime to identify terrorists and protect the ports and trade from a terrorist attack. Indeed, it is difficult to imagine what standard background checking system could identify a potential terrorist. Background checking based on criminal record risks serious injustice in denying access to employment to vulnerable sectors of the society and failing to reintegrate them back into society (see Lucken and Ponte 2008).

The need to implement the maritime security regime in a compressed time-frame had generated concern not only around the conditions attached to the introduction of the MSIC, but also around the specific areas of the port that needed an MSIC to enter. There was a demand by the OTS that all entering a passenger pier should have an MSIC or be accompanied by someone who did. This was seen as both impractical and was argued to show a misunderstanding of the port environment by the regulator. One security officer recounted his conversations with the OTS around access:

> I said in the airport you only have to have an ASIC card on the airport apron, not the whole terminal. So I said (to the OTS), 'if you're going to be fair about this, if you want us to employ at our main passenger pier an access regime for five thousand people walking through the front door you take your ASIC point and have it at the front door of every airport and see what problems you have with everyone walking in, whether they need an escort to walk onto the airport, every person going in on it.' ... They seemed to think that they could take the aviation model and put that over the maritime [context] and everything would be fine and they're just two totally different environments. ... I mean airports are fairly rigid. They're there and they're in this box building ... and that's where you have to protect. Yes, we can have our ship to shore interface which is the centre of gravity for us, but you know we've got ports everywhere and we've got an enormous amount of people coming in and going and their working environments and it's totally different. (30, p.10)

Different seaports arrived at different conclusion about who should, and should not, need an MSIC. Strictly speaking, MSICs were only required in security sensitive areas of the port and at the port as a whole if the security threat assessment level was lifted from a level 1 (normal level) to a level 2, a level where there was considered to be a heightened risk of a non-site-specific security threat. The smallest port in the study felt that MSICs should be required at all times in all areas, even at level 1:

> Well if you're not going to comply, don't come ... all the people who have MSICs we get them to wear it, even at level 1. Because it's port security, so I thought, you know, there's no big deal in wearing an MSIC. They've got to wear an ID anyway. (So your standards in a sense are above what's required?) Yeah, so basically when you go to level 2, there's very little to do ... at a level 2, we would say, 'anybody without an MSIC either must leave or you must be accompanied by somebody with an MSIC.' Whereas if you turn around and say, 'oh we're going to level 2 now' and everybody says, 'oh gee, my MSIC's at home' that's a hell of a lot of use to you! If you've got to wear ID anywhere, why not wear your MSIC? It's the same with us – I've got my MSIC on one side and my maritime ID on the other. ... I don't see it as a problem. I really think that it should be compulsory even at a level 1 for everywhere. (60, p.10)

Some larger ports, however, were concerned to keep the number required to have an MSIC under control. A wide array of contractors needed access to larger ports to work at repairing port infrastructure and to deliver cargo and to require each to have an MSIC visible at all times whilst at the port, even when the level of threat was low at level 1, would be both costly and a logistical headache. The population of contractors was always shifting as people moved in and out of employment and the number potentially needing an MSIC could be considerable. One port had success in limiting the number of MSICs required and had decided that most entering the port would not be required to have an MSIC, only a port access card. This port had made the decision that an increase to level 2 was unlikely and had argued successfully to the OTS that only a port access card should be required for most people to enter the port.

This example of a port arguing for a lesser standard of security than was present in security plans at commensurate ports was rarely encountered in this study. Most often the trajectory was for security requirements to increase, not decrease. Overall, as the argument for biometrics above illustrates, the trajectory was for ever- increasing security demands. The impact on some, particularly foreign seamen, was considerable:

> … Most of the time in this new security regime era, the crew are actually not allowed ashore. … Some of the ports are so strict on that that they won't even allow the crew to come down and stand on the shore alongside the ship unless they've been issued with a MSIC card. They're foreign, they've got to stay on the ship, that's what it is like. They stay on the ship, 15 hours later the ship leaves. (42, p.21)

Security brought order and control. Order and control could be both beneficial and problematic not only for foreign sailors, but also for other regulatory concerns of the port. In terms of safety, strict access and greater order was seen predominantly to bring safety dividends. One manager commented:

> We've implemented all the measures in as practical manner as we can, and they serve the useful purpose to the industry. Occupational health and safety is probably the biggest winner out of all this because we had an open berth and people could drive a truck up to the side of a ship unannounced and do whatever. Once we'd put the fence around and [controlled] access to the secured area, significant health and safety risks were minimised. So, and of course in introducing the maritime security identification card, we piggy backed an occupational health and safety induction (onto that). (41, p.20)

But speedy access to avoid an injury at times of emergency could be a problem. Occasionally, there was the need for swift repairs (often involving welding or 'hot work') to ships or containers. The access to the ships was made more difficult by the security regime and, in particular, because the port and stevedoring companies had separate security plans that were not coordinated. This meant that stevedoring companies would require 24-hour notice under their security plan before necessary repair work could be undertaken that would create a potential safety risk to those in the vicinity. These companies argued that the OTS would consider them in breach of their plan if they were flexible in allowing repair workers through to the dock. There was a conflict in regulatory requirements between the state-based OHS regime and the Federal security regime. As Commonwealth (Federal) law overrode state law the security regime prevailed.

This problem of coordination was recognised by the OTS. A review process in 2007 had led to a port-wide risk assessment regime being implemented where all facilities on the port (so called Marine Industry Partners or MIPS) were encouraged to coordinate their security activities through publication of a 'Good Practice Guide'. However, the primary concern here was to enhance security, not to resolve conflicts with other regulatory demands. At one port there were new committees being set up to try to deal with inconsistencies in regulations and disparate demands that arose across the port. However, each regulatory regime had generated a new committee, essentially with the same participants. Emergency management, security, safety and environment each had generated new demands for coordination and hence for a new committee to be created. Over time it was expected that these separate committees would be consolidated, but the increased workload was notable.

Overall, the new security regime had come at some considerable cost. These costs were met by both the ports themselves and each operator at the port required to develop their own security plan. For the larger ports, these costs could be in the 'tens of millions' (30, p.22). What was noteworthy was that this cost was borne largely by state and territory governments; the level of additional funding provided by the Commonwealth Government for port security, for example at small ports (as it had done for small airports), was non existent. Costs mounted for both the hardware and technology as well as for personnel. As with the airports the costs of security personnel could be considerable, a demand for 24-hour surveillance, for example, required employing five new security guards at approximately $100,000 per person.

The cost needed to be understood in light of the size of the operation. Small operators faced lower costs but given their capacity to pay could find themselves no longer viable. One manager commented:

> … We've got a single man who runs a line boat. He's a one man business. He was required to produce his security plan and have it approved by the Department of Transport (OTS), to undergo audits and if he was running close to the line it could have been enough to push him over the edge. But that's the requirement of the Code and the Act and he therefore had to comply or get out of the business. (41, p.3)

Money spent on security was money that could not be spent elsewhere. Ports pointed to projects that had been pushed aside or slowed down, such as the upgrading of amenities for recreational craft, because of the demand for increased security. Despite the challenges of implementing the new security regime, what was striking was that over time there was an embracing of the counter-terrorism security regime and of the technology. Ports and MIPs such as stevedoring companies embraced security. This begs an obvious question about why they eventually took to security with such enthusiasm. From a regu-latory point of view it might be assumed that the reason was that the risk of a terrorist attack had been reduced, that is that their enthusiasm related to the purpose of the regime. The ports in this study, though, appeared somewhat ambivalent about whether the regime had indeed reduced the likelihood of an attack. This ambivalence related to both the likelihood of attack as well as their capacity to prevent an attack. Most felt the level of threat their port faced in terms of an attack was not able to be assessed. Further, they could try to reduce this unknown level of threat, but gaps would inevitably remain:

> Well, what's the chance of a terrorist act? So basically you can only cover so many bases. If you really want to get into some place, you can. And if you're willing to die to do it, then it's relatively simple. ... It becomes a way of life [the security regime], the more people are aware of it the harder it will be, because you might just need that little bit of information that somebody noticed, passed on to prevent some-thing [happening]. But in the end, I think it would be, easy, fairly easy to do a lot of damage. (60, p.15)

What was achieved was 'target hardening' that is to deflect the problem else-where. Security personnel at ports did consider their workplaces to be under threat from attack. However, heightened security meant that an attack was more likely outside of the port environment – and to be someone else's problem:

> Why we do this? Because we're not under threat? Well we are. But it's the protec-tion measures that delineate, I suppose, and mitigate the threat. For instance, we put so many measures in our passenger pier, that we've mitigated the threat to outside the front gate. ... now the threat's in the parking area in front of the pier. It's not my land, not my area, it's the Council's. [I say] 'Council you've got a problem.' 'Oh why have we got a problem?' 'Because we've mitigated our threat, the threat's now outside ...' (30, p.29)

The nebulous nature of the threat of attack meant that the sense of security was just as important at ports as it had been at airports. Security was to be found in surveillance, screening, fences and other forms of security technology:

> I think any security measures give people some understanding that their work envi-ronment's safer than what it was before. And while people are unhappy that there's gates there and they've got to go through a guard or they've got to have swipe

access, the feeling inside is much more, 'I feel safer' than having an open plan. And I mean you read the newspaper and people are going to do this. Well, when they see big fences and lights and that and they have a lot of comfort in that. (30, p.24)

This sense of security in the face of a nebulous threat alone, though, does not explain the level of enthusiasm for the security regime. The reason for the level of support was because of the advantages that flowed from order and control. Order and control brought many advantages, such as increased safety noted above. Order could also bring benefits to environmental risks, reducing waste and pollution.

Both larger ports in this study also highlighted the business efficiencies that flowed from the need under the new security regime to notify the port in advance of a ship arriving by sea or a freight delivery by land. A port manager explained:

All of a sudden people had to really think – hey, I've got to get my containers in! And then from the port's point of view you weren't holding the ship up – the ship has advance notice [of] what's coming down. If it's 24 hours (notice) for cargo you can't bring any more cargo in. So definitely from an efficiency side it (the security regime) helped. (53, p.16)

Order also bought relief from 'nuisance' demands. Harbourmasters, port managers and supervisors could control access to the port, even reduce political demands. One harbourmaster recalled with some relish controlling the demands of local politicians to grandstand with their mates and refusing access to an inter-state politician who had failed to give advanced notice of a visit to his port:

In the past, we had a minister ... and he would bring all his members down, his friends down, there'd be alcohol drunk on the port, and the port, actually the port manager went down there and he told him in no uncertain terms and foul language to bugger off. ... We just ring DoTARS now. ... There's a lot of advantages that came in from that (security regime). And we've had a minister from another state just got up by the gate, rang me and said, 'Do you want to let me in?' 'No, sorry, I say, you haven't informed us. You haven't got the correct documentation, go away.' 'But I'm the Minister of other state!' 'I don't care, you could be God. Go away. Off you go.' (53, p.7)

The new security also had seen a marked decline in vandalism and theft. This had led to a decline in insurance premiums, not only for one of the ports but also for the private stevedoring companies that leased port land. Preventing terrorism had brought tangible benefits.

Overall, the significant authority of the security regime had provided both ports and private companies with a powerful tool of control. It could be used to further social goals, such as safety, but also to simplify decisions, reducing accountability by keeping 'troublemakers' out. The controls included reducing access to union officials with the security regime being a powerful weapon in an ongoing industrial war.

Ultimately, the benefits of the security regime lay not principally in security, but in a plethora of other domains. It was in the level of control it afforded to those charged with improving security that its attraction was found. This distortion of purpose was well understood by one security manager:

> ... What's in fact happening is that people are using the security regime for their own purposes to streamline their business processes and blaming it on security. And in fact they're quite open in saying, 'We are being required to do this by the Department of Transport.' Which is nonsense, the Department of Transport doesn't tell them what to put in the plan, they just authorise a plan. [But] the people who have caused the problem are pointing at [the] Department of Transport. The Department of Transport say, 'Hey, it's not our plan. We just approved it. If you want to change it you change it.' But they don't want to change it because it's there for their own purposes, non-security purposes. (41, p.12)

Here, the orientation of the OTS in looking for greater security was important to understand. All the ports in this study argued that their relationship with the OTS was good, despite a rocky beginning. The local regulator, distinct from headquarters, was seen as professional and helpful. But, this did not change the basic orientation of the regulator towards tighter and tighter security. The seaport discussed above, which wanted to have a lesser level of security, had to argue vociferously that it was appropriate for their circumstances. In contrast, placing ever tighter levels of control in a security plan was rarely, if ever, questioned. Hence tight control used for a range of purposes unrelated to security could flourish.

This trajectory towards tighter control under a security plan and the level of threat seen to reside in the regulator, the OTS, could spur a contest of authority between regulators. Customs had traditionally been considered the regulator with arguably the greatest level of authority at the ports. This dominance was now under threat. Competition for authority between multiple regulators appeared in different guises whether enforcement officers were armed, for example, or whether they had the authority to stop a ship from coming to port. The following exchange in an interview with various port staff illustrates this dynamic well:

> Interviewee 1: ... There's a bit of friction between DoTARS and Customs. Customs seems to be getting more and more patrols, they've got armed people onboard, and I notice in the meetings as well, you know, Customs started it, DoTARS started it.
> Interviewee 2: You know, they come stepping into our area.
> Interviewee 1: Yeah. And you could see that from day one that that was going to happen. Interviewer: Right.
> Interviewee 1: But see you'll get – like customs can stop a ship from sailing. (Department of) Immigration, AQIS[10] can stop a ship. AMSA[11] can stop a ship from sailing, and DoTARS. There's five regulators here ...
> Interviewee 2: Fisheries.

Interviewee 1: And Fisheries can stop a ship, yeah, that's another one. Six. ASIO, seven. Federal Police, you know, they can stop it as well.
Interviewee 2: And we can.
Interviewee 1: Yeah, there's about eight of those different organizations that can stop that ship from sailing, for their own different things you know. (53, p.28)

Clearly, subject to such an array of controls the life of a ship captain became considerably more complex than it was. In the same interview the port managers reflected on the growing challenges for sea captains, at a time when the number of sailors on a merchant vessel had declined dramatically over three or four decades from an average of around 100 to little more than 10. Ultimately, the seaport security regime, a relative latecomer to the counter-terrorism environment, had made its presence well and truly felt. There were considerable implementation challenges that were encountered by the ports in this study. As with airports, technology could be problematic and security managers complained about a 'one size fits all' orientation of the security regime. This time it was a complaint levelled against the use of an airport regime in a seaport environment. But the overriding finding of the case studies of the ports was that there was strong support for the regime. This support, however, lay not in the capacity of the regime to reduce the threat of terrorism; indeed, respondents were ambivalent about the capacity of security to prevent an attack. The best they could hope for was displacement, which was their principal goal. But the security regime had tangible associated benefits, from improved safety and environmental standards to the capacity to control every-day irritations from political demands to industrial strife.

Diminished in this shift to security and control were human relationships and community activities. Fishing on the dock was a thing of the past and relationships with foreign sailors largely gone. Improved pollution control might have resulted in fish good enough to eat, but security meant that catching them was now considered to conceal a potential terrorist threat. Finally, the loss of historical marine traditions such as the sharing of knowledge of captains, crew and ships engineers and the decline of the social aspects of the merchant marine, meant that maritime expertise in Australia appeared to be on the wane. In its stead was ever tighter control aided by, sometimes effective, technology.

CONCLUSION

Compliance demands emanating from the counter-terrorism regulatory regime were shaped primarily by the need to protect trade and industry and to secure enhanced political legitimacy for the incumbent government. In the airport context, the primary concerns of the regime were to keep the airlines flying, to capitalise on the demands for security aired in the media, to assuage public anxieties and demonstrate political leadership in the face of threat. Those at airports charged with ever-increasing demands for security screening or other forms of surveillance were well positioned to understand both the wastage of resources applied to reduce the risk of a terrorist attack in some areas and also the gaps in security that still remained. For most, the pattern of demands was contoured by the demand to keep the planes flying, ships sailing and the media critics quiet.

The maritime environment did not attract the same level of public scrutiny as did airports. However, here too the compliance demands were shaped by the need to retain trade with the US (and so protect US borders) and respond to local political demands for the seaports to enhance security. For seaports, however, the strong trade union presence (albeit somewhat diminished) meant that compliance demands were shaped not only by local industry pressure, but also by union demands, particularly in the nature of background checking of those able to work in the seaport environment.

This political and economic character to compliance demands should not lead to an assumption that air and seaports felt they were not a target for attack. There were arguments made that the security regime was too heavy handed, particularly at smaller airports. However, most felt there was a need for improved security and that the threat of terrorism was real. The challenge, however, was that this actuarial risk of attack could not be accurately gauged. Each site aspired to create layers of security: multiple obstacles that a would-be terrorist would need to overcome before they were successful. But these layers were always incomplete. Further, the layers were not uniformly distributed but shaped by the demands of the industry to keep planes flying and trade moving. So, a narrative of attack was generated and the security plans shaped around this narrative.

This narrative was assisted by the regulator, the OTS. Whilst port experience with the regulator was difficult in the early weeks and months after the regimes were put in place, over time a good working relationship was developed. Both air and seaports came to respect the OTS and to feel that, on the whole, that most (but not all) of their demands were reasonable. However, as the relationship improved, the emphasis subtly shifted from preventing an attack to negotiating what the detailed requirements of compliance actually were.

The security plans at both types of port shared similar – visible – features. Each element needed to resonate with what the public and the media would consider as 'good' security. This led to an almost generic quality to the 'individualised' plans, fences, screening, access control, surveillance and policing. Both port environments were the target of security companies keen to capitalise on this burgeoning market for new technology and in both environments the technology could fail to live up to expectations.

Yet, this narrative around the likely method of future attack developed through the dialogue between regulator and regulated was always vulnerable, particularly at airports. It could be exposed by resourceful investigative journalists, by the political opposition or by a subsequent attack overseas. The narrative was then exposed as a fiction and a new set of security demands would arise. This in turn acted as a catalyst for a further round of demands for technological innovations, such as biometric controls on identification cards, for example, or enhanced screening at regional airports. The nature of this vulnerability to increased security demands differed at seaports. They were less visible to the public eye and the sheer volume of trade meant that total surveillance remained a distant vision. Demands for enhanced security could be more easily shaped to meet local needs.

What was striking at seaports was the eventual enthusiasm that existed for the new security regime. Perhaps because the demands were more easily shaped, the controls that eventuated were seen in a range of ways to enhance the efficiency, security and even the safety of the port. Critically, access control was a powerful weapon, particularly because it was underpinned by a well-resourced and politically well-placed regulator. Threatening troublesome politicians or union members with the wrath of the OTS was a powerful tool. The counter-terrorism regulatory vehicle was indeed a useful one to achieve many varied goals.

These growing regulatory demands, however, needed to be considered separately from compliance. Day-to-day demands could create holes in security layers, by sidestepping a suspicious package procedure, by asking for (and obtaining) exemptions for screening or by inventing ways to accommodate local demands for a funeral tradition or for a local businessman to park his private jet. These gaps could be created either in consultation with the regulator or under their gaze. Control was never likely to be total. Whether these gaps created a heightened possibility for an attack was impossible to ascertain, but they did create potential ingredients for future criticisms and media speculation about 'lax security.'

The changes wrought by the counter-terrorism security regime were indeed transformative. They generated a reliance on technology, screening and suspicion in the stead of enhanced relationships of trust. Social pastimes, such as fishing from a dock, and educational pursuits such as school visits could be submerged under the weight of security demands. Security also threatened the authority of the considerable number of other regulators with an interest in air and seaports. Tensions between regulators could rise and competitions in regulatory authority erupt. This transformation in social relationships did not arise from the security regime alone, however. Economic policies of corporatisation and privatisation also changed the nature of established relationships, as did the growing use of technology in both the maritime and airline industries, technology which enhanced efficiency and productivity rather than increased security. The irony here is that this emphasis on control and efficiency and the technology that assisted it was spurred in part by the demand for reassurance by the public that it was safe to travel by air and reassurance to workers that the port was a safer workplace.

NOTES

1. The OTS was referred to using several different names by both air and seaports, the OTS, DoTARS (The Department of Transport and Regional Services, the department that housed the OTS) or simply the Department of Transport. For this reason, these terms are all used in this chapter to denote the regulator.
2. Each quotation from interviews undertaken as part of this research is referenced by a transcript number and by the specific page of the transcript where the quotation appears.
3. This was a reference to John Howard, the Prime Minister at the time of interview.
4. Regular public transport. RPT aircraft are those on a regular schedule as opposed to charter aircraft that fly only when paid to do so by the individual or group chartering the aircraft.
5. General aviation refers to private planes that are flown by their owners and charter flights. General aviation did not have the same level of requirements under the counter-terrorism regime. General aviation could, and often was, co-located with RPT aircraft although at different locations on the airport site.
6. Since this research took place full body screening and screening of cargo has moved to a more prominent position with Australia aiming to follow the lead of the US where 100 per cent screening of cargo on passenger flights was required from 1 August 2010.
7. A security firm.
8. Small boat.
9. As noted above, the regulator was named as both The Department of Transport and Regional Services (DoTARS) that referred to the department as a whole and the Office of Transport Security (OTS), a more accurate term relating to the particular office within the department that had responsibility for the security regulatory regime. Occasionally, interviewees would also use the generic term the Department of Transport for the same regulator.
10. Australian Quarantine and Inspection Service.
11. Australian Maritime Safety Authority.

8. Finance, compliance and the ambiguity of actuarial risk

The financial reforms that emanated from HIH, in both the insurance and investment regimes (as discussed in Chapter 5 pp. 123–39), affected a far broader range of businesses than either the major hazard or counter-terrorism reforms. In the case of prudential reforms to insurance, they had the potential to influence purchasing decisions concerning insurance cover for their business. The insurance reforms discussed above (pp. 124–32) had the potential to increase the cost to business of purchasing insurance from an Australian-based insurer, hence making the decision to source insurance overseas more attractive. The corporate law reforms (CLERP 9) primarily affected public companies within Australia, but changes to accounting practices, such as the move to International Financial Reporting Standards (IFRS), affected all business sectors, public and private, government and not-for-profit.

The assessment of the impact of both prudential and financial regulatory reforms undertaken in this research was restricted. This research primarily analysed the impact of the prudential and financial reforms on the facilities studied in the previous chapters: namely the major hazard facilities, sea and airports. For this reason, the analysis undertaken here should be viewed with these particular sectors in mind. However, to understand the impact of these reforms it became essential to place them within the broader financial regulatory framework and industry setting. To assist in this, interviews were also undertaken with the Insurance Council of Australia (ICA), the peak body representing the Insurance industry and the Institute of Chartered Accountants of Australia (ICAA), one of the professional bodies representing accountants. This contextualisation allowed a much more nuanced understanding of the particular experiences the MHFs and ports studied in Chapters 6 and 7 had as they grappled with the financial reforms first hand and the prudential reforms through their experiences in gaining insurance in the post-HIH era. In turn, the analysis of the experience of these sites shed light on the challenges that are faced by reforms aimed at ensuring a robust financial and prudential regulatory environment.

Critically, the nature of risk and regulation in the financial sphere needs to be understood in light of the essence of actuarial risk in the context of finance and the complexity of its calculation. There were several elements that impinged on such a calculation. The first was to understand the way the calculation spanned both the abstract and the concrete. At the most abstract level, the assets and liabilities of the businesses studied in this research existed primarily as numbers on a ledger or on the computer. Here the transactions of a business were financial, that is, they involve the switching of figures between the businesses, their debtors and creditors (such as insurers, finance companies, banks and the like). A distinction was made by the sites between losses that may occur here (so called financial losses) and cash losses. Cash losses and gains were considered more 'real' and were anchored in the product or service at the heart of the business, the sales of a particular chemical from an MHF or the receipts from airlines to an airport (for example, through landing charges). A negative assessment in both areas could threaten a business, but financial losses were more restricted and might represent no more than a change in the way a particular asset or liability should be calculated: 'they are not cash losses, they are financial losses' (49, p.29)[1] stated one in response to a question of the impact of new accounting rules. An assessment of the solvency of a business, then, required teasing apart what was a tangible threat or tangible asset as opposed to a figure that may, or may not be realised as 'real' sometime in the future.

The second element here was the way that financial losses materialised as cash losses. The actual process by which financial losses materialised into cash losses and the particular point at which they did so was ambiguous and opaque. The interaction between the financial and realised gains and losses necessarily made the calculations of actuarial risk, such as the level of solvency or of profit subject to various interpretations. These differences in calculation or application of a particular rule could be entirely legitimate, that is, they may not represent a wilful misrepresentation of the risks or profits involved. So, for example, during interviews there was discussion about the collapse of HIH and arguments made by some that HIH could have traded its way out of its particular predicament. The following was a good example of this, where an interviewee argued, 'I mean they obviously tried to paper over all the cracks at the end and tried to trade their way out of the problem,' that is, they tried to re-orientate the *financial* representation of the company (the figures on a budget sheet or figures on a screen) to allow it to be represented as solvent. He continued, '... and I think there are still some people who think they might have actually achieved that if they had enough time,' (9, p.9) according to this view, time would have allowed the tangible assets to have materialised from the financial projections constructed by accountants and accepted by auditors.

The necessary corollary here was that there needed to be public and market confidence in the figures presented. Assessments of value, solvency and business prospects in essence comprised an analysis of figures (in a manner allowed for in the particular regulatory standard) and confidence in those figures, that they provided a reasonable account of the particular business's prospects, which in turn meant the figures represented something of value. Figures needed to be understood as more than empty representations, merely arbitrary figures on a page.

The paradox here is that 'just financial losses' generated by a change of a regulatory standard may also be viewed an oxymoron – if that new standard as required by regulatory reform was indeed an attempt to capture more accurately the worth of a business. There was ambiguity created here where changes to regulatory standards that altered a financial assessment of a business needed to be understood both as 'more accurate' and 'not real' at the same time.

This ambiguity in the calculation of actuarial risk was the space where prudential, accounting and auditing standards attempted to construct an assessment of the liabilities and assets of a business and, in the case of prudential standards, the capacity an insurer had for meeting insurance claims into the future. This was the place where actuarial risk assessments were made by accountants, actuaries and accepted by auditors that attempted to capture the impact and probability of various liabilities and profits arising and collectively a representation of the capacity of a business trading profitably into the future.

But there is a further complication here. From a philosophical standpoint, the demands made by the financial regulators were not designed to inform the Government or even the public per se about actuarial risk. Under a capitalist democracy, financial regulators are not akin to a financial police force. Their purpose is to allow the market to keep business competitive and productive. The ultimate 'regulator' here is the market, that space where buyers and sellers jockey for advantage and investors enter to multiply their capital. The market, however, depends on risk *taking* and, because of this, attempts by governments and regulators to tighten definitions of financial risk can be viewed as misplaced. As Pat O'Malley (2004) has argued it is uncertainty, not risk, that underlies entrepreneurialism. Interviewees, too, pointed to the need for vibrant markets that thrived on individuals pushing the boundaries, of individuals taking risks, and where failure was not only inevitable but desirable:

> [If you] want the system to work, then failure on the part of some of them [businesses] is a necessary ingredient to having good outcomes, otherwise you will have mediocre performance, no one will be stretching themselves ... you are in a race, some of the athletes push themselves too far in the endeavour to win, or they make their run too early and they're not there at the end, but without them in the race you've got no competition, you never going to get better times. It's no different in a commercial environment as well, so that's why I think we have to be careful in that if one of them falls over we don't, in the effort to address the problems that arose around that, kill the whole system. (31, p.3)

From this perspective, then, the process by which financial gains and losses materialise was necessarily opaque to ensure the productive functioning of the market system. Ambiguity provided the requisite environment for the taking of risk that could allow competition to flourish. If the calculation of risk, particularly through regulatory standards, were to be too clear then the incentive to question that calculation might be lost and with it the risk-taking that was understood to lie at the heart of the productivity of competitive markets. Hence, businesses were seen to depend on some ambiguity in order to trade their way to greater profitability or, in the case of lean times, out of difficulty.

The fact that the corporate collapse of HIH Insurance involved an insurance entity meant that some understanding of the nature of insurance was also required to allow a reflexive analysis of the impact of reform that took account of the norms of that industry. This added a level of complexity to this particular corporate collapse and its consequences. At a fairly basic material level it was important to understand that insurance requires (at least) three players: firstly the insurance broker who acts as an intermediary to find (secondly) an insurance underwriter who is willing to shoulder the liability should the event insured against eventuate. Thirdly are reinsurers who are approached by underwriters to take on some of their liabilities in exchange for a fee (an arrangement that takes place through a reinsurance contract).

In addition, there were two other financial practices at play here: risk spreading and hedging. Risk spreading requires a sufficient spreading of the liability burden amongst a given population in order for the funds to be amassed to pay off claims. Hence within a particular line of insurance, a sufficient pool of money needs to be amassed (for example gained through premiums) in order to be able to pay out on claims in a timely manner. For this reason, if a calculation was made that potential claims might be costly (as is often the case of low probability but high-impact risks) and the potential population at risk was small then an insurer may well make the decision that they would not insure for this particular form of risk. In this case, if the insurance cover was seen as necessary and in the public interest then the Government needed to step in and, for example, require risk spreading over a wider population or to provide the insurance themselves (for example through various state insurance offices). For this reason, the insurance industry and governments have a close relationship.

The second component to understand both in the context of insurance and finance more generally was hedging. At a very simple level, hedging can be understood as an arrangement where two parties come together with one party placing their money on a position that a particular liability will not be realised and the other that the same liability will be realised. A business may enter a hedging arrangement, for example through a contract that fixes the price for certain raw materials it knows it will need at a certain point in the future. The business saves money if the cost of raw materials rises above the contract price[2] when the time for purchase arrives. Hedging (in this case through a futures contract) can be used to provide some certainty when the price of raw materials is volatile. Hedging has a somewhat ambiguous nature, though. On the one hand, it can be seen as a conservative strategy since it reduces financial risk, yet on the other hand it can also be viewed as a gamble with the finances used to hedge various positions akin to a series of bets that the value of a particular good will rise or fall.

The insurance industry also can be likened to a series of hedging arrangements. At an extremely simple level it can be understood as follows. A person who has never had a car accident decides to take out comprehensive car insurance. In doing so they are 'hedging' against the possibility of a future accident, even though they have never experienced such a loss. They are willing to pay out a certain amount so that in the eventuality of an accident they will not be liable for the costs incurred. The insurance company (or more accurately the underwriter) takes the other side of the hedge. They are accepting money ('a bet') that the owner will not have an accident or that some other misfortune will not befall the car. But they may then also hedge this position. So, the underwriter may then take a pool of money gained from such premiums and purchase reinsurance (another 'bet') that allows it to cover an eventuality such as a hailstorm where a great number of those insured will claim all at the same time. In this case, through the purchase of reinsurance, the underwriter is 'making a bet' that the hailstorm will occur, the reinsurer that it will not.

It will be clear from the above example that the insurance relationships from client, to broker, to underwriter and to reinsurer can be understood both as an exercise in risk spreading and as an exercise in hedging. The insurance industry emerges as a complex amalgam of relationships aimed at spreading and hedging risk. In the case of insurers in the private sector, such as HIH, they are also, however, profit-maximising entities. As profit-maximising entities, they may change their character depending on the regulatory framework they are working under and the particular market conditions they face. At one extreme they appear not as an insurance company at all, but as an investment house. So, up until the time of the collapse of HIH Insurance, the premiums paid to insurers by clients could not, and did not, cover the costs of HIH's liabilities. This was common practice throughout Australian insurers; the profitability of the industry as a whole did not stem from their premiums, but was made through the investment market. Premiums provided money (a cash flow) that could be invested in a whole array of the opportunities the investment market held. The profits from investments then paid both for claims made on insurance contracts and provided the profits for the business as a whole.

The character of the industry altered dramatically as a response to the HIH collapse. The Insurance Council explained:

One of the market consequences of HIH failing and a lot of other things happening at the same time was that … for the last four years, or three and a half at least, the insurance industry all around the world has produced underwriting profits, which [are] profits before investment income on its core business. It has not done that in my memory since the early 70s. … For 30 years [before that] the industry has lived off investment income, basically. So it wasn't HIH alone. I mean [this] was the way the whole market worked. And because it's a global market with very few barriers to access, and you're faced with global price competition, I mean you're up against 'London's doing it, Bermuda's doing it, everyone else.' So you can stand in the market and say, 'I'm not going to match all these prices' [but] people [will] say 'fine, you know, well we won't insure with you.' So price competition tends to drive down the overall market. HIH was the ultimate of price cutters in this market, they drove the market prices for the liability insurance business in particular to a floor and that led to the valid crisis. (9, p.9)

INSURANCE

This context both in terms of the complex nature of actuarial risk in the financial arena and the character of the insurance industry provides an important backdrop to understanding the impact on the case study sites of the insurance reforms. To an extent, their experience reflects and extends the discussion begun in Chapter 6 where consideration was given to whether insurers acted as a secondary regulator in the case of major hazard risk. The discussion in that chapter highlighted that MH risk reduction was most often not a central consideration of a particular insurance contract, and whilst there could be some benefits arising out of the concern of insurers about a client's capacity to manage and reduce their risk, they tended to be some-what tangential to those of MHF managers and not to drive their compliance activities. The audits often were largely rather perfunctory and the impact on premiums insignificant. Of greater importance to the site was the capacity they had to combine lines of insurance or the leverage they exerted over insurance costs by virtue of their purchasing power (if it were a multinational operation, for example) … Both these factors could reduce the cost of insurance to a particular site. Yet, the connection between the risk management practices of the site and the premium paid cases, on the whole, was rather remote.

Overall, there were two elements that drove the insurance practices of the case study sites at the MHFs, seaports and airports studied: namely cost and the convention in a particular insurance line. So, for example at the time of writing much insurance in the case of aviation was underwritten in London, hence the airports in this study (particularly those larger airports) looked to London to underwrite their facilities for aviation-related insurance. It was here that the expertise to write such insurance was to be found. Alternatively, general insurance was commonly underwritten in Australia with Australian insurers prominent and trusted.

The dominant concern of the case study sites from the point of the financial officers interviewed was with the cost of insurance. In turn, the cost of insurance related to the competitiveness of the insurance market, the skills of the broker and the capacity of a particular site such as port or airport to combine its insurance requirements, together with the needs of other sites owned by the same operator. The experience of the reforms to insurance companies and the higher costs that may have resulted were experienced by the sites as a harder insurance market, one where insurance companies could be less inclined to take on particular risks and to charge higher premiums. Ultimately, it was difficult in this research to disentangle whether higher costs of insurance were driven by the conditions of the insurance market (brought about through a lack of competition) or whether the tighter regulations had increased costs that were then passed down to insured clients.

The difficulty and cost in attracting sufficient cover in the wake of the HIH collapse led some sites to take a number of steps to increase their attractiveness or to decrease their overall insurance requirements. For example, during 2002–03 one site had their insurance broker restructure their risk in their major portfolio area (Industry Special Risk (ISR)) into smaller units to make it more attractive to insurers: 'We basically had to split it [ISR] up into two or three segments [after HIH] to actually get the reinsurance market to cover us' (52, p.7) they commented.

This same site found an opportunity in the challenging insurance environment to reassess its risk and insurance profile. In light of the cost and difficulty of gaining insurance cover, insurance costs would no longer be considered as 'a cost of doing business' as they had in the past but would be carefully assessed to see if they were entirely necessary to the overall running of, in this case, a seaport. This business brought in a consultant to analyse its operations to assess the need for cover based on the cost of the liabilities involved. The port decided as a result that in some areas the costs of insurance outweighed the benefits. Hence, certain assets would remain uninsured[3] as the cost of insurance was simply too high and any outlay, should it be necessary, sufficiently manageable for the business to cover its own liabilities in that area.

An important element in terms of what the case study sites needed to do to obtain sufficient insurance cover was in understanding the impact of different business structures as well as any change in ownership. For example, an airport in a mining town gained preferable premiums for its insurance needs because of its relationship to the mining company. Its insurance costs were much lower than would otherwise have been the case. Privatisation of an asset (such as an airport) by government or sale of a site from one company to another could have major ramifications for the cost of insurance for that facility. In one MHF, the sale of the business by a major multinational, with a comprehensive experience in MH risk, to an Asian consortium, with a much lower level of experience, brought with it particular challenges in renegotiating insurance cover. The previous owners had principally self-insured against much of the MH risk they faced, because the size of their combined assets could cover any liability that arose. Now, under new ownership, the MHF required a third party to cover their MH liability. Nonetheless, there were advantages from their earlier experience with the previous owners and they had been able to gain preferable premiums because of their historical experience in controlling MH risk:

> When we came off the back of [the previous owner] we didn't realise how significant a player we were in the insurance marketplace. A lot of large companies retain a lot of risk so they actually buy a very little risk [i.e. by purchasing insurance]. With us, we've got a significant placement in the marketplace so there's an appetite to insure us … We are a major hazard facility … but what's interesting is when we've had the underwriters in here to look at our business, we run a fantastic program and they're keen to insure the business because they know of all the programs we've run, all the safety standards, that if there's ever an issue hopefully it's going to be well contained. And the likelihood of a major disaster is very unlikely. So we insure for a worst case scenario. Can a plane drop on one of our major sites? Absolutely … the potential impact if it hits the wrong tanks, we're in trouble. But again, take that scenario away [and] the rest of it is very safe. (44, p.13)

As the quote above illustrates, large, well-resourced businesses often can decide (legislation permitting) to cover their own liabilities. Further, the combination of a hardened insurance market and a changed ownership structure could also mean that self-insurance, for certain businesses with sufficient assets, was a clear option. The growing assets involved in the increased level of self-insurance across a number of lines of risk at one MHF led them to consider setting up a separate insurance entity within their broader operations. This led to a further decision, namely, whether to set up this arrangement within Australia or overseas. It was at this point that the post-HIH regulatory framework did impinge directly on their decision-making. This business argued that the increased demands from the regulator made the path to setting up a separate insurance entity within the business uneconomic. They felt that the regulatory requirements were out of proportion to the risk for self-insurers since the insurance business would be set up where the insurer was only insuring their own broader business activities – that is, they were client, broker and underwriter. The concern of APRA with protecting the policyholder by ensuring the underwriter had the means to pay takes a particular flavour in this context. The particular form being considered here by this MHF was what was known as Direct Offshore Foreign Insurer (DOFI). The finance officer explained:

We may set up an insurance company. For a number of reasons you might do that offshore somewhere. If you do that though, there's talk that APRA want to regulate insurance companies like that. But in essence it would be our own in-house insurance company; we would not insure any other third party company. In which case we'd argue why would APRA care about the fact that we are taking money out of the business, parking it somewhere, and using it for a rainy day in case one of the plants has a claim? So rather than us paying multimillion dollars to (our current insurer), we might want to take half of that and put in our own insurance company and insure the other half of the risk with the external insurer. So APRA is saying, 'well hang on, if you do that we might want to regulate how you run this insurance company.' ... But the bureaucracy attached to that would be cost prohibitive. So it would mean that it would be uneconomical for us to actually go out and set up an insurance company. (44, p.27)

The debate over Direct Offshore Foreign Insurers (DOFIs) that emerged after the main tranche of post-HIH reforms to insurance was an important one. From a regulatory point of view the omission of DOFIs from the reforms post-HIH created a loophole, a means by which businesses in Australia could avoid the prudential regulations that emerged in the wake of HIH, by purchasing insurance directly from overseas. The Insurance Council of Australia argued, however, that their concern centred on the loss of business to Australian Insurers. These factors lay behind further reform. The *Financial Sector Legislation Amendment (Discretionary Mutual Funds and Direct Offshore Foreign Insurers) Act* 2007 came into force on 1 July 2008. This required DOFIs to meet the standards as set out in the post-HIH amendments to the Insurance Act 1973. There were exemptions allowed for, however, in the Insurance Amendment Regulations 2008 (Item 4, Part 2, sections 4 to 4E). These exemptions included insurance contracts for: (a) high-value insureds; (b) atypical risks; (c) other risks that cannot be placed in Australia; and (d) those required by foreign laws. These exemptions were designed to meet some of the concerns of the MHF in this study.

Yet, the increased breadth of coverage of Australian regulations aimed to protect Australian insureds, which could be considered a paternalistic view and had the potential to conflict with the individualistic orientation of a market philosophy which places a dominant priority on competition and consumer choice (cf. Haines and Gurney 2003). It was not surprising then, that the tenor of the insurance reforms and their increasing breadth to include DOFIs raised the concerns of the competition regulator, the Australian Competition and Consumer Commission (ACCC). The concern of the ACCC was the potential for the reforms to nurture a 'closed shop' in Australian underwriting and general insurance (a concern shared by the National Insurers Brokers Association) which might then encourage collusion and higher prices between underwriters, even to the point of price fixing (Pratten 2008).

This concern of the ACCC regarding the increasing breadth of the financial

reforms, the tension between the individualism of the market and the pater-
nalism of government intervention can also be seen to reflect the two elements
of political risk. Political risk as we have seen is comprised of the need to keep
the economy vibrant and to encourage entrepreneurial risk-taking, whilst also
assuring the citizenry of their safety and security.

The discussion at the beginning of this chapter on the need for ambiguity
in financial calculations sheds further light on the relationship between actuarial risk in finance and entrepreneurial risk-taking. Actuarial risk calculations
around finance seek to clarify the potential for certain liabilities to come to
fruition whilst entrepreneurial risk-taking thrives in a grey zone of uncertainty.
The insurance industry (underwriters and reinsurers) bridge both camps; as
entrepreneurial businesses they desire ambiguity, yet as insurers they require
clarity. Their desire for clarity stems from their fear of exposure to risk that
they may not have realised they were liable for. One example of this was exposure to asbestos liabilities:

> [The problem you have in the insurance industry] is the growth in latent risks. I
> mean asbestos is obviously the most common example of that now, where insurance
> companies sold policies for a $100 in the 1950s covering asbestosis risk, paying out
> hundreds of millions of dollars on that one policy 50 years down the track. It was
> risk that they never understood and never assessed. … [In the future] we don't really
> know what [other risks] are now going to be [exposed] either, but we know that
> they're out there. (9, p.24)

The fear of the unknown generated extensive requirements for the insured
businesses to provide information to the insurer about the risks of the business
to which the insurer was exposed. This process could be time-consuming, with
the financial officer of one small airport stating, 'Each year we do a pretty
detailed insurance renewal process … there's like fire protection equipments,
security protection equipment, just for your property insurance. There's a
million questions they ask. Basically (the process) knocks all my October out'
(13, p.9).

Here, too, there were risks that underwriters in the private sector were not
willing to cover. In this case it was the risk of cyclone damage. For this reason,
a state insurer was chosen to cover the risk of property damage at this airport
in the north of Australia.

The most pertinent example of exposure to the unknown and the with-
drawal of cover relevant to this study arose in the wake of September 11. The
combined impact of this event and the collapse of HIH Insurance resulted in
Australian insurers withdrawing their cover for a terrorist attack. They argued
that they did not realise the significant impact that such cover could have on
their bottom line. This was unacceptable to government, and seen as a failure
of the private insurance industry at the time when the Australian government

needed to reassure the population and business that they were covered. An attack on an iconic building, such as the Sydney Opera House would be both costly and a blow to Australian pride. Government also needed to ensure that its own budgetary resources were not too exposed in the event of a terrorist attack.

The concerns of the insurance industry need to be viewed in light of the discussion at the beginning of the chapter. The main problem was one of a lack of capacity to spread the risk, should an attack occur on an iconic building. Finding other property owners to share the burden of insurance against a terrorist attack was difficult, 'Let's say you own a poultry processing plant in Dubbo, well no terrorist is ever going to go out there and blow up all your chickens!' (9, p.7) quipped one Insurance Council director. The chicken farmer would not, without compulsion, pay for the insurance cover of the Opera House. In short, the capacity for the industry to spread the risk was seriously limited.

Without the capacity to spread the risk sufficiently in order to amass enough resources, and in light of the regulatory need for terrorist cover to be provided, the Government stepped in. It was made mandatory for insurers to include terrorist risk in their policies as stipulated in the *Terrorism Insurance Act 2003*. Under the Act, insurers could not exclude such risk from their contract. However, the Government set up a reinsurance pool, which combined both private and public monies under the Australian Reinsurance Pool Corporation (ARPC). The ARPC had the capacity, when fully set up, to provide aggregate cover to a maximum of $10.3 billion. Part of this pool was paid for through increases to insurance premiums, that is, it was paid for by the consumer. The pool was thus a public private partnership[4] and envisioned to be temporary. It was reviewable every three years (the most recent in 2009) with the expectation that at some time in the future the private market would be able to both price the risk of terrorist attack with some degree of accuracy and to be able to have amassed sufficient funds to be able to cover their liabilities, should such an attack occur. At the time of this research, however, government involvement in the reinsurance pool was still seen as necessary.

What was demonstrated in this research, though, was the labile nature of political and economic considerations that shaped where liability for risk should lie. Government involvement in coverage in the event of a terrorist attack needed to be carefully considered in light of the other risks where, in the wake of the HIH collapse, insurance cover was removed. Chapter 5 described the reforms to the laws of negligence that recommended insurance companies be allowed to reduce their liability through the use of signed waivers (Ipp 2002). Signed waivers could then transfer the risk of an activity from the owner of a business (and their insurer) to the consumer. Here the consumer would be required to cover the costs of their medical expenses should they be injured, for example, in the case of a specified event (such as an accident during a horse trekking experience). Hence, liability for risk was constantly shifting as government need to reassure the public or the industry waxed and waned.

Overall, despite the reforms to the regulation of the insurance industry the Insurance Council remained troubled by the liabilities of their industry in the light of ambiguity around the limits of coverage within insurance contracts. Because of this, they had recommended to the Government that some form of policy holder protection scheme be set up to provide a basic safety net, a scheme they argued was common to OECD countries. The absence of such a scheme created uncertainty for the industry, unsure of when it might be required to pay into another compensation scheme when the next crisis erupted.

The fluid nature of risk exposure, though, needs to be understood in light of the final area of uncertainty, namely the pricing of the actuarial risk itself. Uncertainty around exposure created uncertainty around the pricing of risk, as it was not possible to price a risk of which underwriters were unaware. Clearly, concerns such as a rise in global terrorism and the risks associated with climate change brought with them challenges of how to price insurance adequately. The need to be alert to future risks was an everyday reality for underwriters and reinsurers:

> Whenever you have an event, whether it's a natural disaster, man made disaster, a new sort of head of damage that gets invented by some creative lawyers or ordered by the courts. ... the industry sits down and evaluates the implications of that for its pricing models, for its exposures, for its reinsurance models. ... that's a constant process that goes on every day of the week. I mean we know one company that's looking at it's pricing of household insurance policies for buildings that are built in bushfire prone areas, because they're now trying to work out, is there a need for a different pricing model? (9, p.3)

The insurance industry response to the collapse of HIH and the regulatory reforms that resulted were shaped by their role as a service industry that could spread risk and one that could allow both consumers and the industry to hedge their potential liabilities. They did this in part through their interaction with government. Through this relationship, the industry sought to reduce their uncertainty and place some liabilities with government, thus enhancing their own profitability.

Too much government involvement, though, was unwanted. The history of insurance demonstrates the impact of nationalisation of certain forms of insurance on the private industry. HIH Insurance, for example, was badly affected when the state stepped in to provide workers' compensation insurance. The fear of greater government intervention meant, that when HIH collapsed, there was a need for the insurance industry to demonstrate its integrity to protect itself against unwelcome intervention and any loss of confidence by the public in the industry which also might result in demands for greater state involvement. To do so, the industry as a whole needed to isolate HIH as a rogue business. The Insurance Council reflected:

> The biggest risk to the industry when HIH went down was the industry's own reputation and we carried the sort of burden for the industry right throughout the Royal Commission process and everything else. I think the media and everyone else concluded that it was a rogue company run by a few rogue people and this wasn't representative of the way the rest of the industry was managed or run. From that point of view I suppose it helped us with the members because we managed to deliver that message for them. (9, p.14)

The impact of the reforms to the insurance regulatory framework was understood at two levels, at the level of the case study sites and at the level of the insurance industry. The impact on the case study sites was muted and hard to distinguish from general increases in the cost of insurance overall. The sites certainly responded to cost increases, while at the same time insurance became more than a cost of doing business to something that needed to be analysed and assessed to determine whether the cost could be reduced (through economies of scale or reduction in the risk insured) or the liabilities covered through the resources of the business itself, in the form of self-insurance.

The response by the insurance industry needed to be viewed as both the response of a service that was concerned that it could provide policyholders with the necessary funds should they be needed, but also as a business that could retain its market share and enhance its future success. There were a range of threats to business profitability that the industry faced from risks that were suddenly realised and that could have a devastating effect (such as the need to fund the losses from a terrorist attack), increased levels of self-insurance and the possibility that a catastrophic loss of the legitimacy of private insurance might see even greater levels of government intrusion in the form of government-provided insurance in areas that profit could be made.

FINANCE

At one level, understanding the impact of the financial reforms arising from the *Corporate Law Economic Reform Program (Audit Reform & Corporate Disclosure) Act 2004* (CLERP 9), on the businesses studied in this research was much more straightforward than assessing the indirect impact of the prudential reforms above. Each of the businesses in this research had to prepare a statement of accounts that needed to be compiled according to revised rules and needed to engage an auditor to audit their accounts, again according to a revised set of rules as set out in the reforms.

Yet, the impact of the reforms was not as significant as might have been expected. The reason for this was quite simple, that is the CLERP 9 reforms primarily targeted public companies, those owned by shareholders and listed on the Australian Stock Exchange. The case study sites in this research comprised a combination of privately-owned sites (the MHFs and some airports) corporatised government entities (seaports) and local government-owned facilities (some sea and airports) and finally not-for-profit entities (some airports) owned by a larger entity (such as a mine). With the exception of privately-owned businesses, the purpose of the case study sites in this research was not to generate profit per se but rather to fulfil a service (for example, air transport services, trade infrastructure) for a particular community, state or the country as a whole. It was clear, however, that some of these not-for-profit and government owned facilities could, in fact, make a profit, but this revenue would be used for public purposes, rather than received by individuals as private income.

The presence of a number of businesses in the study that were owned privately, some by private equity consortiums and some by a single owner[5] raised three important issues with respect to regulatory reform. The first of these was the possibility that the level of private ownership of major firms was rising because of the increasingly onerous requirements of corporate governance that arose from CLERP 9 (Reserve Bank of Australia 2007), as was argued to be the case in the US following the introduction of Sarbanes Oxley, the equivalent corporate governance reforms in that country (Talley 2009). The second was the light that the increase in private equity ownership shed on the emphasis in CLERP 9 on independence as the bulwark against financial mismanagement or misappropriation by executives. Finally, the growth of private equity ownership funded by superannuation funds highlighted the ever-increasing need for high returns on equity – a concern that Palmer (2002) saw as underlying the collapse of HIH Insurance itself.

Clearly, such a small sample cannot provide solid evidence regarding the influence of each of these issues on the growth of private equity ownership, on the impact of this ownership structure on the likelihood of further collapses, or the effectiveness or otherwise of the CLERP 9 and associated reforms in controlling or influencing the activities of private business. Nonetheless, the interviews did provide some insight into the consideration given by businesses to their increased regulatory responsibilities. The research highlighted problems with emphasis in reform on independence between executive and oversight functions as a cornerstone of corporate governance, particularly when the need for investment to reap ever-increasing returns was taken into account.[6] Certainly, for firms that were privately-owned increased regulatory obligations was an issue of concern. One manager commented on the benefits of private ownership:

> If I was running a public company you've got all that hassle on top of all the things that we're running, you've got all that other pressures of compliance and disclosing 'how much money did I earn?' All that sort of stuff ... I think that this is one of the great attractions of private capital going into a public company is that you don't have to put up with a lot of the other nonsense. ... (49, p.32)

Raising the costs associated with running a public company increases the attractiveness of a company to a private equity buyout that could then reap the profits from reduced compliance costs. However, there are other considerations here. The 'push' factor for private equity, the increased amount of funds available to pursue private equity arrangements also needs to be taken into account alongside the 'pull' factors of businesses' lower compliance costs. The argument here was that to understand the rise of private equity, account must be taken of the supply of private equity capital and the demands it makes in terms of investment conditions and the expectation of high returns. Private equity, it was argued, allowed for a closer alignment between the interests of the owners and management in running the business and the business as a whole. That is, for private businesses dependence could bring better results than independence (Reserve Bank of Australia 2007).

This contrast in the value placed on independence between private and public companies was important to understand. Independence was a key element of CLERP 9 and contrasted with the ethos within private equity ownership with its emphasis on the importance of the dependence of the private equity owners on the firms they own. The argument raised by private equity investors was that they can take a long-term view of a firm's profitability, and will do so, because of their close relationship and dependency on the firm to succeed (Reserve Bank of Australia 2007). As Chapter 5 highlighted, there is value on owners' dependence upon outcomes both in public, as well as private, ownership arrangements (Bhidé 2009; Clarke and Dean 2005). In contrast, independence and transparency were fundamental to the CLERP 9 reforms. According to the philosophy behind these reforms, what was needed to protect investors was a strong regime of independent audit and evaluation.

To tease apart this inconsistency between private ownership (where dependency was valued) as opposed to public ownership (where independence was seen as paramount) required close attention be paid to the character of finance and the ambiguity of actuarial assessments of financial risk. In particular, it was important to understand in the financial arena the importance of not only the numbers produced in accounting statements but also how assurance was provided that those numbers were meaningful in terms of the business's underlying value and prospects.

The entry point to this analysis was comments made with respect to the element of the reforms that affected all the case study sites, namely the shift to International Financial Reporting Standards (IFRS) that accompanied the CLERP 9 reforms. IFRS took effect in Australia through the development of Australian versions of these international rules known as AIFRS. At one level, the move to AIFRS represented little more than simply a change in reporting rules. This change in accounting rules, as discussed in the introduction to the chapter, was argued to mean very little in terms of changes to the commercial value of a particular firm or enterprise. Different numbers on the budget sheet were argued to be merely financial gains or losses; they did not have a material impact on the profitability or otherwise of the operation. This was despite the numbers involved being quite considerable. A financial manager at one seaport commented:

> As a result of that our assets went from $40m to $180m ... It looked like we grew our business overnight by $130m, and we thought 'you beauty!' ... What it has done though I suppose on the flipside of that is all of our returns: return on asset, return on equity, has gone down a blazes because we've increased our value so much. (52, p.7–8)

For this government-owned entity it was a matter of educating their political masters about the significance of the change. The financial managers needed to make sure that the increased value of the business was understood to be 'real' on paper only and that the poor return on equity did not mean that there was any substantial fall in productivity at this particular port.

Yet, such a significant change in numbers raised questions about what such numbers actually represented and the relationship they bore to the solvency or otherwise of a particular business.[7] The meaningfulness of the new sets of figures compiled under AIFRS rules was contested by some, despite part of the reason for the implementation of AIFRS being to increase the transparency and communicability of sets of accounts through the standardisation of accounting rules (Pearce 2005; cf. Jones and Higgins 2006). One of the private companies amongst the case study sample was critical of the changes and argued that they were less meaningful than previously had been the case. That is, they communicated less about how well the business was actually travelling, 'It's been a nightmare to be perfectly honest. The implementation of AIFRS has been a huge burden for companies of our size, smaller companies. And in reality we believe the outcomes of the reporting are less meaningful to our users' (56, p.2).

This financial officer recounted how accounts had been prepared and not signed off because of differences in opinion between auditors and accountants about the way values on certain assets should be counted. These differences of opinion had resulted in accounts being prepared twice, with the added expense that this entailed. In this study, the aspiration that the AIFRS would actually result in standardisation of reporting was at some distance from the reality (see also Jones and Higgins 2006).

However, further questions needed to be asked about the reason why standardisation would be desirable from the point of view of enhancing corporate governance. These questions returned to the substance that underpinned the reported figures. Ideally, standard reporting would mean the value associated with the figures could be more clearly assessed both within a particular company over time and between companies. Again, however, this emphasis on substance contrasted with the views of interviewees that these changes were 'merely financial.'

Ultimately, the discussion in the interviews around the introduction of AIFRS when examined closely underscored the essence of financial reporting as comprising a set of figures and assurance that those figures represented something of value. Ideally, financial reporting required both elements. To critics, the shift to AIFRS mistook 'standardisation' with substance, that is, that the figures represented something of value (Clarke and Dean 2005). For proponents, accounts compiled according to a standard set of rules should be able to be compared to one another in a meaningful manner. At one level, the consequential nature of the AIFRS changes could be seen to be enhanced by their emphasis on a principled rather than a prescriptive approach.

A principled approach, however, meant that interpretations of a set of accounts could vary, a variation that troubled ASIC. The requirement to generate a set of accounts resting on key principles meant that there might be a legitimate difference in interpretation. The Institute of Chartered Accountants argued, 'Where you get principles-based standards you can come up with more than one answer' (35, p.8). ASIC, however, was concerned with the production of more than one answer from the same rules as it detracted from the transparency of accounts. The ICAA continued:

> ASIC had originally came out [during the implementation of AIFRS] and implied that well as far as they were concerned there was only one answer and it was the one they agreed with and that was it. Now I notice they've come back and acknowledged that there [can be], in fact, within these standards, [differences] because they're principle-based ... two people could get slightly different views. Now not radically different, right but there are interpretations and, in some of the standards, there are options. (35, p.8)

Yet, there could be subtle shifts in emphasis here. On the one hand, the emphasis could lie on whether there could be different views about the right interpretation of a particular rule; on the other hand there could be different interpretations about whether one interpretation was a more meaningful representation of a business state of affairs than another. In one case the emphasis was on the rule (or principle), the other on what it should represent. From a Weberian standpoint, in the former case the emphasis was on formal rationality and the latter on a substantive concern with representing meaning through the presentation of figures.

The interviews illustrated the bureaucratisation of the process of implementation of the new rules and the institutionalisation of AIFRS rules through a focus on adherence to proper process in completing a set of accounts. The implementation of the AIFRS was assisted in large part by the advice to business accountants from two sources, their professional bodies and their auditors. Professional bodies such as the ICAA were seen as major sources of support and education by keeping accountants abreast of the new changes that were brought in and the philosophy underpinning those changes. In addition, though, were the resources provided by the auditor firms themselves to assist in-house accountants when compiling their figures. These resources could be seen to orientate the business accountant or finance officer towards compliance with the rule, rather than consideration of its meaning. Each of the major auditing firms provided templates of how to comply with particular accounting rules, as one financial officer explained:

> For a lot of accounting standards you rely a lot on your auditors. For example, this document here (shows document) you may think that [it] looks lovely and I know all the accounting standards and all that, but there's a trick that all accounts have got … basically you follow through [a template] that tells you how to lay it all out so it meets all the accounting standards. …
> Interviewer: So who puts this document out?
> Our auditors … each accounting firm will have their own one of those documents. So if I hadn't had that you would need another one of me. … And that's not a real good one (pointing to the template). If you see the [competitor's] one, it's actually got another line over here that tells you that line there relates to Australian Accounting Standard number 1005, paragraph two. So then if you got a question, 'why the hell didn't you put that in?' you go to the Australian Accounting Standards and you can read it and you can understand it. (13, p.21)

This process of institutionalisation of accounting standards may provide the context where the adherence to the rule becomes prioritised over the substance, namely that the figures represent a meaningful statement of the business accounts (see also Clarke and Dean 2005). Whether this is the case or not depends on how well the regulatory standards (in this case requirement for compliance with the AIFRS) that lie behind the figures actually capture the value of the underlying business.

The shift towards AIFRS with its emphasis on generating more substance to reporting was mirrored in the broader CLERP 9 reforms. The essence of these broader reforms was to enhance the meaningfulness of the accounts by drawing on independent assurance. The regulatory reforms pertaining to public companies were designed to enhance meaning through assuring investors that independent actors would make more truthful judgements about company worth. The key independent actors were the auditors, who were clear on their role. The ICAA argued that 'our members are in the business of providing services around assurance' (35, p.3). The role of the auditor was to provide a service to the shareholder and the market by assuring them that the accounts represented a 'true and fair' view of the company's financial position. The ICAA continued:

> It's about providing third party assurance when you provide assurance in auditing reports. So that's got to be independent without fear or favour – telling it as it is. And the way it happens is we say we can confirm that the rules that are set down, being the accounting standards if you like, are being applied appropriately using what are our auditing standards [say] to determine it essentially. (35, p.18)

In terms of listed companies, the auditor provides this assurance. But in the case of HIH Insurance the auditors failed to communicate to investors and the broader public the parlous state of HIH finances. In the wake of the collapse, the question then arose of who would keep the auditors honest? The ICAA were clear, what kept auditors honest were their professional ethics and their obligation to their clients. This definition of client is critical; the client was the shareholders not executive management or the business as a whole:

> If you come to a profession with a sense that it's purely a money making enterprise and that's all you're interested in, then you're not going to have good outcomes, right? So that's why ethics [is important] ... without fear and favour on those things [that] are the fundamental basis [to our work]. I mean why would you put it in your motto? It emphasises just how important that is. And the public – you get a social franchise around having a registered company auditor status because it enables you to do things. But the quid pro quo for that is that the public expects you to do the right thing. (35, p.19)

Here, the emphasis was on the need for discretion and for auditors to use that discretion in the public interest. The principle of the accounting rule then would seem to be the paramount consideration. But, behind this discretion and shaping its use were the law and the courts. Ultimately, the ICAA acknowledged the difficulty for accountants in general and auditors (as the legitimating body of meaningful accounts) because of this. They understood that if a decision of the professional body was that a misrepresentation by an accountant or auditor had occurred that was then overturned by the court, the court decision prevailed:

> Well it [the tension between the law and professional ethics] puts us in a constrained position in the sense that we're subject to criticism for not doing enough, when some of the time we've got one hand behind our back because we clearly can't take

action when matters are before the courts. We've had good legal advice that tells us
that ... So you've really got to leave it to the court to determine whether they did
something right or wrong and then we can act accordingly. (31, p.14)

There was a complex relationship between trust and distrust that lay behind
the financial regulatory regime. The CLERP 9 reforms could be seen to
increase the distrust of auditors on the one hand by shifting to standardised
accounts and constraining discretion. On the other hand, the continued emphasis on principle not prescription meant accountants and auditors retained some
discretion. Professional ethics together with templates provided to accountants
to assist them with the new changes ideally provided the basis for accounts
that communicated accurately the value of a business to its owners. However,
in the case of a dispute it would be the courts and not the profession that would
decide what was and was not acceptable accounting and auditing practice.

Additional elements within CLERP 9 such as the separation of audit from
non- audit services, the rotation of audit partner and the separation between the
audit partner and the company could all be seen as signals of both the need for
independence but also of distrust of those providing that assurance. Yet,
heightened requirements around demonstrating independence, based on
distrust, had the capacity to slow down the business. It led to prescriptive rules
that determined what comprised independence and what did not. So, the
demand for the separation of audit from tax services required financial officers
to explain the same set of accounts to more than one party, 'it's always hard
when you get a change of personnel or anything like that, you know what I
mean? ... It is extra work for me, extra compliance work' (49, p.3) argued one
firm's accountant. Further, CLERP 9's requirement for a detailed history of
business relationships to ensure there was no conflict of interest between the
auditor, their relationship to the business being audited and the owners (the
shareholders) also created the demand for new monitoring systems to be set
up:

> Certainly the costs have been very substantive associated with implementation of
> CLERP 9 ... I think one's got to look at not CLERP 9 per se but some of the things
> running from it. ... Firms have had to set up sophisticated systems to deal and moni-
> tor with all these financial relationships. (35, p.9)

Mistrust, then, could cost time and money. Some of these elements of mistrust
were considered necessary, others less so. Ultimately, though, the levels of
mistrust expressed in the reforms could not replace the need for independence
of thought and will by the auditors:

> A lot of these things revolve around the strength of character of the individual and
> the independence of mind of the individual. I'm sure if you go and talk to a lot of
> directors about independence of directors there would be some people that are

totally independent, but they are not independent. They are independent [on paper] you can be totally independent and tick all the boxes. Nominally independent, but have they got the rigour of thought? Have they got the strength of character? Will they stand up when it counts? (35, p.4)

In terms of a system of accounts, an assessment of actuarial risk around the profitability of an enterprise depended on the numbers and the assurance process. In turn, assurance was based on a complex and sometimes contradictory amalgam of trust and distrust of both businesses and auditors. The relationship between trust and distrust in turn framed what was in the regulations as an expression of the independence needed to provide adequate assurance.

But this amalgam could shift and did so under the CLERP 9 reforms, where distrust was afforded greater emphasis. But, even after these reforms, assurance premised on the trustworthiness of accountants and auditors remained both essential and problematic. For example, the ICAA argued that the complex nature of contemporary finance required accountants to be skilled and have discretion, 'in the complex environment in which we live today, in which the capital markets operate, the ability for people to exercise judgement in a principle-based environment is more important than it ever was' (35, p.4). Yet, assurance might be provided and accepted but misplaced. The complexity of the capital markets also created situations where financial innovation might see the resulting figures containing little of assistance to the investor:

When you look back on it too, accounting standards didn't move with the times. We had new technology and other developments, things that were occurring [but] we had a set of accounting standards that were based on what an old manufacturing company looked like. Thirty years later WorldCom comes along, swapping time over copper wires with a whole lot of different people. How do you account for that? There wasn't enough to really deal with some of that. ... (31, p.7)[8]

Despite the failures of auditors in the case of HIH Insurance and the ultimate demise of Arthur Andersen, the demand for skilled professional accountants increased as complexity in accounts increased, partly as a result of greater distrust of accountants and auditors. The ICAA pointed to the paradox that in the years post-HIH in Australia and post-Enron and WorldCom in the United States the demand for accountants increased significantly. Assurance remained and remains still central to the calculation of actuarial risk in the financial context.

This close relationship between the figures and the need for assurance creates a vulnerability to assessments of actuarial risk in the financial context. The MHFs, sea and airports and the ICAA all pointed to the challenge associated with collusion and dishonesty in financial management. The view was 'You'll never legislate against dishonesty successfully' (35, p.4) and 'Once you've got collusion, you're in trouble … you've got two people who want to do fraud, they're going to do fraud' (44, p.40). The inadvertent and the opportunistic could be reduced (at a cost) but not the well-planned and intentional fraudulent activity.

Yet, the nomenclature of fraud and collusion also brings back the problem that not only might the figures themselves be ambiguous, but also the motive behind their representation in one manner or another. A figure in a set of accounts may deliberately exist to create an opportunity for a business to trade its way out of difficulty. The same figure may be an expression of hope or an exercise in deceit for the purpose of relieving a company of its assets. A fascinating distinction was explained again by the ICAA:

> When they talk about fraud today, a lot of what they're talking about is financial reporting fraud as opposed to someone pulling money out from the bank. Are you with me? And it's because they've misstated earnings or they've misstated revenue and you know, you have [a problem]. (35, p.9)

In this quote the figures themselves have an ambiguous quality. They both are and are not real. Another example of ambiguity relates to what appears as an asset. At some level, efficiency in the calculation of assets for the purposes of compiling the accounts meant that items were left uncounted and unrepresented:

> We count all our nuts and bolts in our engineering stores and our finished goods. We did a study where for the engineering stores 5% of our equipment in the stores are big ticket items worth, worth about 80% of the costs, yet, [the auditors] were telling us, you have to count everything. So we're counting these little washers worth a dollar each, 50 cents each and we're going – hang on, this is crazy! We challenged them for a couple of years and they wouldn't come to the party so we finally did a study and we said, 'well hang on, we are no longer doing this. We're telling you this is just inefficient, we are spending hours and dollars monitoring something which has a very small financial impact.' So we then stopped asking. We just said [to ourselves], 'look, we don't believe we need to do this. We don't see the value in it and here's a business proposal and justification for it.' And I got the CFO to sign off on it. So we just stopped doing it. So things that we really think are an imposition we are happy to challenge. Does that fall outside the boundary of the accounting standards? I suspect not. (44, p.42)

What was represented by the numbers themselves, then, changes over time as assets materialised and dematerialised. These changes took place both at the level of nuts and bolts that could dematerialise and in terms of the assessment of the future. The same firm that stopped counting nuts and bolts had just entered into hedging contracts, in order to protect its bottom line in the case of a (then) worsening exchange rate. The figures here were significantly larger, but the emphasis was that they were only numbers:

We've reached agreement with our board given where the Australian dollar is, where the oil price is, we thought hedging was a good idea, so we've hedged a particular layer of risk, which we haven't in the past. ... We've engaged [accounting firm] to help us account for it appropriately. So it's significant dollars, but again there are only zeros at the end of the numbers. Once the processes are in place, whether you're talking two million or a twenty million [it's fairly straightforward]. At the moment I think we've got a hundred million of a particular currency. But again they're only in numbers. (44, p.24)

Ultimately, then, the emphasis on independence, transparency and standardisation within the CLERP 9 reforms could not dispel continued ambiguity around account figures and what they represented. For some, including the privately owned businesses in this study the answer was to generate greater dependence of the owners directly on business outcomes as exemplified by private rather than public ownership. The emphasis on independence itself was seen to be somewhat misplaced. For others, the accountants and auditors, independence was fundamental. Yet, the accounting profession depended on independent assurance of accounts being valued. Further, there were limits placed on their independent decisions about accounting principles, through decisions made by the courts about whether the discretion of their members was consistent with a legal interpretation of accounting standards.

Finally, the analysis returns to the need for ambiguity in actuarial calculations of finance. This need emerged from several quarters. Firstly, it arose because of the demand that accounts focus not on the rules but the substance of a business's worth. As Clark and Dean (2005) have argued the emphasis here should be not only on the figures or even the principles but the account given as to why the figures best represent the worth of a business. Such an approach requires flexibility in enumeration of the accounts as well as considerable judgement by both accountant and auditor. Secondly, ambiguity arose because of the labile nature of business success where profitable businesses could emerge from difficult times, perhaps because of optimism expressed through a set of accounts, and conversely where apparently healthy finances could suddenly be perceived of as a fiction. The uncertainty of actuarial risk itself provides fertile ground for business ingenuity and resilience (Bernstein 1996; O'Malley 2004). Yet, this uncertainty is unsettling, particularly when confidence in business is low. Here the final tension arises, namely that the purpose of business in the private sector is to pursue profit:

The reality is businesses ... we're not here to land planes, or move passengers, we're in business to make money. Now whether you like it or not, or the public likes it or not, businesses are in business to make money. No other reason. Absolutely there's no other reason that you're in business. ... I believe in the great churn of economic enterprise to keep the country going, but all these things [regulations] are just creating a great weight on it. (49, p.18)

Ultimately, the public is ambivalent about such motives, an ambivalence that demands in the aftermath of a collapse a political response, reassurance that substance will be injected back into financial accounts and the public protected from venal business practice.

CONCLUSION

This chapter on the impact of both the insurance and financial reforms has centred on the ambiguity of the calculation of actuarial risk in the financial context, an ambiguity that was consistent with an understanding that reforms in this area are closely intertwined with political risk. This ambiguity arose as calculations of actuarial risk were pulled between the demand for clarity, certainty and reassurance on the one hand and the need for entrepreneurial risk-taking on the other. In the wake of the collapse of HIH Insurance, requirements for increased clarity and transparency in accounting and actuarial assessments arose. This was pursued through the standardisation of accounting principles through the adoption and development of international financial reporting standards within Australia (AIFRS). Standardisation was accompanied by increased demand for the independence of auditors from the business they audited to ensure that they could provide the assurance that the shareholders and investors required.

Even on its own terms, the standardisation route to transparency and clarity was seen as somewhat problematic by accountants and by the businesses themselves as misguided. Firstly, the different figures in the accounts that resulted from regulatory changes could be dismissed as merely financial and as such reflecting little of substance regarding real changes to underlying business health. Secondly, the emphasis on principle in the reforms based on the need to pursue a substantive representation of the accounts could result in different views about what the figures actually should be. Standardisation did not mean that comparable figures would, or should, be forthcoming.

But, for regulators to accept that there could be genuine differences in views around what figures should be required, the producers of different views (that is, the accountants and auditors themselves) needed to be trusted. The CLERP 9 reforms were premised on mistrust (based on the experience of the collapse of HIH Insurance) and aimed to increase the trustworthiness of the accounts, their compilers (the accountants) and their auditors by ensuring greater independence of auditors from the businesses.[9] A lack of independence was argued to undermine assurance and the trustworthiness of accounts. This materialised in quite prescriptive rules around what constituted adequate independence and to an extent diverted attention away from the importance of ethics within the profession itself. Indeed, the profession ultimately was subject to court decisions about whether its judgement was or was not valid. This ambivalence around the trustworthiness of the assurers of accounts generated further ambiguity around what the account figures actually represented. Finally, the importance of independence itself could be challenged by both business and commentators. Independence could generate disinterest and an emphasis on adherence to rules and principles that became an end in themselves, rather than driven by a vital interest in the fortunes of the particular business. Each of these elements could cloud the pursuit of transparency and clarity in accounts. Transparency and independence then appeared to have some limits as a means to enhance assurance and meaningful accounting practice.

From another perspective, ambiguity was precisely what was seen as necessary for the pursuit of self-interest through the market and for the market to generate wealth. Here, ambiguity was not something to be dispelled rather it needed to be embraced. Entrepreneurs, it was argued, depended on some level of uncertainty and freedom to pursue business opportunities. Further, government also was dependent on such entrepreneurialism for revenue and to reduce the burden for government services. Government, too, could be seen to require ambiguity in the calculation of actuarial risk in the financial arena. Again, ambiguity was evident in the distinction made between financial accounts and their underlying basis in actual profit and loss. From an entrepreneurial standpoint, this distinction could be used productively to allow a struggling business to recover over time, rather than see it go under and for all investment in the enterprise to be lost. Further, hedging could be entered into to bolster financial statements, arrangements that might smooth profitability but that might also bring unexpected gains. In short, ambiguity or the 'grey zone' where financial gains and losses materialised and dematerialised provided a space where entrepreneurs could exploit the opportunities of the market.

This grey zone that forms the boundary between financial and cash losses, however, generates significant challenges for a regulator. A financial regulator that acts too conservatively and intervenes in a business 'too soon' can be argued to threaten a viable business and might even be found responsible for investor losses.[10] Alternatively, if the regulator is judged to have intervened 'too late' they risk being criticised for being weak or having been captured by the market. The difficulty for the regulator, too, can be seen to result from their role not as financial police but as a guardian of a fair and vibrant market where productive gains can be made, but where losses too are inevitable. This ambiguity of their role, too, exacerbates perceptions in the case of corporate failure that they have either been too heavy handed (interfering too much in the market) or too weak and not preventing losses. Both can threaten their legitimacy.

The continued emphasis on independence and transparency in reforms despite their mixed impact on the accounting and auditing process and in light of the value placed by some on dependence requires some explanation.

Perhaps these values represent more socio-cultural norms than they do principles that would enhance the calculation of actuarial risk. Independence and transparency from a normative orientation frame a world where all can be included and no one kept in the dark. They speak of equality. For this reason the emphasis on the need for independence in market valuation would seem likely to continue as a move away from such values would raise socio-cultural risks quite independently from their capacity to deliver more accurate actuarial risk calculations.

The centrality of the insurance industry to this analysis provided additional insights into the nature of regulation in the financial arena. The insurance industry comprises private for-profit businesses but also is in the business of assurance. Like government, it looks for both certainty and ambiguity in the calculation of actuarial risk. It also sits in a particular position vis-à-vis government. As private enterprise the insurance industry exploited the uncertainties and opportunities of financial actuarial calculations to make money. HIH pursued the limits of uncertainty in actuarial calculation and failed. Yet, in the wake of the collapse, regulation premised on the need for greater clarity and certainty in the ability of the businesses to cover their liabilities were resisted, particularly when seen as a threat to their business by virtue of their international competitors. This saw the industry push government, successfully, to include foreign insurers in the local regulatory regime, which directly affected some of the businesses in this research who were looking to international partners to shore up their liabilities from self-insurance schemes.

However, insurance emerged as more than just a business. It shared with government responsibility for compensating the citizenry (its policyholders) in times of difficulty. This shared responsibility with government was mutually beneficial in allowing government to divest itself of some liabilities whilst also providing, in some areas but not others, the opportunity for profit. Because of this close connection with government, it also needed to assure both its clients and the government that it could cover its liabilities. Failure to reassure customers could threaten business; failure to reassure the government might see higher levels of intrusion into business affairs.

The insurance industry faced a more difficult environment post-HIH where it had been shaken by the collapse and a number of unrealised liabilities, in particular its vulnerability to liabilities arising from terrorist attacks post September 11. It was only through a relationship with government that insurance companies were willing to cover terrorism risks. Government might mandate insurance cover, but it also needed to be involved in providing adequate reinsurance cover.

For the MHFs, sea and airports studied in this research project, their main concern was to ensure adequate coverage and to keep the cost of insurance as low as possible. Their insurance needs were diverse, as were their access to levers they could use to reduce their insurance costs. The impact of the reforms following HIH, however, could not be teased apart from the general conditions of the insurance market. Both these elements combined to increase challenges in finding adequate cover at an acceptable cost. In response, sites scrutinised their insurance costs and found ways to reduce them by drawing on economies of scale, where possible, by purchasing insurance across sites in the same company. This may well have benefited both insurer and industry. But, it also could be achieved by increased use of self-insurance, a move that reduced the potential market for private insurance companies.

NOTES

1. Each quotation from interviews undertaken as part of this research is referenced by a transcript number and by the specific page of the transcript where the quotation appears.
2. But obviously loses money if the price of raw materials falls below the contract price.
3. Of course, this also depended on whether insurance cover was mandatory under government legislation.
4. This arrangement was found in approximately 18 other countries internationally according to an Australian Government Terrorism Insurance Act Review 2009 see http://www.treasury. gov.au/contentitem.asp?NavId=&ContentID=1640 Chapter 1.
5. One MHF was sold to a public company after completion of the data collection at that site.
6. The latter may well have been affected by the global financial crisis of 2008–09 but the long-term trajectory suggests pressure for increased returns will remain an important consideration for financial managers into the future.
7. Clearly, there was the need to review the accounts for an extended period after the change to AIFRS to be able to assess changes within the parameters of the new rules. However, the key question here is whether they represent the underlying financial actuarial risks of the firm with a greater degree of accuracy. The discussion below suggests that this proposition was contested by the case study sites.
8. It is interesting to note that this interview took place before the recent (2008–09) financial crisis.
9. This fell short, though, of the conflict of interest where the business pays the auditor to audit their own books.
10. At the time of writing the chapter, ASIC, the securities regulator, was being criticised for intervening in a company, Westpoint, too early and causing its demise, illustrating this dilemma of the regulator well. See A. Ferguson (2010) 'Critical time for ASIC under siege'. *The Age*. Melbourne June 22, 2010. http://www.theage.com.au/business/critical-time-for-asic-under-siege-20100621-ysc9.html. June 30, 2010.

9. Conclusion

The analysis of regulation presented in this book demonstrates the need for a comprehensive and dynamic appreciation of the challenges that regulation is required to address. These challenges are diverse and encompass political and social as well as actuarial risks. Such diversity demonstrates the limits of studying compliance without considering the goals that infuse reform and of scrutinising reform without taking account of whether and how compliance occurs. In the wake of the three events analysed in the chapters above, regulatory reforms cascaded from parliaments through to regulatory agencies and finally made their presence felt at workplaces. Within disparate worksites new infrastructure was created, routines reconfigured and records developed to demonstrate compliance. In this process, improvements were made that could reduce the risk of future disaster, a demonstration that regulatory reform can result in a 'spiral of progress' as Kahn (1990) hoped. There were clear examples in this study where the lessons of disaster were learnt, leading to enhanced and well-designed regulatory regimes and high levels of compliance. Here, 'Never again' could ring true.

At the level of regulatory technique, the wisdom behind a meta-regulatory approach (Parker 2002), as exemplified by the major hazards regime in Victoria, demonstrated the power of drawing on local knowledge, together with rigorous oversight, as an effective method of reducing the risk of low probability yet high impact events. Yet, there were also examples of failure, which were well understood by the regulatory literature with examples of ritualistic (for example, Power 1997) and creative compliance (for example, McBarnet and Whelan 1999) together with examples of both overzealous (for example, Yeung 2004) and weak enforcement (for example, Clinard and Yeager 1980).

The strength of this study, however, did not lie in its capacity to add to the existing literature on what regulatory methods work best and what problems might be expected to accompany any one approach, important as this literature is. Rather, the analysis here points to three conclusions. Firstly, this study highlights the importance of the particular focus of a regulatory regime. Substance matters. Secondly, the analysis above suggests that a focus on techniques of regulation and accompanying enforcement strategies should not downplay the importance of politics in determining regulatory outcomes and what methods and resources are made available to the regulator. Politics matters. Finally, this study has explored the way regulation is often well-characterised as instrumental law, that is, it is narrow in scope. The arguments developed through this book are that this instrumental framing neither arises from a single focus, nor does it generate commitment to a single goal. Rather, regulation is designed to achieve multiple risk reduction goals, from actuarial and socio-cultural to political. It is in this complex of goals that the paradox of regulation arises and where its strengths and limitations can be understood.

This study illustrates well the importance of substance, that is, the stated aims of a particular regulatory regime. The disparate areas analysed here: major hazards, counter-terrorism and financial regulation posed particular, and often unique, challenges. Meta-regulation in the form of the safety case approach (explored in Chapters 5 and 6) was an effective method for reducing the actuarial risk of explosion at major hazard facilities provided that the necessary expertise was present, channels of communication open and the regulator sufficiently resourced. But, a meta-regulatory approach to counter-terrorism at air and seaports, for example, made far less sense. This was because there were few 'stop rules' that could determine when security was sufficient. The intentional nature of a terrorist attack, the labile purposes attached to the regime (to reassure the public, enable political legitimacy, keep the airlines flying and trade flowing) meant security escalated not only in response to the potential for an attack, but also to goals that had a complex relationship to security.

The second conclusion relates to the political nature of regulation. Politics, both in the formal sense of the actions of governments and the bureaucracy and in the informal sense of the strategies employed to maintain or gain power pervaded the empirical analysis presented above. The way each event was framed by the political elite at the time of each disaster, their instigation of and response to formal inquiries in each of the respective domains (as described in Chapter 4), shaped the regulatory response seen as necessary. Further, the absence of political attention – for example in New South Wales following the Longford Gas explosion – saw regulatory reform there flounder and resources employed by sites in anticipation of a new regime wasted. Political attention and support was both necessary to, but could be problematic for, effective reform.

Politics was important not only in the first wave of reforms, but also in propelling subsequent amendments to legislation and regulation. In each of the areas – major hazards, counter-terrorism and finance – industry, professional associations, the media and opposition parties shaped further reform efforts. What was striking here was the dynamic nature of regulatory reform. Regulatory reform was an iterative, relational, occasionally collaborative, often contested, but above all a continuing enterprise. When prominent on the public and media agenda, or when propelled to prominence by virtue of political gains that were desired by members of the government or opposition, the wheels of reform churned relentlessly. It is important too, to understand politics associated with compliance. A regulatory regime (such as security) that commanded significant authority could result in unintended consequences since this authority was, in itself, a desirable asset. Industrial battles could be won in the name of security, for example, or miniature fiefdoms develop to secure higher levels of control and influence over a particular worksite. The lessons here, then, are that measures taken in the name of regulatory compliance cannot be assumed as essentially virtuous. Again, context and content matter.

INSTRUMENTALISM REVISITED

The major contribution of this book, though, is in its development of the political and instrumental nature of regulation through an analysis of risk. The analysis in Chapter 2 confirmed that regulation was well-characterised by its political and instrumental nature. However, it was in teasing apart the dimensions of that instrumentalism through the analysis of risk in Chapter 3, and subsequently through the data itself, that the complexity and dynamism within that framing – as a tightly prescribed means to a narrowly defined end – was revealed. The characterisation of regulation as 'problem focussed' and best when narrowly and clearly targeted (seen as the essence of 'good regulation') requires careful attention. Instrumentalism in practice did not mean singular in purpose, rather the opposite. An instrumental frame to law and regulation was animated by multiple risk management goals, variously actuarial, socio-cultural or political risk (or indeed all three).

The actuarial underpinning to instrumentalism is important to emphasise. Here, the audience for regulation, both of reform and enforcement, was the worksite where compliance was expected with the aim being the reduction of actuarial risk. That is, the primary expectation was that the risk of catastrophic fire or explosion, terrorist attack or financial misrepresentation and fraud leading to corporate collapse would be reduced by compliance with the reformed regulatory regime. A clear actuarial focus could provide strength to a regime where the resources of the regulator and of those working at the site level could be well-directed and effective. Yet, this same process of narrowing the focus in order to sharpen the actuarial lens more clearly necessarily brings with it the potential for avoiding onerous new regulatory responsibilities. Where this was associated with a commensurate reduction in actuarial risk there was little reason for concern. But, this was not necessarily the case. The exporting of actuarial risk (through relocation of a MHF) by writing insurance offshore, or through privatising a previously publicly held company all could incubate risks leading to future disaster.

Here, again, content mattered. In the case of major hazard risk the actuarial risk was complex but apprehensible within an actuarial frame. In contrast, actuarial risk assessments of financial investments or terrorist attacks were often vulnerable. In the absence of a firm grasp of actuarial risk, a narrative was developed to frame both the cause of catastrophe and method of amelioration. Such a narrative needed to resonate as much with socio-cultural expectations of what should be in place as to actuarial calculations of the risk itself. The audience for regulation and compliance in the case of these latter two risks, then, shifted from those charged with compliance within the businesses to the public (in the case of counter-terrorism) or to the market (in the case of financial regulation).

However, this narrative still was required to conform to instrumental expectations rooted in an actuarial conceptualisation of regulatory purpose. It was justified through an actuarial logic. Security clearance procedures at airports were not justified by the need to make people feel safe, but by the need to prevent a terrorist attack. CLERP 9 reforms to audit processes and corporate governance were not primarily justified by the need to generate confidence in the market (although they could be) but rather by enhancing the accuracy of financial reports and their transparency to the investing public. Transparency and independence generated confidence. There is an important conclusion to be drawn from this interchangeable quality to actuarial and socio-cultural risk orientations, namely the principle or outcome sought by a regulatory regime may be inspired by either the management of actuarial or socio-cultural risk.

The dominant form of risk management involved in the regulatory reforms analysed here was neither actuarial nor socio-cultural, but political. Political risk, as explored in Chapter 3 comprised two necessary, but occasionally competing elements: a concern to keep the economy growing and with this guarding government revenue; and secondly the need to provide security to reassure the citizenry that they were indeed in a safe pair of (political) hands. This focus on reassurance was where the interchangeable nature of actuarial and socio-cultural risk management took place, since reassurance could be provided by either form of risk reduction or both together. To a considerable extent, this study found that the purpose of regulation was to be found in reform and the capacity for reform to reduce political risk and enhance political fortunes.

But it is necessary to dig a little deeper when understanding the instability of the regulatory regimes studied here. The reasons for instability were various. Firstly, the narrow targeting of regulation inspired by an actuarial orientation could be exposed as providing the means for regulatory arbitrage and creative compliance. Here, reforms would develop to broaden the scope of a regime, witnessed by the extension, some five years after the original changes to the insurance regulatory regime, to encompass insurance written overseas. Secondly, the instrumental framing afforded by a causal narrative based on reassurance could, when exposed to political scrutiny, fail to demonstrate actuarial rigor. In short, the methods of reassurance (such as screening of passengers and hand luggage at major airports) were seen to be vulnerable; the narrative would breakdown, political risk rise and further reform result. Hence, security moved from screening hand luggage to full body screening, from stowed luggage to all cargo, from major airports to small and on occasion even to airstrips where no regular passenger flights ever landed.

This political risk-driven dynamic to regulatory reform then demonstrated the first paradox of regulation, the paradox of reform. The assumption behind regulatory reform primarily is that some actuarial problem exists: unsafe food, insecure airports, fraudulent accounting practices, and so on. The lesson of this research is that the primary problem infusing regulatory reform is the reduction of political risk. The received wisdom that regulation should be problem-focused may well be true, but what was demonstrated here was that it was as much a political as a technical concern.

Nonetheless, progress was possible. But progress required reform to be able to address all three risks. Clearly, the reduction of actuarial risk was important, but reforms needed also to resonate with public expectations and to be compatible with enhanced political legitimacy. This, perhaps, illustrates why a regulatory spiral is the most that can be hoped for. Reform may rarely address each of these three risks adequately. Hence if the reduction of political risk is the primary concern, and where actuarial and socio-cultural risk reduction are, to an extent at least, interchangeable then there is no necessary reason why reform will reduce the risk of a repeat disaster. Nonetheless, reform may still reassure the majority that successful change has been achieved and risks adequately addressed.

In this research, successful reform that addressed each of the three risks in question required a context within which political, actuarial and socio-cultural needs can all be met. The failure of the industrial manslaughter legislation in Victoria, together with the presence of sufficient expertise, provided (in the early years at least) the supportive environment for effective reform and compliance. The reforms to insurance similarly came with strong political support for the regulator, albeit here the funds for regulation were provided by the insurance industry itself, not from government coffers. In both major hazards and insurance reform political breathing space was enabled through ancillary measures. In the former disaster, additional sources of gas supply to the citizens and businesses within the State of Victoria were found. In the case of HIH, the Commonwealth Government set up a scheme to fund the neediest policyholders who suffered in the wake of the collapse and initiated reforms to the laws of negligence that reassured the insurance industry of their own viability. There was a need for sufficient political pressure, together with a degree of latitude to enable reforms to be shaped by the regulator in a manner that retained attention on how actuarial risk reduction could best be achieved.

A political cycle shaped the degree of attention paid to a regulatory regime. This in turn was animated by the dual nature of political risk of economic concern and reassurance. In each of the regimes, the lobbying efforts by business made a material impact on the particular regime. This relationship with industry was not necessarily counterproductive. Indeed, such a relationship could enhance the capacity for regulation to be effective. Issues could be clarified and regulatory demands more clearly communicated. But, clarification also could constrain regulatory autonomy, which – when well deployed – could ensure an enduring focus on actuarial risk concerns. Finally, political sensitivity to lobbying by industry could result in lost opportunities and wasted resources. The efforts undertaken by NSW MHFs in anticipation of a regime that was seriously and unnecessarily delayed saw resources wasted and morale dissipate.

There was, however, another paradox at play here, which might be termed the paradox of compliance. Much regulation is premised on the notion that the actuarial risk is real, that it has a tangible quality. Actuarial risk management contains the assumption of the real. The analysis of this book demonstrates that whilst this may be the case, what is 'real' and also what risk is 'realised' is complex. Again, the reforms pertaining to major hazard risk provided the clearest case of tangible risk. Here, a faulty risk assessment that persisted over time would lead to disaster. The actuarial potential underlying the assessment of that risk was non-negotiable. But, even here socio-cultural concerns were critical and illustrate the importance of understanding actuarial, socio-cultural and political risk as ideal typical. That is, the emphasis on an adequate actuarial risk assessment that could identify all necessary hazards at a particular MHF necessarily involved addressing socio-cultural concerns. Issues of respect, of the need to value the opinions and concerns of all present at an MHF concerning hazards and amelioration were important. Yet, socio-cultural concerns, retaining harmony and smoothing relationships at work, could detract from addressing actuarial risk. Here, what is evident is both the independent and interdependent nature of these two ideal types of risk.

The paradoxical outcomes of compliance with counter-terrorism regulation at sea and airports where greater rigor around compliance could be found at a remote port servicing a small island than at a capital city port, revealed that the purpose of this regime remained ambiguous and actuarial risk assessments insecure. Various narratives around the risk and its causal sequence developed to provide the security and assurance required. But, the purpose of this regulatory regime was continuously shifted between reassurance and keeping trade and tourism vibrant and airlines flying. The purpose moved but the attention to the regime did not. This base provided fertile ground for unintended and apparently 'irrational' outcomes.

Perhaps the most elusive, even capricious, of the actuarial risks in this study were the financial. The assessments made about the levels of actuarial risk posed by a particular business necessarily encompassed assessments about levels of entrepreneurial (desirable) and excessive (undesirable) risk-taking. But the line between the two could, and did, shift. To some extent, excessive levels of actuarial risk in the arena of finance were only firmly established as 'real' once they were actually realised. This is not to say that it was illusory – indeed far from it. But calculations around financial risks necessarily involve figures, calculations and confidence. Put rather crudely (perhaps too crudely), figures plus confidence represents real value, the same figures without the confidence quickly lose that value. Yet, such confidence could also be misplaced. Hence, we see the fickle nature of financial value; it can be there at one point in time and not there in the next; it can be alternatively real and illusory. Indeed, changes to financial risk assessments required through reforms to financial standards were understood as somewhat unreal assess-ments of underlying value. Perhaps this is because financial risk inevitably involves risk calculations of a socio-cultural and political nature. Confidence and assurance here are inevitably bound up with the management of socio-cultural and political risk.

The role of political risk management in establishing financial value brings attention back to the central role played by uncertainty in regulation. As the analysis in Chapter 3 (in the discussion of political risk) and in Chapter 8 (with the analysis of the impact of the financial reforms) demonstrates, entrepre-neurial activity that is necessary to the reduction of political risk also thrives on ambiguity in actuarial risk calculations. Uncertainty is too important to dispel. It is worth exploring here a different emphasis on traditional notions of creative compliance with the emphasis on the benefits, rather than the detri-ments, to such creativity. Creativity may provide the means to achieve alter-native (desirable) goals. This brings the discussion back to comments made by John Palmer in his assessment of the actions of the prudential regulator APRA in the wake of the collapse of HIH (Palmer 2002). As Chapter 4 highlighted, Palmer pointed to the very real pressures of the market for unsustainable returns on investment, for ever-increasing values to provide superannuants their income in retirement and shareholders their expectation for 'proper' returns (Chapter 4 p. 93). This uncertainty, though, provides fertile ground for the demands for certainty, for reassurance. Narratives around financial risk and its amelioration develop, together with techniques for spreading and hedg-ing these risks. The demand for reassurance and certainty is met by financial technology and regulation.

The interplay between certainty and uncertainty that is found within political risk management needs careful assessment. Very real consequences can arise where those with least power, the most dispensable, are made to bear the consequences of excessive risk-taking and those with greater influence reap the benefits of entrepreneurial activity. Attention to political risk management may provide a way to understand the dynamic of regulation and compliance, but careful assessment of the consequences of that activity on just outcomes for particular groups in society is a separate and critically important consideration. Again, context matters.

Important as it is, this relationship between political legitimacy and regulation should not consume all our attention. Certainly, we should be cognisant of the finding that political commentators and analysts who provide strategies for governments (and indeed businesses (Haines 2009b)) to enhance their legitimacy through regulation may well end up achieving the opposite effect. The explicit promulgation of regulation for the purpose of short-term political gain breeds cynicism, a condition that may well propel politicians to produce greater and greater volumes of 'problem solving' regulatory regimes that necessarily are fallible and transient in the political gains they bring. So, although political risk lies at the heart of regulation it cannot be the focus for those analysing the best use for regulation.

So, then, finally what can regulation achieve and what can it not? My argument here may be somewhat surprising, namely that regulation is almost too powerful. It can deliver alluring and significant, if transient, political benefits. It can see actuarial gains and it can reassure. Inevitably, however, it promises more than it can deliver – particularly when pitted against determined opposition in the form of destructive market forces or those determined to wreak havoc. It is a human process and, as such, people, processes and purpose all are important to the outcome. In each of the areas analysed above, the presence of good processes that had the best chance of delivering effective outcomes required good people. Clearly, some problems were more suited to amelioration through regulatory reform and enhanced compliance (with the instrumental orientation that encompasses) than others. In particular, the limits to a regulatory approach to both terrorism and financial security should be acknowledged. Such methods may complement, but should not replace, alternative approaches to enhance social integration and assist in the quest for an equitable, sustainable and vibrant society.

Appendix: research methods

This research project was designed to analyse both regulatory reform and regulatory compliance in order to ascertain the possibilities and problems within the regulatory project. To do so, it was as important to assess the constraints and enablers for reform success as it was to understand the nature and effectiveness of compliance on the ground. This was both an analytical and empirical research project that drew comparatively on three arenas (major hazards, counter-terrorism regimes at sea and airports and financial regulation (specifically corporate law reform and reforms to the regulation of general insurance)). The material reviewed and the arguments developed in Chapter 2 and Chapter 3 resulted from iterations in my thinking as developed through my reading and also several papers on this work (Haines 2009a; 2009b; Haines, Sutton and Platania-Phung 2008). The analysis of the regulatory and risk literatures presented in this book extends and reformulates this earlier analysis of these literatures whilst also benefitting from earlier analyses of the data.

The analysis presented in Chapters 4 to 8 required collection of extensive primary and secondary resource materials. Chapter 4 drew extensively from Royal Commission reports into the Longford explosion (Dawson and Brooks 1999) and the collapse of HIH Insurance (Owen 2003). The analysis of the Longford explosion was also supplemented by analysis of parliamentary proceedings in the Victorian, NSW and NT parliaments where the explosion was cited. This material also assisted in the analysis of reforms following Longford in each jurisdiction. In addition, Andrew Hopkins' (2001; 2002a) work on the Longford explosion and subsequent trial were of considerable importance to the analysis of the explosion and the subsequent reforms. Additional material analysed for the reforms to financial regulation and the impact of the HIH collapse included publicly available material provided by the major regulators ASIC and APRA. These included their submissions to the HIH Royal Commission as well as a report by John Palmer (2002) into the role played by APRA in the collapse of HIH. The material into the aftermath of the September 11 terrorist attacks involved analysis of transcripts of the Commonwealth Parliament of Australia (both from the House of Representatives and the Senate). Publicly available reports from responsible government agencies (including the Department of Foreign Affairs and Trade

(DFAT), AFP, OTS and Customs) were reviewed as well as key documents as accessed through the Parliamentary Library from their chronology of events Chronology of Legislative and Other Legal Developments from 11 September 2001 (available at http://www.aph.gov.au/library/intguide/law/terrorism.htm). The material used in the analysis of September 11 also included two reviews into aviation security, one undertaken by the Joint Committee of Public Accounts and Audit: Review of Aviation Security in Australia Official together with the Committee Hansard of the Public Hearings and an Independent Review undertaken by Sir John Wheeler (2005).

For each regulatory arena interviews were undertaken with regulators responsible for the areas of risk covered by the three events: Victorian WorkSafe (Major Hazards Unit), NSW WorkCover and NT WorkSafe for reforms relevant to the Longford Gas Explosion; the Commonwealth Department of Transport and Regional Affairs (DOTARS) later renamed the Office of Transport Security (OTS) and the Australian Customs Service (Customs) with regards to the terrorist attacks and finally the Australian Securities and Investments Commission (ASIC) and the Australian Prudential Regulatory Authority (APRA). In each of the relevant chapters interviews are identified by the bureaucracy involved, except in the case of ASIC where Malcolm Rogers (Executive Director of Regulation) asked that the comments be attributed to him personally and not to ASIC. The Australian Federal Police refused a request for a formal interview relating to the reforms to counter-terrorism security but did meet informally to provide some understanding of the regulatory reforms that pertained to sea and airports. Public documentation from each agency was also analysed. Ancillary interviews to understand the reforms were also undertaken with consultants in the major hazard area.

The analyses of compliance in the three areas involved studies of several major hazard facilities, air and seaports. Analyses of compliance were then undertaken at six MHFs (five chemical plants and an oil refinery) in Victoria, two MHFs in NSW (both chemical plants) and one in the NT. These involved between one and five interviews on each site (depending on the level of access provided), analyses of annual reports and written documentation provided by the sites' managers. The latter could include their risk management methodology. The analysis of MHF compliance also included 12 months of observations of community group meetings in Victoria between MHFs, regulators and community members that supplemented analysis of three of the MHFs included in the overall study. Material for one of the case study sites comprised primarily informal conversations with managers during community group meetings, as well as 12 months of observations of a community group specifically concerned with this one facility. The Victorian regulator also provided details of all significant incidents and enforcement action at MHFs from 2003–08, which was used to supplement material provided by the sites themselves during the interviews. Licence length and licence conditions, another indication of compliance, were accessed and publicly available. There were ten airports (five in NSW, two in the NT and three in Victoria) and three ports in the analysis of compliance with the security regime. Sea and airports varied from large facilities with extensive international demands for trade and passenger movements to small regional sites with domestic concerns. Interviews with between two and three site personnel were undertaken for each of these sites, combined with analysis of documentation, largely annual reports. In the case of airports too, there was analysis of government enquiries where airport management had been required to appear before committees. Interviews were between one and three hours in length. Attendance at two security conferences each dedicated to dialogue between sea and airports, politicians and regulators provided important contextual information to the challenges of compliance. As noted in Chapter 8, the material for compliance with financial regulations was more limited. This analysis primarily involved interviews with financial officers at each of the MHFs, air and seaports. Secondly, additional interviews were undertaken with the Insurance Council of Australia to understand the perspective of the Australian Insurance Industry on the reforms and with the Institute of Chartered Accountants of Australia (ICAA). There were a total of 60 interviews with 73 individuals undertaken, with three of these being follow-up interviews.

Bibliography

Allan, G. (2006) 'The HIH Collapse: A Costly Catalyst for Reform'. *Deakin Law Review*, 11 (2):137–59.

Auditor General (2004) 'HIH Claims Support Scheme – Governance Arrangements'. Department of the Treasury: Australian National Audit Office. Available at http://www.anao.gov.au/uploads/documents/2003-04_Audit_Report_51.pdf, accessed 16 July 2009.

Australian Broadcasting Corporation (ABC) (1999) 'Esso has Cover-up Strategy: Longford Disaster Allegations'. *7.30 Report*. 16 April 2009. Available at http://www.abc.net.au/7.30/stories/s23848.htm, accessed 15 September 2010.

Australian Bureau of Statistics (2005) 'Crime and Safety, Australia'. Available at http://www.abs.gov.au/AUSSTATS/abs@.nsf/productsbyCatalogue/669C5A997EAED891CA2568A900139405/, accessed May 20 2010.

Australian Law Reform Commission (2002) 'Principled Regulation: Federal Civil and Administrative Penalties in Australia'. Commonwealth of Australia. Available at http://www.austlii.edu.au/au/other/alrc/publications/reports/95/, accessed 4 July 2010.

Australian Prudential Regulation Authority (2005) 'Prudential Supervision of General Insurance – Stage 2 Reforms: Risk and Financial Management'. Commonwealth of Australia. Available at http://www.apra.gov.au/RePEc/RePEcDocs/Archive/discussion_papers/dp0016.pdf, accessed 17 July 2009.

Australian Prudential Regulation Authority (2006) 'Prudential Supervision of General Insurance Groups'. Commonwealth of Australia. Available at http://www.apra.gov.au/Policy/upload/Prudential-supervision-of-general-insurance-groups-discussion-paper.pdf, accessed 17 July 2009.

Australian Prudential Regulation Authority (2008a) 'Probability and Impact Rating System'. Commonwealth of Australia. Available at http://www.apra.gov.au/PAIRS/upload/PAIRS_Final_May_2008_External_Version. pdf, accessed 16 July 2009.

Australian Prudential Regulation Authority (2008b) 'Refinements to the General Insurance Prudential Framework – Final Response to Industry'. Commonwealth of Australia. Available at http://www.apra.gov.au/General/upload/Response-paper-Refinements-June-2008.pdf, accessed 17 July 2009.

Australian Prudential Regulation Authority (2008c) 'Supervisory Oversight and Response System'. Commonwealth of Australia. Available at http://www.apra.gov.au/PAIRS/upload/SOARS_Final_May_2008_External_Version.pdf, accessed 16 July 2009.

Australian Securities and Investments Commission (2009) 'CLERP 9: Corporate reporting and disclosure laws'. Commonwealth of Australia. Available at http://www.asic.gov.au/asic/asic.nsf/byheadline/CLERP+9?openDocument#how, accessed 27 July 2010.

ASX (2007) '2006 Australian Share Ownership Study'. Available at http://www.asx.com.au/about/pdf/2006_australian_share_ownership_study.pdf, accessed 13 May 2009.

Ayres, I. and Braithwaite, J. (1992) *Responsive Regulation: Transcending the Deregulation Debate*. New York: Oxford University Press.

Baldwin, R. (2004) 'The New Punitive Regulation'. *The Modern Law Review*, 67 (3):351–83.

Baldwin, R. and Black, J. (2008) 'Really Responsive Regulation'. *The Modern Law Review*, 71 (1):59–94.

Baldwin, R. and Martin, C. (1999) *Understanding Regulation: Theory, Strategy and Practice*. Oxford: Oxford University Press.

Banks, G. (2005) 'Regulation-making in Australia: Is it broke? How do we fix it?' *Public Lecture Series, Australian Centre of Regulatory Economics (ACORE)*. Faculty of Economics and Commerce, ANU. 7th July 2005.

Beazley, K. (2005) 'A Nation Unprepared: Australia in the Fourth Year of a Long War'. *Address to the Sydney Institute*. Sydney, 4 August.

Beck, U. (1992) *Risk Society: Towards a New Modernity*. London: Sage.

Bedsworth, L.W. and Kastenberg, W.E. (2002) 'Science and Uncertainty in Environmental Regulation: Insights from the Evaluation of California's Smog Check Program'. *Science and Public Policy*, 29 (1):13–24.

Bernstein, P.L. (1996) *Against the Gods: The Remarkable Story of Risk*. New York: John Wiley and Sons.

Beyea, J. and Berger, D. (2001) 'Scientific Misconceptions among Daubert Gatekeepers: The Need for Reform of Expert Review Procedures'. *Law and Contemporary Problems*, 64 (2&3):327–72.

Bhidé, A. (2009) 'An Accident Waiting to Happen'. *Critical Review*, 21 (2–3):211–47.

Bishop, J. (2001) 'Speech to the House of Representatives: Matters of Public Importance, HIH Insurance'. *House of Representatives, Hansard Parliamentary Debates* Thursday, 24 May 2001. Available at http://parlinfo.aph.gov.au/parlInfo/genpdf/chamber/hansardr/2001-05-24/0125/hansard_frag.pdf;fileType%3Dapplication%2Fpdf, accessed 14 May 2009.

Black, J. (1997) *Rules and Regulators*. Oxford: Clarendon Press.

Black, J. (2002) 'Critical Reflections on Regulation'. *Australian Journal of Legal Philosophy*, 27:1–35.

Black, J. (2005a) 'The Development of Risk-Based Regulation in Financial Services: Just "Modelling Through"?' In: Black, J., Lodge, M. and Thatcher, M. (eds). *Regulatory Innovation: A Comparative Analysis*. Cheltenham, UK and Northampton, MA, USA: Edward Elgar, 156–80.

Black, J. (2005b) 'What is Regulatory Innovation?' In: Black, J., Lodge, M. and Thatcher, M. (eds). *Regulatory Innovation: A Comparative Analysis*. Cheltenham, UK and Northampton, MA, USA: Edward Elgar, 1–15.

Black, J. (2006) 'Managing Regulatory Risks and Defining the Parameters of Blame: A Focus on the Australian Prudential Regulatory Authority'. *Law & Policy*, 28 (1):1–30.

Blake Dawson Waldron (2004) 'The BDW Guide to CLERP 9: Practical Guide to the Corporate Law Economic Reform Program (Audit Reform and Corporate Disclosure) Act 2004'. Available at http://www.blake dawson.com/Templates/Publications/x_publication_content_page.aspx?id =51825, accessed 27 July 2009.

Boin, A. and t'Hart, P. (2003) 'Public Leadership in Times of Crisis: Mission Impossible?' *Public Administration Review*, 63 (5):544–53.

Borradori, G. (2003) *Philosophy in a Time of Terror: Dialogues with Jurgen Habermas and Jacques Derrida*. Chicago: University of Chicago Press.

Bourdieu, P. (2001) *Practical Reason*. Cambridge: Blackwell.

Braithwaite, J. (1985) *To Punish or Persuade: Enforcement of Coal Mine Safety*. Albany: State University of New York Press.

Braithwaite, J. (2000) 'The New Regulatory State and the Transformation of Criminology'. *British Journal of Criminology*, 40 (2):222–38.

Braithwaite, J. (2003a) 'Meta Risk Management and Responsive Regulation for Tax System Integrity'. *Law & Policy*, 25 (1):1–16.

Braithwaite, J. (2003b) 'Through the Eyes of the Advisors: A Fresh Look at High Wealth Individuals'. In: Braithwaite, V. (ed). *Taxing Democracy: Understanding Tax Avoidance and Tax Evasion*. Aldershot: Ashgate, 245–68.

Braithwaite, J. (2008) *Regulatory Capitalism: How it Works, Ideas for Making it Work Better*. Cheltenham, UK and Northampton, MA, USA: Edward Elgar.

Braithwaite, J. and Drahos, P. (2000) *Global Business Regulation*. Cambridge: Cambridge University Press.

Braithwaite, V. (2009) *Defiance in Taxation and Governance: Resisting and Dismissing Authority in a Democracy*. Cheltenham, UK and Northampton, MA, USA: Edward Elgar.

Brown, P. and Tarca, A. (2005) '2005 – It's Here, Ready or Not: A Review of the Australian Financial Reporting Framework'. *Australian Accounting Review*, 15 (2):68–78.

Brunsson, N. (2002) *The Organization of Hypocrisy*. Abstrakt: Copenhagen Business School Press.

Calavita, K., Pontell, H.N. and Tillman, R. (1997) 'The Savings and Loans Debacle, Financial Crime and the State'. *Annual Review of Sociology*, 23:19–38.

Cantor, R. (1996) 'Rethinking Risk Management in the Federal Government'. *Annals of the American Academy of Political & Social Science*, 545:135–43.

Carroll, J. (2006) *House of War: The Pentagon and the Disastrous Rise of American Power*. Melbourne: Scribe.

Carroll, P. (2008) 'The Regulatory Impact System: Promise and Performance'. In: Carroll, P., Rex, D.-S., Silver, H. and Chris, W. (eds). *Minding the Gap: Appraising the Promise and Performance of Regulatory Reform in Australia*. Canberra: ANU E-Press with The Australian and New Zealand School of Government, 17–32.

Carson, W.G. (1974) 'Symbolic and Instrumental Dimensions of Early Factory Legislation: A Case Study in the Social Origins of Criminal Law'. In: Hood, R. (ed). *Crime, Criminology and Public Policy: Essays in Honour of Sir Leon Radnowicz*. London: Heinemann, 107–38.

Carson, W.G. (Kit) (1985) 'Policing the Periphery: the Development of Scottish Policing 1795–1900'. *Australian and New Zealand Journal of Criminology*, 17 (4):207–32.

Chen, R. and Hanson, J. (2004) 'The Illusion of Law: The Legitimating Scripts of Modern Policy and Corporate Law'. *Michigan Law Review*, 103 (1):1–149.

Christoff, P. (2006) 'Post Kyoto? Post Bush? Towards an Effective "Climate Coalition of the Willing"'. *International Affairs*, 82 (5):831–60.

Clarke, F. and Dean, G. (2005) 'Corporate Governance: A Case of "Misplaced Concreteness?"'. *Advances in Public Interest Accounting*, 11:15–39.

Clarke, F., Dean, G. and Oliver, K. (2003) *Corporate Collapse: Accounting, Regulatory and Ethical Failure*. Cambridge: Cambridge University Press.

Clarke, L. and Short, J.F.J. (1993) 'Social Organization and Risk: Some Current Controversies'. *Annual Review of Sociology*, 19:375–99.

Clinard, M.B. and Yeager, P.C. (1980) *Corporate Crime*. New York: Free Press.

Coglianese, C. (2003) 'Management-Based Regulation: Prescribing Private Management to Achieve Public Goals'. *Law and Society Review*, 37 (4):691–730.

Coglianese, C. and Nash, J. (eds). (2006) *Leveraging the Private Sector: Management-Based Strategies For Improving Environmental Performance*. Washington: Resources For The Future.

Coonan, H. (2003) 'Closure of the HIH Claims Support Scheme'. The Treasury, Commonwealth of Australia. Available at http://www.treasury. gov.au/content/hih_claims.asp?titl=HIH&ContentID=689, accessed 16 July 2009.

Council of Australian Governments (2007) 'Best Practice Regulation'. *A Guide for Ministerial Councils and National Standard Setting Bodies.* Available at http://www.coag.gov.au/ministerial_councils/docs/COAG_best_practice_guide_2007.pdf, accessed 5 July 2010.

Curran, D.J. (1993) *Dead Laws for Dead Men: The Politics of Federal Coal Mine Health and Safety Legislation.* Pittsburgh, PA: University of Pittsburgh Press.

Cullen H.L. (1990) *The Public Inquiry into the Piper Alpha Disaster*, Cmnd 1310, HMSO.

Darian-Smith, E. and Scott, C. (2009) 'Regulation and Human Rights in Sociolegal Scholarship'. *Law & Policy*, 31 (3):271–81.

Dawson, D. and Brooks, B. (1999) 'The Esso Longford Gas Plant Accident: Report of the Longford Royal Commission'. Melbourne: Government Printer for the State of Victoria.

De Marchi, B., Funtowicz, S.O. and Ravetz, J.R. (1996) 'Seveso: a Paradoxical Classic Disaster'. In: Mitchell, J.K. (ed). *Tokyo, the Long Road to Recovery: Community Responses to Industrial Disaster*: United Nations Press.

Department of Defence (2003) 'Australia's National Security: A Defence Update'. Commonwealth of Australia. Available at http://merln.ndu.edu/ whitepapers/Australia-2003.pdf, accessed 15 September 2010.

Department of Foreign Affairs and Trade (2003) 'Advancing the National Interest: Australia's Foreign and Trade Policy White Paper'. Commonwealth of Australia. Available at http://homepage.ntu.edu.tw/~lbh/ ref/Statandyearbook/others/32.pdf, accessed 29 April 2009.

Department of Foreign Affairs and Trade (2004) 'Transnational Terrorism: The Threat to Australia'. Commonwealth of Australia. Available at http://www.dfat.gov.au/publications/terrorism/, accessed 29 April 2009.

Douglas, M. (1966) *Purity and Danger: An Analysis of the Concepts of Pollution and Taboo.* London: Routledge, reprinted 1996.

Douglas, M. (1992) *Risk and Blame: Essays in Cultural Theory.* London: Routledge.

Durkheim, E. (1964) *The Division of Labour in Society.* New York: Free Press.

Eckert, H. (2004) 'Inspections, Warnings, and Compliance: the Case of Petroleum Storage Regulation'. *Journal of Environmental Economics and Management*, 47 (2):232–59.

Eggert, H. and Ellegard, A. (2003) 'Fishery Control and Regulation Compliance: a Case for Co-Management in Swedish Commercial Fisheries'. *Marine Policy*, 27:525–33.

Environmental Assessment Institute (2006) 'Risk and Uncertainty in Cost Benefit Analysis: Toolbox paper'. Available at http://www.scribd.com/doc/ 15014896/Risk-and-Uncertainty-in-Cost-Benefit-Analysis, accessed 15 September 2010.

Erikson, K.T. (2005) *Wayward Puritans: A Study in the Sociology of Deviance*. Boston: Pearson Education.

Espeland, W. (1998) *The Struggle for Water: Politics, Rationality and Identity in the American Southwest*. Chicago: University of Chicago Press.

Ferguson, N. (2008) *The Ascent of Money: A Financial History of the World*. New York: The Penguin Press.

Ferguson, A. (2010) 'Critical Time for ASIC under Siege'. *The Age*. Melbourne, 22 June 2010. Available at http://www.theage.com.au/business/ critical-time-for-asic-under-siege-20100621-ysc9.html, accessed 30 June 2010.

Fife-Yeomans, J. (2008) 'Ray Williams, You're kidding'. *The Daily Telegraph*. Sydney, Australia. Available at http://www.news.com.au/ dailytelegraph/opinion/story/0,22049,23050718-5001031,00.html, accessed 14 May 2009.

Fischhoff, B. (1996) 'Public Values in Risk Research'. *Annals of the American Academy of Political & Social Science*, 545:75–84.

Fisher, E. (2007) 'Risk Evaluation through the Lens of Administrative Constitutionalism'. In: Fisher, E. (ed). *Risk Regulation and Administrative Constitutionalism*. Oxford: Hart, 1–47.

Fox, D.R. (1999) 'Psycholegal Scholarship's Contribution to False Consciousness about Injustice'. *Law and Human Behaviour*, 23 (1):9–30.

Fraser, N. (1992) 'Rethinking the Public Sphere'. In: Calhoun, C. (ed). *Habermas and the Public Sphere*. Cambridge: MIT Press, 109–42.

FRC (2002) 'Adoption of International Accounting Standards by 2005'. In: Financial Reporting Council (ed). *Bulletin of the FRC*. July 3 2002. Available at http://www.frc.gov.au/bulletins/2002/04.asp, accessed 12 July 2010.

Freeman, J. (1999) 'Private Parties, Public Functions and the New Administrative Law'. *Administrative Law Review*, 52 (3):813–58.

Freidman, J. (2009) 'A Crisis of Politics, not Economics: Complexity, Ignorance and Policy Failure'. *Critical Review*, 21 (2–3):127–83.

Freidman, T. (1999) *The Lexus and the Olive Tree*. London: Harper Collins.

Friedrichs, D.O. (1996) *Trusted Criminals in Contemporary Society*. Belmont California: Wadsworth Publishing Company.

Freudenburg, W.R. (1993) 'Risk and Recreancy: Weber, the Divison of Labor and the Rationality of Risk Perceptions'. *Social Forces*, 71 (4):909–32.

Gable, R.S. (1992) 'Regulatory Risk Management of Psychoactive Substances'. *Law & Policy*, 14 (4):257–76.

Garland, D. (2001) *The Culture of Control: Crime and Social Order in Contemporary Society*. Chicago: University of Chicago Press.

Garnaut, R. (2008) 'Interim Report to the Commonwealth, State and Territory Governments of Australia', *Garnaut Climate Change Review*, 1–63. Available at http://www.garnautreview.org.au/domino/Web_Notes/Garnaut/garnautweb.nsf, accessed 19 September 2008.

Gerth, H.H. and Mills, C.W. (eds) (1991 [1948]) *From Max Weber: Essays in Sociology*. London: Routledge.

Gezelius, S.S. (2002) 'Do Norms Count? State Regulation and Compliance in a Norwegian Fishing Community'. *Acta Sociologica*, 45:305–14.

Gezelius, S.S. (2003) *Regulation and Compliance in the Atlantic Fisheries*. Dordrecht: Klewer Academic Publishers.

Gibbs, D. (1996) 'Integrating Sustainable Development and Economic Restructuring: A Role for Regulation Theory?' *Geoforum*, 27 (1):1–10.

Giddens, A. (1991) *Modernity and Self-Identity: Self and Society in the Late Modern Age*. Cambridge: Polity Press.

Giddens, A. (1995) *Politics, Sociology and Social Theory: Encounters with Classical and Contemporary Social Thought*. Cambridge: Polity Press.

Giddens, A. and Pierson, C. (1998) *Conversations with Anthony Giddens: Making Sense of Modernity*. Cambridge: Polity Press.

Glasbeek, H. (2002) *Wealth by Stealth: Corporate Crime, Corporate Law, and the Perversion of Democracy*. Toronto, Canada: Between the Lines.

Gobert, J. (2005) 'The Politics of Corporate Manslaughter – the British Experience'. *Flinders Journal of Law Reform*, 8 (1):1–38.

Government of Victoria (2007) 'Victorian Guide to Regulation'. *Incorporating Guidelines made under the Subordinate Legislation Act 1994 and Guidelines for the Measurement of Changes in Administrative Burden (Second Edition)*: Department of Treasury and Finance. Available at http://www.dtf.vic.gov.au/CA25713E0002EF43/WebObj/VictorianGuidetoRegulation2007/$File/Victorian%20Guide%20to%20Regulation%202007.pdf, accessed 5 July 2010.

Grabosky, P. (1994) 'Green Markets: Environmental Regulation by the Private Sector'. *Law & Policy*, 16 (4):420 48.

Grabosky, P. (1995) 'Counterproductive Regulation'. *International Journal of the Sociology of Law*, 3:347–69.

Grabosky, P. (1997) 'Inside the Pyramid: Towards a Conceptual Framework for the Analysis of Regulatory Systems'. *International Journal of the Sociology of Law*, 25 (3):195–201.

Gray, W.B. and Scholz, J.T. (1993) 'Does Regulatory Enforcement Work? A Panel Analysis of OSHA Enforcement'. *Law & Society Review*, 27 (1):177–213.

Gunningham, N. (2009) 'Environmental Law, Regulation, Governance: Shifting Architectures'. *Journal of Environmental Law*, 21 (2):179–212.

Gunningham, N. and Grabosky, P. (1998) *Smart Regulation: Designing Environmental Policy*. Oxford: Clarendon Press.

Gunningham, N. and Johnstone, R. (1999) *Regulating Workplace Safety: System and Sanctions*. New York: Oxford University Press.

Gunningham, N., Thornton, D. and Kagan, R.A. (2005) 'Motivating Management: Corporate Compliance in Environmental Protection'. *Law & Policy*, 27 (2):289–316.

Guruswamy, L. (1991) 'The Case for Integrated Pollution Control'. *Law and Contemporary Problems*, 54 (4):41–56.

Gusfield, J.R. (1963) *Symbolic Crusade: Status Politics and the American Temperance Movement*. Illinois: University of Illinois Press.

Habermas, J. (1979) *Legitimation Crisis*. London: Heinemann.

Habermas, J. (1989a) 'Social Action and Rationality'. In: Seidman, S. (ed). *Jurgen Habermas on Society and Politics: A Reader*. Boston: Beacon Press, 142–64.

Habermas, J. (1989b) 'Technology and Science as Ideology'. In: Seidman, S. (ed). *Jurgen Habermas on Society and Politics: A Reader*. Boston: Beacon Press, 237–65.

Habermas, J. (1989c) 'What Does a Crisis Mean Today? Legitimation Problems in Late Capitalism'. In: Seidman, S. (ed). *Jurgen Habermas on Society and Politics: A Reader*. Boston: Beacon Press, 266–83.

Habermas, J. (1996) *Between Facts and Norms*. Cambridge: Polity Press.

Habermas, J. (1998) 'Learning by Disaster? A Diagnostic Look Back on the Short 20th Century'. *Constellations*, 5 (3):307–20.

Haines, F. (1997) *Corporate Regulation: Beyond 'Punish or Persuade'*. Oxford: Clarendon Press.

Haines, F. (2005) *Globalization and Regulatory Character: Regulatory Reform after the Kader Toy Factory Fire*. Dartmouth: Ashgate.

Haines, F. (2007) 'Crime? What Crime? Tales of the Collapse of HIH'. In: Pontell, H.N. and Geis, G. (eds). *International Handbook of White-Collar and Corporate Crime*. New York: Springer, 523–39.

Haines, F. (2009a) 'Regulatory Failures and Regulatory Solutions: A Characteristic Analysis of the Aftermath of Disasters'. *Law & Social Inquiry*, 34 (1):31–60.

Haines, F. (2009b) 'Vanquishing the Enemy or Civilizing the Neighbour? Controlling the Risks from Hazardous Industries'. *Social & Legal Studies*, 18 (3):397–415.

Haines, F. and Gurney, D. (2003) 'The Shadows of the Law: Contemporary Approaches to Regulation and the Problem of Regulatory Conflict'. *Law & Policy*, 25 (4):353–80.

Haines, F. and Hall, A. (2004) 'The Law and Order Debate in Occupational Health and Safety'. *Journal of Occupational Health and Safety: Australia and New Zealand*, 20 (3):363–73.

Haines, F. and Sutton, A. (2003) 'The Engineers Dilemma: a Sociological Perspective on the Juridification of Regulation'. *Crime, Law & Social Change*, 39 (1):1–22.

Haines, F., Sutton, A. and Platania-Phung, C. (2008) 'It's All About Risk Isn't It? Science, Politics, Public Opinion and Regulatory Reform'. *The Flinders Journal of Law Reform*, 10 (3):435–53.

Hall, P.A. and Soskice, D. (2001a) 'Introduction'. In: Hall, P.A. and Soskice, D. (eds). *Varieties of Capitalism: The Institutional Foundations of Comparative Advantage*. Oxford: Oxford University Press, 1–68.

Hall, P.A. and Soskice, D. (2001b) *Varieties of Capitalism: The Institutional Foundations of Comparative Advantage*. Oxford: Oxford University Press.

Hancher, L. and Moran, M. (1998) 'Organising Regulatory Space'. In: Baldwin, R., Scott, C. and Hood, C. (eds). *A Reader in Regulation*. Oxford: Oxford University Press, 148–73.

Hansard (2001a) 'House of Representatives: Official Hansard'. Commonwealth of Australia, Monday, 17 September. Available at http://www.aph.gov.au/hansard/hansreps.htm#2001, accessed 29 April 2009.

Hansard (2001b) 'Senate: Official Hansard'. Commonwealth of Australia, Monday, 17 September. Available at http://www.aph.gov.au/hansard/hanssen.htm#2001, accessed 29 April 2009.

Harvey, D. (1989) *The Condition of Postmodernity*. Cambridge: Blackwell.

Heimer, C.A. (2008) 'Thinking about How to Avoid Thought: Deep Norms, Shallow Rules, and the Structure of Attention'. *Regulation and Governance*, 2 (1):30–47.

Hilgartner, S. (1992) 'The Social Construction of Risk Objects: Or, How to Pry Open Networks of Risk'. In: Short, J.F.J. and Clarke, L. (eds). *Organizations, Uncertainties and Risk*. Boulder: Westview Press, 39–53.

Holley, C. and Gunningham, N. (2006) 'Environment Improvement Plans: Facilitative Regulation in Practice'. *Environmental and Planning Law Journal*, 23:448–64.

Holloway, D.A. and van Rhyn, D. (2005) 'Effective Corporate Governance Reform and Organisational Pluralism: Reframing Culture, Leadership and Followership'. *Advances in Public Interest Accounting*, 11:303–28.

Hood, C. (1998) *The Art of the State: Culture, Rhetoric and Public Management*. Oxford: Clarendon Press.

Hopkins, A. (2001) *Lessons from Longford: the Esso Gasplant Explosion*. Sydney: CCH Books.

Hopkins, A. (2002a) 'Lessons from Longford: the Trial'. *Journal of Occupational Health and Safety: Australia and New Zealand*, 18 (6):3–71.

Hopkins, A. (2002b) 'Safety, Culture, Mindfulness and Safe Behaviour: Converging Ideas'. *National Research Centre for OHS Regulation*.

December, 2002. Available at http://ohs.anu.edu.au/publications/pdf/ wp%207%20-%20Hopkins.pdf, accessed 15 September 2010.

Hopkins, A. and Larsson, T.J. (2002) 'Has Victoria's Major Hazard Watchdog Been Muzzled?' *Safety Science Monitor*, 6 (1).

Hutter, B.M. (2001) *Risk and Regulation*. Oxford: Oxford University Press.

Hutter, B.M. (2005) 'The Attractions of Risk-Based Regulation: Accounting for the Emergence of Risk Ideas in Regulation'. *Discussion Paper No. 33*: ESRC Centre for Analysis of Risk and Regulation, The London School of Economics and Political Science.

Institute of Foresters of Australia (2009) 'Submission to the 2009 Victorian Bushfires Royal Commission'. *Australian Forestry*, 72 (3):117–45.

Ipp, D. (2002) 'Review of the Law of Negligence'. The Treasury, Commonwealth of Australia, available at http://revofneg.treasury.gov.au/ content/Report2/PDF/Law_Neg_Final.pdf, accessed 17 July 2009.

Ipp, D. (2007) 'The Politics, Purpose and Reform of the Law of Negligence'. *Australian Law Journal*, 81:456–64.

Jones, S. and Higgins, A.D. (2006) 'Australia's Switch to International Financial Reporting Standards: a Perspective from Account Preparers'. *Accounting and Finance*, 46 (4):629–52.

Jordan, A., Wurzel, R.K.W. and Zito, A. (2005) 'The Rise of "New" Policy Instruments in Comparative Perspective: Has Governance Eclipsed Government?' *Political Studies*, 53:477–96.

Kagan, R.A., Gunningham, N. and Thornton, D. (2003) 'Explaining Corporate Environmental Performance: How Does Regulation Matter?' *Law and Society Review*, 37 (1):51–90.

Kahn, A.E. (1990) 'Deregulation: Looking Backward and Looking Forward'. *Yale Journal on Regulation*, 7:325–54.

Kasperson, R.E. and Kasperson, J.X. (1996) 'The Social Amplification and Attenuation of Risk'. *Annals of the American Academy of Political & Social Science*, 545:95–105.

Kazan-Allen, L. (2005) 'Asbestos and Mesothelioma: Worldwide Trends'. *Lung Cancer*, 49 Supplement 1:S3–S8.

Keeney, R.L. (1996) 'The Role of Values in Risk Management'. *Annals of the American Academy of Political & Social Science*, 545:126–34.

Kindleberger, C.P. and Aliber, R. (2005) *Manias, Panics, and Crashes*. Fifth Edition with a new forward by Robert Solow (ed.). New Jersey: John Wiley & Sons.

Koehler, D.A. (2007) 'The Effectiveness of Voluntary Environmental Programs – a Policy at a Crossroads?' *The Policy Studies Journal*, 35 (4):689–722.

Kramer, H. and Sprenger, J. (1486) *Malleus Maleficarum*: On line edition. Available at http://www.malleusmaleficarum.org/, accessed 15 September 2010.

Krueger, A.B. (2007) *What Makes a Terrorist? Economics and the Roots of Terrorism*. Princeton: Princeton University Press.

Kunreuther, H. and Slovic, P. (1996) 'Science, Values and Risk'. *Annals of the American Academy of Political & Social Science*, 545 (116–25).

LaMontagne, A.D., Shaw, A., Ostry, A., Louie, A.M. and Keegal, T.G. (2006) 'Workplace Stress in Victoria: Developing a Systems Approach'. Melbourne: Victorian Health Promotion Foundation.

Latour, B. (2005) *Reassembling the Social: An Introduction to Actor-Network-Theory*. Oxford: Oxford University Press.

Leiss, W. (1996) 'Three Phases in the Evolution of Risk Communication Practice'. *Annals of the American Academy of Political & Social Science*, 545 (85–94).

Levi-Faur, D. (2005) 'The Rise of Regulatory Capitalism: the Global Diffusion of a New Regulatory Order'. *The Annals of the American Academy of Political and Social Science*, 598 (1):12–32.

Lin, G.A., Beck, D.C., Stewart, A.L. and Garbutt, J.M. (2007) 'Resident Perceptions of the Impact of Work Hour Limitations'. *Journal of General Internal Medicine*, 22 (7):969–74.

Long, S. (2003) 'The World Today – HIH Verdict Released'. *ABC Online*. *Available* at http://www.abc.net.au/worldtoday/content/2003/s833577.htm, accessed 14 May 2009.

Lucken, K. and Ponte, L.M. (2008) 'A Just Measure of Forgiveness: Reforming Occupational Licensing Regulations for Ex-Offenders Using BFOQ Analysis'. *Law & Policy*, 30 (1):46–72.

Lupton, D. (1999) *Risk*. London: Routledge.

Lynn, C. (2008) 'WorkCover Bullying and Harassment'. Hansard, Legislative Council, Parliament of New South Wales, 10651. 28 October.

Main, A. (2003) *Other People's Money: The Complete Story of the Extraordinary Collapse of HIH*. Sydney: Harper Collins.

Majone, G. (1998) 'The Rise of the Regulatory State in Europe'. In: Baldwin, R., Scott, C. and Hood, C. (eds). *A Reader on Regulation*. Oxford: Oxford University Press, 192–215.

Makkai, T. and Braithwaite, J. (1998) 'In and Out of the Revolving Door: Making Sense of Regulatory Capture'. In: Baldwin, R., Scott, C. and Hood, C. (eds). *A Reader on Regulation*. Oxford: Oxford University Press, 173–91.

Mares, I. (2003) *The Politics of Social Risk: Business and Welfare State Development*. Cambridge: Cambridge University Press.

Marshall, S., Mitchell, R. and Ramsay, I. (2008) 'Varieties of Capitalism, Corporate Governance and Employment Systems in Australia'. In: Marshell, S., Mitchell, R. and Ramsay, I. (eds). *Varieties of Capitalism, Corporate Governance and Employees*. Melbourne: Melbourne University Press, 1–18.

Marvel, H.P. (1977) 'Factory Regulation: A Reinterpretation of Early English Experience'. *The Journal of Law and Economics*, 20 (2):379–402.

Marx, K. (1990) *Capital: Volume 1*. London: Penguin Classics.

McBarnet, D. and Whelan, C. (1999) *Creative Accounting and the Cross-eyed Javelin Thrower*. New York: J. Wiley.

McCright, A.M. and Dunlap, R.D. (2003) 'Defeating Kyoto: The Conservative Movement's Impact on U.S. Climate Change Policy'. *Social Problems*. 50 (3):348–73.

McNichol, J. (2006) 'Transnational NGO Certification Programs as New Regulatory Forms: Lessons from the Forestry Sector'. In: Djelic, M.L. and Sahlin-Andersson, K. (eds). *Transnational Governance: Institutional Dynamics of Regulation*. 2006: Cambridge University Press, 349–71.

Meidinger, E.E. (2006) 'The Administrative Law of Global Private–Public Regulation: the Case of Forestry'. *European Journal of International Law*, 17:47–87.

Meyer, J.W. and Rowan, B. (1977) 'Institutional Organizations: Formal Structure as Myth and Ceremony'. *American Journal of Sociology*, 83 (2):340–63.

Miller, K. (1991) 'Piper Alpha and the Cullen Report'. *Industrial Law Journal*, 20 (3):176–87.

Mittleman, J. (1994) 'The Globalisation Challenge: Surviving at the Margins'. *Third World Quarterly*, 15 (3):427–43.

Morgan, B. (2003) 'The Economization of Politics: Meta-Regulation as a Form of Nonjudicial Legality'. *Social & Legal Studies*, 12 (4):489–523.

Morgan, B. and Yeung, K. (2007) *An Introduction to Law and Regulation: Text and Materials*. Cambridge: Cambridge University Press.

Morris, N. and Hawkins, G.J. (1970) *The Honest Politician's Guide to Crime Control*. Chicago: University of Chicago Press.

Murphy, R. (2001) 'Nature's Temporalities and the Manufacture of Vulnerability: A Study of a Sudden Disaster with Implications for Creeping Ones'. *Time and Society*, 10 (2/3):329–48.

Newman, P. (1999) 'UK Legislation, Cultural and Legislative Differences between the Organisations to Implement Seveso II'. Greece November, 1999. Available at http://mahbsrv.jrc.it/Proceedings/Greece-Nov-1999/A4-NEWMAN-z.pdf, accessed 15 September 2010.

Nyborg, K. and Telle, K. (2006) 'Firms' Compliance to Environmental Regulation: Is There Really a Paradox?' *Environment and Resource Economics*, 35 (1):1–18.

OECD (n.d.) 'OECD Guiding Principles for Regulatory Quality and Performance'. Available at http://www.oecd.org/dataoecd/19/51/37318586.pdf, accessed 5 July 2010.

Offe, C. (1984) *Contradictions of the Welfare State*. Cambridge: MIT Press.

O'Malley, P. (2004) *Risk, Uncertainty and Government*. London: Glasshouse Press.

Owen, J.N. (2003) 'Report of the HIH Royal Commission'. Commonwealth of Australia. Available at http://www.hihroyalcom.gov.au/finalreport/index.htm, accessed 15 September 2010.

Packham, D. (2009) 'Victorian Bushfires Stoked by Green Vote'. *The Australian* February 10th. Available at http://www.theaustralian.news.com.au/story/0,25197,25031389-7583,00.html, accessed 23 March 2009.

Palmer, J. (2002) 'Review of the Role Played by the Australian Prudential Regulation Authority and the Insurance and Superannuation Commission in the Collapse of the HIH Group of Companies'. *Report the Messrs Corrs Chambers Westgarth From John Palmer, FCA. Available* at http://www.apra.gov.au/Media-Releases/loader.cfm?url=/commonspot/security/getfile.cfm&PageID=5206, accessed 13 May 2009.

Parker, C. (1999a) 'Compliance Professionalism and Regulatory Community: The Australian Trade Practices Regime'. *Journal of Law and Society*, 26 (2):215–39.

Parker, C. (1999b) 'The Greenhouse Challenge: Trivial Pursuit?' *Environmental and Planning Law Journal*, 16 (1):63–74.

Parker, C. (2002) *The Open Corporation: Effective Self-Regulation and Democracy*. Cambridge: Cambridge University Press.

Parker, C. and Lehmann Neilsen, V. (2006) 'Do Businesses take Compliance Systems Seriously? An Empirical Study of the Implementation of Trade Practice Compliance Systems in Australia'. *Melbourne University Law Review*, 30:441–94.

Paterson, J. (2000) *Behind the Mask: Regulating Health and Safety in Britain's Offshore Oil and Gas Industry*. Aldershot: Ashgate Dartmouth.

Pearce, C. (2005) 'The Importance of Cross-Border Cooperation in an Environment of Global Capital Markets'. Parliamentary Secretary to the Treasury: IFRS Regional Policy Forum 24 October 2005. Available at http://www.treasurer.gov.au/DisplayDocs.aspx?pageID=&doc=speeches/2005/016.htm&min=cjp, accessed 15 September 2010.

Pearce, F. and Tombs, S. (1990) 'Ideology, Hegemony, and Empiricism – Compliance Theories of Regulation'. *British Journal of Criminology*, 30 (4):423–43.

Pearce, G. (2007) *High & Dry: John Howard, Climate Change and the Selling of Australia's Future*. Camberwell, Vic.: Viking.

Pettit, T. (2007) 'Will a National Port Regulator Solve Congestion Problems in Australian Ports?' *Maritime Policy & Management*, 34 (2):121–30.

Popper, S.W., Lempert, R.J. and Bankes, S.C. (2005) 'Shaping the Future'. *Scientific American*, 292 (4):66–71.

Powell, W.W. and DiMaggio, P.J. (eds) (1991) *The New Institutionalism in Organizational Analysis*. Chicago: University of Chicago Press.

Power, M. (1997) 'The Audit Society: Rituals of Verification'. New York: Oxford University Press.

Pratten, C. (2008) 'Re: Opinion Concerning the Effect on Insurance Arrangements BTW Insurance Brokers & Direct Offshore Foreign Insurers'. Australian & New Zealand Nationwide Insurance Services. Available at http://www.ruralandgeneral.com.au/dofi_exemptions_iais. php, accessed 24 June 2010.

Quinlan, M. and Bohle, P. (1991) *Managing Occupational Health and Safety in Australia*. South Melbourne: Macmillan.

Reason, J. (1997) *Managing the Risks of Organisational Accidents*. Aldershot: Ashgate.

Rees, J.V. (1994) 'Hostages of Each Other: The Transformation of Nuclear Safety Since Three-Mile Island'. Chicago: University of Chicago Press.

Regulation Taskforce (2006) 'Rethinking Regulation: Report of the Taskforce on Reducing Regulatory Burdens on Business'. A Report to the Prime Minister and Treasurer. Available at http://www.regulationtaskforce.gov.au /finalreport, accessed 28 August 2010.

Reichman, N. (1998) 'Moving Backstage: Uncovering the Role of Compliance Practices in Shaping Regulatory Policies'. In: Baldwin, R., Scott, C. and Hood, C. (eds). *A Reader on Regulation*. Oxford: Oxford University Press, 325–46.

Renn, O. (2008) *Risk Governance*. London: Earthscan.

Reserve Bank of Australia (2007) 'Private Equity in Australia'. Financial Stability Review. Available at http://www.rba.gov.au/publications/fsr/2007/ mar/html/private-equity-aus.html, accessed 28 June, 2010.

Roos, L. and Roos, N.P. (1972) 'Pollution, Regulation and Evaluation'. *Law & Society Review*, 6 (4):509–30.

Rose, N. and Miller, P. (1992) 'Political Power beyond the State: Problematics of Government'. *British Journal of Sociology*, 43 (2):173–205.

Rosoff, S.M., Pontell, H.N. and Tillman, R.H. (2004) *Profit Without Honor: White Collar Crime and the Looting of America (Third Edition)*. Upper Saddle River, New Jersey: Pearson Prentice Hall.

Sayer, A. (1997) 'Essentialism, Social Constructionism, and Beyond'. *The Sociological Review*, 45 (3):453–87.

Scott, C. (2004) 'Regulation in the Age of Governance: the Rise of the Post-Regulatory State'. In: Jordan, J. and Faur, D.L. (eds). *The Politics of Regulation: Institutions and Regulatory Reforms for the Age of Governance*. Cheltenham, UK and Northampton, MA, USA: Edward Elgar, 145–74.

Senate Legal and Constitutional Legislation Committee (2002) 'Consideration of Legislation Referred to the Committee: Security Legislation Amendment (Terrorism) Bill 2002 [No.2]; Suppression of the Financing of Terrorism

Bill 2002; Criminal Code Amendment (Suppression of Terrorist Bombings) Bill 2002; Border Security Legislation Amendment Bill 2002; Telecommunications Interception Legislation Amendment Bill 2002'. Commonwealth of Australia. Available at http://www.aph.gov.au/senate/committee/legcon_ctte/completed_inquiries/2002-04/terrorism/report/report.pdf, accessed 6 May 2009.

Senate Select Committee (2002) 'A Certain Maritime Incident'. Commonwealth of Australia. Available at http://www.aph.gov.au/Senate/committee/maritime_incident_ctte/report/, accessed 8 July, 2010.

Shah, A.K. (1996) 'Creative Accounting in Financial Reporting'. *Accounting, Organisations and Society*, 21 (1):23–39.

Shearing, C. (1993) 'A Constitutive Conception of Regulation'. In: Grabosky, P. and Braithwaite, J. (eds). *Business Regulation and Australia's Future*. Canberra: Australian Institute of Criminology, 67–73.

Shearing, C. and Wood, J. (2003) 'Nodal Governance, Democracy and the New "Denizens"'. *Journal of Law and Society*, 30 (3):400–19.

Short, J.F.J. and Clarke, L. (1992) 'Social Organization and Risk'. In: Short, J.F.J. and Clarke, L. (eds). *Organizations, Uncertainties and Risk*. Boulder: Westview, 309–21.

Slovic, P. (1987) 'Perception of Risk'. *Science*, 236:280–85.

Snider, L. (2000) 'The Sociology of Corporate Crime: An Obituary'. *Theoretical Criminology*, 4 (2):169–206.

Somogyi, S. (2005) 'Regulation of the Insurance Industry'. *AON Re Hazards Conference*. Gold Coast, Queensland. 21–23 August. Available at http://www.apra.gov.au/Speeches/upload/Regulation-of-the-Insurance-Industry.pdf, accessed 16 July 2009.

Sparrow, M.K. (2000) *The Regulatory Craft: Controlling Risks, Solving Problems and Managing Compliance*. Washington DC: Brookings Institution Press.

Spigelman, J.J. (2006) 'Tort Law Reform: An Overview'. *Tort Law Review*, 14 (1):5–15.

Stewart, M. (2008) 'The Model Made Me Do It'. *The Big Money. Available* at http://tbm.thebigmoney.com/print/747, accessed 20 March 2009.

Stigler, G.T. (1971) 'The Theory of Economic Regulation'. *The Bell Journal of Economics and Management Science*, 2 (1):3–21.

Stiglitz, J. (2001) 'Forward'. In: Polanyi, K. (ed). *The Great Transformation: the Political and Economic Origins of our Time with a New Introduction by Fred Block*. Boston: Beacon Press, vii–xvii.

Stiglitz, J. (2009) 'The Anatomy of a Murder: Who Killed America's Economy?' *Critical Review*, 21 (2–3):329–39.

Sunstein, C. (1990a) *After the Rights Revolution: Reconceiving the Regulatory State*. Cambridge, MA: Harvard University Press.

Sunstein, C.R. (1990b) 'Paradoxes of the Regulatory State'. *The University of Chicago Law Review*, 57 (Spring):407–41.

Sunstein, C. (2003) 'Terrorism and Probability Neglect'. *The Journal of Risk and Uncertainty*, 26 (2/3):121–36.

Sunstein, C. (2005) *Laws of Fear: Beyond the Precautionary Principle*. Cambridge: Cambridge University Press.

Sutton, A. (2000) 'Drugs and Dangerousness: Perception and Management of Risk in the Neo-Liberal Era'. In: Brown, M. and Pratt, J. (eds). *Dangerous Offenders: Punishment and Social Order*. Oxford: Routledge, 165–80.

Sutton, A. and Haines, F. (2003) 'White Collar and Corporate Crime'. In: Goldsmith, A., Israel, M. and Daly, K. (eds). *Crime and Justice: An Australian Textbook in Criminology*. Sydney: Lawbook Company, 141–58.

Talley, E.E. (2009) 'Public Ownership, Firm Governance and Litigation Risk'. *University of Chicago Law Review*, 76 (1):335–66.

Tankebe, J. (2009) 'Policing, Procedural Fairness and Public Behaviour: a Review and Critique'. *International Journal of Police Science & Management*, 11 (1):8–19.

Teubner, G. (1998) 'Juridification: Concepts, Aspects, Limits, Solutions'. In: Baldwin, R., Scott, C. and Hood, C. (eds). *A Reader on Regulation*. Oxford: Oxford University Press.

Thornton, D., Kagan, R.A. and Gunningham, N. (2008) 'Compliance Costs, Regulation, and Environmental Performance: Controlling Truck Emissions in the US'. *Regulation and Governance*, 2 (3):275–92.

Tilley, N. (1980) 'Popper, Positivism and Ethnomethodology'. *The British Journal of Sociology*, 31 (1):28–45.

Tombs, S. (2002) 'Understanding Regulation?' *Social & Legal Studies*, 11 (2):113–33.

Tyler, T.R. (2006a) 'Psychological Perspectives on Legitimacy and Legitimation'. *Annual Review of Psychology*, 57:375–400.

Tyler, T.R. (2006b) 'Restorative Justice and Procedural Justice: Dealing with Rule Breaking'. *Journal of Social Issues*, 62 (2):307–26.

Tyler, T.R. and Blader, S.L. (2003) 'The Group Engagement Model: Procedural Justice, Social Identity, and Cooperative Behaviour'. *Personality and Social Psychology Review*, 7 (4):349–60.

Viscusi, W.K. (1992) *Fatal Tradeoffs: Public and Private Responsibilities for Risk*. New York: Oxford University Press.

Wailes, N., Kitay, J. and Lansbury, R.D. (2008) 'Varieties of Capitalism, Corporate Governance and Employment Relations under Globalisation'. In: Marshall, S., Mitchell, J.K. and Ramsay, I. (eds). *Varieties of Capitalism, Corporate Governance and Employees*. Melbourne: Melbourne University Press, 19–38.

Walker, C. (2008) 'The Mirage of Rail Reform: Building Regulatory Capacity in Policy Sectors'. In: Carroll, P., Deighton-Smith, R., Silver, H. and Walker, C. (eds). *Minding the Gap: Appraising the Promise and Performance and Regulatory Reform in Australia*. Canberra: ANU E-Press and The Australian and New Zealand School of Government, 51–62.

Walker, R., Robinson, P., Tebbutt, J., Lin, V., Bisset, P., Burns, R. and Schauble, J. (2006) 'Emergency Management Risk Communication Project'. School of Public Health La Trobe University Final Report to the Department of Human Services (Victoria). Available at http://www.health.vic.gov.au/environment/downloads/risk_communication.pdf, accessed 16 April 2009.

Wallis, S. (1997) 'Financial System Inquiry Final Report'. The Treasury, Commonwealth of Australia. Available at http://fsi.treasury.gov.au/content/FinalReport.asp, accessed 17 July 2009.

Weber, M. (1964 [1947]) *The Theory of Social and Economic Organization*. Edited with an Introduction by Talcott Parsons. New York: The Free Press.

Weber, M. (1991 [1925]) *Max Weber on Law in Economy and Society*. Edited and annotated by Max Rheinstein. New York: Simon & Schuster.

Weber, M. (1991 [1948]) 'Politics as a Vocation'. In: Gerth, H.H. and Mills, C.W. (eds). *From Max Weber: Essays in Sociology*. London: Routledge.

Weick, K., Sutcliffe, K. and Obstfeld, D. (1999) 'Organising for High Reliability: Processes of Collective Mindfulness'. *Research in Organizational Behaviour*, 21:81–123.

Wells, C. (ed) (2001) *Corporations and Criminal Responsibility*. Oxford: Oxford University Press.

Wheeler, J. (2005) 'An Independent Review of Airport Security and Policing for the Government of Australia'. Available at http://www.customs.gov.au/webdata/resources/files/SecurityPolicingReview.pdf, accessed 20 August 2009.

Wheelwright, K. (2004) 'Prosecuting Corporations and Officers for Industrial Manslaughter – Recent Australian Developments'. *Australian Business Law Review*, 32:239–53.

Wickham, G. (2006) 'Foucault, Law, and Power: A Reassessment'. *Journal of Law and Society*, 33 (4):596–614.

Wickham, G. (2010) 'Sociology, the Public Sphere, and Modern Government: a Challenge to the Dominance of Habermas'. *The British Journal of Sociology*, 61 (1):155–75.

Willis, H.H. (2005) 'Analyzing Terrorism Risk'. Testimony presented before the House Homeland Security Committee, Subcommittee on Intelligence, Information Sharing and Terrorism Risk Assessment 17 November, 2005. Available at http://www.rand.org/pubs/testimonies/2005/RAND_CT252.pdf, accessed 15 September 2010.

Willis, H.H., Morral, A.R., Kelly, T.K. and Medby, J.J. (2005) 'Estimating Terrorism Risk'. Rand Center for Terrorism Risk Management Policy. Available at http://www.rand.org/pubs/monographs/2005/RAND_MG388.pdf, accessed 15 September 2010.

Windeyer, R. (2006) 'Transport Security as an Integral Part of a National Security Plan and Ensuring Business Continuity'. Presentation at the *Australian National Security Summit*. Sydney, 15 November 2006.

WorkSafe, Victoria (2009) 'What is a Safety Case?' Available at http://www.workcover.vic.gov.au/wps/wcm/connect/WorkSafe/Home/Safety+and+Prevention/Your+Industry/Major+Hazard+Facilities/About+the+industry/What+is+a+safety+case/, accessed 8 July 2009.

Wright, E.W. (2006) 'National Trends in Personal Injury Litigation: Before and After "Ipp"'. *Tort Law Journal*, 14 (3):233–52.

Wynne, B. (1996) 'May the Sheep Safely Graze? A Reflexive View of the Expert-Lay Knowledge Divide'. In: Lash, S., Szerszinski, B. and Wynne, B. (eds). *Risk, Environment and Modernity: Towards a New Ecology*. London: Sage, 44–83.

Yeung, K. (2004) *Securing Compliance: A Principled Approach*. Oxford: Hart.

Acts and Regulations

Index